GEORGE WASHINGTON
IN NEW YORK

BY

ALLAN BOUDREAU

AND

ALEXANDER BLEIMANN

EDITED BY

DAVID DEUTSCH

The publication of this volume was made possible
in part by a grant from the
Abraham Felt Memorial Fund

Copyright © 1987 by
THE AMERICAN LODGE OF RESEARCH, F. & A.M.

All rights reserved. No part of this publication, including the photographs or graphics, may be reproduced or transmitted in any form or by any means, electronic or mechanical including photocopying, recording or by any information storage and retrieval system, without the written permission of the Authors and The American Lodge of Research, Free and Accepted Masons of the State of New York, except where permitted by law.

Library of Congress
Catalog Card Number
87-91308

ISBN 0-925658-02-2

Published by
The Masonic Book Club
and
The Illinois Lodge of Research

Not-for-Profit Corporations of Illinois
1989

Printed in the
United States of America

Quiz Graphic Arts   Ord, Nebraska 68862

GEORGE WASHINGTON IN NEW YORK

Washington's Coat of Arms

George Washington drew the cypher or monogram for the doors of his coach, his initials surmounted by a griffin.

Washington's Bookplate

TABLE OF CONTENTS

		PAGE
	Introduction	i
	List of Illustrations	ii
	Acknowledgements	iii
	George Washington Masonic Monument	v
	Buildings Familiar to George Washington	vi
Chapter I	The Early Years, 1756 to 1776	1
Chapter II	George Washington in the Hudson River Highlands	9
Chapter III	Pennsylvania and The Grand Lodge of Pennsylvania	35
Chapter IV	Upstate New York	52
Chapter V	Washington as President Elect, and His Inauguration, 1789	72
Chapter VI	Washington as President, 1789-1790	90
Chapter VII	Washington's Tour of New England	102
Chapter VIII	Washington's Tour of Long Island	117
Chapter IX	Washington's Tour of Rhode Island	128
Chapter X	Brief Masonic History	137
Chapter XI	Washington's Masonic Correspondence	152
Chapter XII	Washington and the Society of the Cincinnati	162
Chapter XIII	The Washington Masonic Lodges	181
Chapter XIV	The George Washington Masonic National Memorial	199
	Bibliography	202
	Index	212

INTRODUCTION

George Washington's relations with New York State, and especially New York City, were more continuous, more intimate, and certainly more important than with any other state, except his native state, Virginia.

Even before Washington's first visit to New York City in 1756, he was well known in New York State. "Major Washington's defeat near the Ohio by the French" had been reported to the New York Assembly in 1754, and his name appears frequently in the following years.

Some of the most important events in Washington's life occurred in New York State. It was here that he experienced his first great ovation as the head of the army. It was here that he received a copy of the Declaration of Independence. It was here that he gained valuable experience in the early battles of the Revolution. It was here that he suffered the agony of Arnold's perfidy and Andrés death. It was here that he instituted the first secret service which resulted in the death of Nathan Hale. It was here that he refused a kingship and replied to the famous Newburgh addresses. It was here that he proclaimed the cessation of hostilities. It was here that he planned masterful campaigns like the Sullivan-Clinton campaign and the Yorktown campaign. It was here that he received news of the signing of the Treaty of Peace. It was here that he saw the last of the British forces leave the shores of the New Republic. It was here that he bade an affectionate farewell to his officers. It was here that he helped to organize the Society of the Cincinnati and became its first head. And it was here that he was inaugurated as the first President of the United States and set the new government in motion in New York City, the first national capital.

LIST OF ILLUSTRATIONS

PAGE

George Washington's Coat of Arms	Frontispiece
George Washington's Coach Monogram	Frontispiece
George Washington's Bookplate	Frontispiece
George Washington, Master of Alexandria Lodge No. 39	iv
Morris-Jumel Mansion	3
Map of West Point, 1779, made by General Thaddeus Kosciusko	14
Military Map of Newburgh and New Windsor, N.Y. (1779-1793)	18
General George Washington's Headquarters at Hasbrouck House (Newburgh, N.Y.)	22
Military Map of Washington's campaign in 1781 from the Hudson River leading to the Battle of Yorktown	31
Temple Hill Monument	34
Dedication page of Sermon on December 28, 1778	40
Title page of Sermon on December 28, 1778	41
George Washington by Charles Wilson Peale	49
George Washington Masonic Shrine at Tappan, N.Y.	53
Masonic Apron presented to George Washington by Watson and Cassoul	60
Draft of Washington's Letter to Watson and Cassoul	64
Van Courtlandt Manor in Van Courtlandt Park, N.Y.C.	69
Fraunces Tavern (Museum and Library), N.Y.C.	70
Electoral Vote (chart) in the first presidential election in 1789	74
First Presidential Mansion — Franklin House on Cherry Street, New York City	78
Wall Street in 1780 showing Federal Hall	79
Railing from balcony of Federal Hall, New York City	84
Inauguration of George Washington as the first President of the United States, N.Y.C.	85
St. John's Masonic Bible	86
St. Paul's Chapel, Parish of Trinity Church	91
George Washington by Joseph Wright	93
Macomb House on Broadway, New York City, the second presidential Mansion	118
George Washington by John Trumbull	129
Tuoro Synagogue in Newport, R.I.	133
Washington's reply to King David's Lodge No. 1, Newport, R.I.	135
Masonic Apron presented to George Washington by General and Marquis de Lafayette	138
Membership Certificate from Holland Lodge, New York	141
George Washington's Eagle of the Society of the Cincinnati	169
The New York Directory, 1786	175
George Washington Masonic National Memorial, Alexandria, VA	198

ACKNOWLEDGEMENTS

The authors are indebted to the staffs of the New York Public Library, The New-York Historical Society, Fraunces Tavern Museum, the New York State Library, the George Washington Masonic National Memorial Association, Anderson House Museum of the Society of the Cincinnati, the Mount Gulian Society, the Library of Congress, the National Parks Service, the Parish of Trinity Church, the Washington Headquarters at Newburgh, New York, the George Washington Masonic Shrine at Tappan, New York, The Metropolitan Museum of Art in New York City, the Art Commission of the City of New York, the Chancellor Robert R Livingston Library of the Grand Lodge, F. & A. M., of New York, The Pierpont Morgan Library, the Federal Hall National Memorial, and the Tuoro Synagogue in Newport, Rhode Island, for providing manuscript material, books, illustrations and other assistance whenever required.

Special thanks are due to the Honorable Hamilton Fish Jr. for his work *George Washington In The Highlands* which was first published in 1932; to Bernard Kusinitz, the historian for both the Tuoro Synagogue and St. John's Lodge No. 1, F. & A. M., in Newport, Rhode Island; to Phyllis Barr, Archivist of the Parish of Trinity Church in the City of New York; to William A. Brown, Librarian of the George Washington Masonic National Memorial in Alexandria, Virginia; to John D. Kilbourne, Director of the Library and Museum of Anderson House of the Society of the Cincinnati; to Barbara Peters, Director of the Mount Gulian Society; to Gerald D. Foss for his work on *George Washington In New Hampshire;* to Wendell K. Walker, Grand Secretary of the Grand Lodge of New York; to Douglas Southall Freeman for his seven volume work on *George Washington;* and to Mrs. Sidney Leader and the Abraham Felt Memorial Fund.

The authors wish to express special gratitude to David Deutsch, the Assistant Editor, whose professionalism in editing this work helped in its success and excellence.

A.B.

Heroic Bronze Statue of Illustrious
BROTHER GEORGE WASHINGTON

George Washington Masonic Monument
Flushing Meadows Corona Park
Queens, New York

This statue was designed by Brother Bryant Baker, noted New York sculptor, as the model for the colossal bronze statue that was cast at the Gorham Company in Providence, Rhode Island and unveiled at the George Washington Masonic National Memorial in Alexandria, Virginia on February 22, 1950.

The statue shows Washington as Master of his Lodge. The Masonic apron he is wearing is an exact reproduction of the Masonic apron presented to Washington at Newburg, New York in 1782. The jewel is identical to the one actually worn by Washington. The face was moulded from the mask of Washington by Jean Antoine Houdon, now in the collections of The Pierpont Morgan Library in New York City. The Physical proportions of Washington are from the measurements taken by Houdon at Mount Vernon in October 1785 for the marble statue of Washington now in the Rotunda of the State Capitol in Richmond, Virginia.

Castings of the heroic Washington were made, under the supervision of the sculptor Donald DeLue, and stand in the Civic Center in New Orleans, Louisiana; the Masonic Home in Wallingford, Connecticut; on the South Lawn of the Indiana Statehouse in Indianapolis, Indiana and in Flushing Meadows Corona Park, New York City.

The original clay model is carefully preserved by the Grand Lodge of the State of New York. It was exhibited at the Masonic Brotherhood Center, New York World's Fair 1964-65, and is on permanent display in Masonic Hall, 71 West 23rd Street, New York City.

George Washington in New York City
Buildings existing in 1989 that were familiar to George Washington

Fraunces Tavern
54 Pearl Street
Lower Manhattan

The original building was erected in 1719 by Etienne Delancy and used as a warehouse and tavern. It was purchased by the Sons of the Revolution in New York State in 1904, and restored to its appearance at the time of the American Revolution.

St. Paul's Chapel
Broadway and
Fulton Street
Lower Manhattan

Built in 1766. Thomas McBean was the architect. St. Paul's Chapel Trinity Church Parish has been restored to the original state in which Washington knew it. The architect, Thomas Nash, (died 1926) supervised the restoration.

Morris Mansion
160th Street and
Edgecomb Avenue
Upper Manhattan

Built about 1765 by Roger and Mary Phillipse Morris. Purchased by New York City in 1903. The Daughters of the American Revolution were given control of the house by the Parks Department for use as a museum. Restored and refurnished.

Washington Headquarters Association, Inc., New York City Department of Parks.

Van Cortland
Mansion
242nd Street and
Broadway
Bronx

Built in 1748 by Frederick Van Cortland. Restored with 17th and 18th Century Dutch, English, and Colonial furnishings, by the National Society Colonial Dames in the State of New York.

CHAPTER I

THE EARLY YEARS, 1756 to 1776

"Last night Colonel Washington arrived here from Philadelphia", the New York City newspaper *Mercury* reported on February 16, 1756, George Washington's first visit to New York City.

At that time, Washington was twenty four years old, six feet three inches tall, an experienced surveyor, a combat seasoned soldier, the squire of Mount Vernon, and a member of the Masonic Lodge in Fredericksburg, Virginia, where he was raised a Master Mason on August 4, 1753.

Washington was a world famous author in 1756. *The Journal of Major George Washington*, the account of his mission as emissary from the Governor of Virginia to the Commandant of the French forces in the Ohio Territory, had been printed by the Governor of Virginia and widely distributed.

This small booklet of about seven thousand words had been read throughout the Colonies. Extracts from it were printed in the Colonial newspapers.

Copies were sent to England where it had been reprinted and read by King and Parliament, and the Officers in the British Army, with the result that General Sir Edward Braddock arrived in America with two regiments of British troops to defend the English border.

Parts of *The Journal* were even translated into French, printed in Paris, and used to justify the French occupation of the Ohio Territory, and to portray the British as the aggressors.

Washington survived Braddock's ill-fated advance against the French at Fort Duquesne in July 1755, where General Braddock was mortally wounded, and most of the senior officers killed or injured by the French and Indians, and even by their own comrades.

Washington, the only surviving officer of rank, after the battle of Monongahela, read the burial service for General Braddock, and supervised the retreat.

George Washington, Colonel of the Virginia Regiment, and the Commander-in-Chief of the frontier militia, made an impressive appearance as he rode through the streets of New York City that winter night.

Garbed in his impressive uniform of buff-and-blue, with a brilliant scarlet and white cloak, accompanied by his aides, servants, and all the horses and trappings of a high military command, George Washington created a sensation as he rode northward across the colonies.

He arrived in New York City by boat, from Perth Amboy in New Jersey, the usual route for travelers coming from the south and west. His first stop in New York City was at a tavern, perhaps the "Crown and Thistle," operated by John Thompson who was familiarly known as "Scotch Johnny." Washington paid 5 shillings 1 pence for lodgings that night.

At that time, New York City had about ten thousand residents, Wall Street was lined with trees, and the City Hall was at 26 Wall Street, on the site now occupied by the Federal Hall National Memorial. Broadway extended only to City Hall Park and was unpaved, muddy in the winter and dusty in the summer.

Washington's host on his first visit to New York City was Beverly Robinson, the son of a former President of the Virginia Colony. Beverly Robinson had married Susannah Phillipse in July 1748. Susannah was the oldest of the two sisters of Frederick Phillipse, the third and last Lord of the Manor of Phillipsboro, what is now Westchester County in New York State.

Washington met Mary Phillipse, the younger sister and co-heiress of Mrs. Robinson. Legend has it that Washington was an admirer of and perhaps suitor to the elegant Miss Phillipse, an unmarried girl who owned 51,000 acres of valuable New York land.

His account book shows that he spent 73 pounds eighteen shillings for horses; three pounds, seven and three for a "Taylors Bill" and smaller amounts for "Servants" and "Treating Ladies to Ye Mn" (microcosm). The Microcosm or World in Minature was a structure of scenery in the form of a Roman temple within which mechanical devices portrayed various activities, such as birds flying, ships sailing, coaches and chariots racing, and even men working in a carpenter's yard.

On February 23, 1756, the New York City newspaper *Mercury* reported, "Friday last (February 20th four days after arriving) Colonel Washington set out from this city to Boston."

No doubt Washington rode up Bowery Lane to Harlem and Kings Bridge. This was the Boston Post Road used by travelers to the north and east.

The purpose of Washington's journey from Virginia to Boston was to confer with William Shirley, then the British Governor of Massachusetts, and the highest military authority in the British Colonies in America.

THE EARLY YEARS, 1756 to 1776

Maryland had raised a small military force under the command of Captain Dagworth who had seen military service in Canada where he held a King's commission as Captain. Dagworthy asserted that, under English Law, any regular officer outranked any colonial officer, and that a Captain even outranked a Colonel.

General Shirley decided in Washington's favor who returned to Virginia with a document that concluded, "it is my order that Colonel Washington shall take command of the troops."

George Washington returned to New York City, where he was a guest of the Robinson's from March 10th to the 14th, borrowing 91 pounds from Robinson to cover unanticipated expenses incurred during the trip and provide funds for the journey southward.

Mary Phillipse eventually married a British Officer, Roger Morris, on January 18, 1758. The Morris home at 160th Street became Washington's headquarters during the last five weeks he spent in New York City in 1776. This colonial mansion is familiar to present day New Yorkers as the Morris-Jumel mansion.

The Morris-Jumel Mansion was built by Lt. Col. Roger Morris in 1765. Morris had come to America in 1746 and during the Braddock expedition in 1755 became a friend of Washington. A loyalist, Morris fled the country at the outbreak of the Revolution,

Morris-Jumel Mansion

and at the end of the war his house and land were confiscated and sold. In 1810 the house became the property of Stephen Jumel, and was restored in Federal period style. After passing through a succession of owners, the house was saved from demolition in 1903 when the City of New York purchased it for $235,000, and by special legislation gave its care to the Washington Headquarters Association of the Daughters of the American Revolution. This group restored the house and again in 1945 renovated and refurnished it. At the same time, the grounds were landscaped.

The Morris-Jumel Mansion, an outstanding example of Georgian architecture, is a two-and-one-half story frame house constructed of rusticated wood planks, with quions at the four corners, in imitation of stonework. Shingles, instead of planks, were used to cover the side that was least likely to be seen by important visitors. The low-hipped roof has a deck surrounded by a Chinese lattice rail balustrade. At the rear, there is a projecting octagonal wing, which was used by Washington as his study in 1776. Of outstanding architectural interest is the giant two-story high entrance portico with its lofty Roman Tuscan pedimented temple front and four tall slender Doric columns. The spacious rooms are handsomely furnished in the styles of the late 18th and early 19th centuries, in consideration of the two distinguished families that lived in the mansion at different periods. The earlier period is carried out on the lower floor, while the American Federal and French Empire of the 19th century is used upstairs, where furniture belonging to the Jumels is displayed. The third-floor rooms, probably utilized formerly as guest chambers, house a collection of early American household utensils. The kitchen and servant quarters are in the basement. The Morris-Jumel Mansion is open to visitors as a historic house exhibit.

Washington's third visit to New York City was May 26-31, 1773, to enroll his stepson, John Parke Custis, in Kings College (now Columbia). On route, Washington visited the Governor of Maryland at Annapolis, dined with the Governor of Pennsylvania in Philadelphia, and with the Governor of New Jersey, Benjamin Franklin's son William, at Burlington. At Basking Ridge, New Jersey, Washington visited with William Alexander, known in America as Lord Stirling by virtue of his claim to the title "Earl of Stirling" not accepted by the House of Lords.

Washington gave President Myles Cooper of Kings College one hundred pounds sterling for his stepson's college expenses, and requested him to keep a fatherly eye on the young man. Custis had a short stay at Kings College. His sister, Martha Custis, died on June 19, 1773, and Custis returned to Mount Vernon. On February 3, 1774, he married Eleanore Calvert in Virginia.

THE EARLY YEARS, 1756 to 1776

The Rev. Dr. Myles Cooper was an ardent and vocal Loyalist. He fled to a British ship in 1775, and returned to England.

During this visit to New York City, Washington recorded in his diary for the evening of May 26th, 1773, "Lodged at a Mr. Farmers" who has never been further identified.

On May 27th, he attended an entertainment given in honor of General Thomas Gage, then Commander of the British troops in North America, who had served with Washington under General Braddock during the campaign against the Indians in 1755.

On May 28th, Washington dined with James DeLancey, the son of Peter DeLancey and Elizabeth Colden, and a business partner of Beverly Robinson. That evening he attended the theater and saw "Hamlet," paying eight shillings for his seat.

On May 29th, he dined with Major William Bayard, and spent the evening "with the Old Club at Hull's." What was the Old Club? The possibility is that this was a Masonic Lodge meeting as the Lodges in New York City at that time met in Hull's and other taverns.

On May 30th, he again dined with General Thomas Gage and "Spent the evening in my room writing."

It is interesting to note that many of the people Washington associated with during this visit to New York City were ardent Loyalists who would lose all their properties by the Act of Attainder passed by the New York Legislature in 1779.

Washington's fourth visit to New York City was on Sunday, June 25, 1775, as Commander-in-Chief of the Continental Army, on his way to Cambridge to take command of the forces besieging Boston. He stepped ashore in New York City at Colonel Leonard Lispenard's near the present Canal Street approach to the Holland tunnel, and dined with members of the Provincial Congress, moving on to Boston before nightfall. Lispenard, at that time, was the Senior Warden of Union Lodge in New York City; Dr. Samuel Bard, the Junior Warden; and Robert R Livingston, the Master. That same evening, the King's Governor, William Tryon, arrived in New York City on his return from England, after a year's absence.

It was reported that the very men who "pourde out flattery and adulation to the rebel General joined the Governor's train, welcomed him to the Colony, and hoped he would remain long in government."

GEORGE WASHINGTON IN NEW YORK

On April 13, 1776, Washington entered New York City for the fifth time, and established his headquarters at what is now the intersection of Varick and Charlton Streets, some two and one half miles north of the Southern tip of Manhattan Island. This house had been the home of Abraham Mortier, the paymaster of the British forces in North America. Martha Washington arrived in New York City later, on April 17th.

Washington's arrival in New York City spurred his Royalist enemies to action. There were many plots against his reputation and some against his life. A member of his own bodyguard, Thomas Hickey, engaged in a plan to mix paris green, a poisonious green powder with Washington's food. The plot was discovered, reportedly by the daughter of Samuel Frauncis. Hickey was hanged for treason on June 28th, 1776, the first of many executions in the Continental Army.

The first weeks preparing for the defense of New York City, confirmed Washington's opinion that it would be impossible to successfully defend the city. No Dorchester Heights, as at Boston, where American cannon could make the wharves of the city their target. New York City's miles of shorefront and large number of Royalist sympathizers who preferred to welcome the British, dictated that the Continental Army must retreat into the countryside where they would be better able to resist.

On May 21st, Washington set out for Philadelphia, pausing to observe the shores of Staten Island which he found he could not hope to defend. Martha preceded her husband to Philadelphia, probably arriving there on May 19th, where she underwent innoculation for smallpox. John Hancock had invited the General and Mrs. Washington to stay at his residence while in Philadelphia, and to have Martha innoculated there. Washington was unwilling to subject a host to inconvenience and possible risk. The exact location of Washington's headquarters in Philadelphia has not been ascertained.

Washington spent his time in Philadelphia in consultation with the Congress. On June 3rd, Hancock expressed to Washington the thanks of Congress for "unremitted attention" to his trust and especially for assistance in making plans for the defense of the Colonies. The General was free, Hancock wrote, to return to his headquarters in New York City.

Leaving Martha in Philadelphia on the 4th of June, Washington was off for New York City, where he arrived at 1:00 o'clock in the afternoon of June 6, 1776. Both good news and bad awaited him. Good because all was quiet and progress had been made on the defenses. Bad news of a defeat at the Cedars, some thirty miles from Montreal in Canada, the death of General John Thomas from smallpox, and the rumors that Howe's fleet had embarked from Halifax for New York City.

During this period, the British Governor William Tryon had established his headquarters on a British ship in New York harbor where Royalists supplied him with fresh provisions and information on the activities in New York City. Tryon awaited the arrival of the British Halifax forces.

On July 9, 1776, Washington received from Philadelphia the resolution of Congress, stating that "The United States of America were free and independent and . . . absolved from all allegiances to the British Crown." Washington announced in his general orders that "the several brigades are to be drawn up this evening on their respective parades, at six o'clock, when the declaration of Congress, showing the grounds and reasons of this measure, is to be read with audible voice."

With the Declaration of Independence, the die was cast for war. That evening, the equestrian statue of King George III at Bowling Green was toppled and broken up with much of the metal carried to Litchfield, Connecticut, and melted into bullets.

On July 19th, the British man-of-war "Eagle" arrived in New York harbor with Vice Admiral Lord Richard Howe, who had command of the British fleet in America. His younger brother, General William Howe, had replaced General Thomas Gage in May 1775 as commander of the British troops in North America. The British forces landed unopposed at Staten Island, and later moved to Long Island, landing at Fort Hamilton and Gravesend Bay, locations too far from the American positions for any effective opposition.

On August 28th, Washington was on Long Island, overseeing the defenses in Brooklyn where the most intensive fighting took place at the Cortelyeau House, Fifth Avenue and Third Street, and at "Battle Pass," in Prospect Park. After three days of combat and heavy losses, the estimate being a total of fourteen hundred killed, wounded, missing, and prisoners of war, Washington's Council of War, the seven Generals, then engaged in the defense of Brooklyn, determined upon retreat.

Washington hastened across the East River, and ordered all boats from the Battery to Harlem to assemble. Under cover of fog and darkness, the men and guns of the defeated army were transported to Manhattan. The next morning, August 30, 1776, the British discovered that the Americans had slipped away, and the opportunity to capture Washington's Army was lost.

Four days later, the British crossed the East River, landing on Manhattan at Kipps Bay, now 34th Street, with the intention of separating the American forces at the southern end of the island from the troops to the north. However, General Israel Putnam was able to march his troops from lower Manhattan along the west road near the Hudson River, to join with the main army at Harlem Heights.

On September 16th, the retreating Americans stiffened, and turned on the advancing British. What at first seemed merely a skirmish, developed into a major engagement. The heaviest fighting occured about where the General Grant National Memorial stands at 122nd Street.

Although Congress had determined that New York City should not be burned to deny its use to the occupying British forces, fire nevertheless did engulf the City on September 21st. The British claimed that the fire had broken out at various places, and that the Americans had set the City on fire. Washington wrote, "Providence, or some good honest fellow, has done more for us than we were willing to do for ourselves."

American defensive positions at 147th Street and 154th Street slowed the British advance northward along the thirteen miles of Manhattan Island. New York City then occupied less than the southern three miles of the island. North of the city was Greenwich, and further north, about five miles from City Hall, the area known as Bloomingdale. The northern end of the island contained few houses at that time, the finest being the Morris mansion which Washington used as his headquarters after the British landing at Kipps Bay and his retreat to White Plains.

Fort Washington at the northern end of Manhattan Island fell to the British Forces on November 16, 1776. The loss of Fort Washington with its garrison of over 2,000 men and a large amount of valuable military supplies was the worst defeat suffered by the American forces during the war. Washington did not return to New York City until the end of the war in 1783 although he was rarely more than a few days march away.

CHAPTER II

GEORGE WASHINGTON
IN THE HUDSON RIVER HIGHLANDS

The importance of the Hudson River Highlands as a natural fortress during the Revolutionary War, controlling navigation on the Hudson River and the Post Roads, between New York and Albany is difficult to overemphasize.

General Washington saw the necessity of using the Highlands as a permanent fortified base for the Continental Armies in the Fall of 1776, and from then on to the end of the war, it was his determined and continuous policy to hold and fortify the Highlands on the Hudson River against attack from the British Army in New York City.

A sense of fairness and accuracy impelled us to write a brief account of the strategic military importance and far-reaching political significance of the events that occurred during the Revolutionary War on that section of the Hudson River, between Verplanck's Point, a few miles south of Peekskill, on the east shore, and Stony Point, on the west, and Beacon and Newburgh twenty miles to the north.

This entire section, known then as well as now as the "Highlands," well may be called the "Cradle of the Republic" both from a military and a political point of view. I use the words "Cradle of the Republic" advisedly, and without apology to Boston, Philadelphia, Saratoga, or Yorktown, for none of these historical shrines in our Revolutionary History, combined both military exploits and political events, compared to that section of the Hudson River which includes Stony Point, Forts Montgomery and Clinton, West Point—the main American stronghold—Washington's chief Headquarters at New Windsor and Newburgh, Temple Hill at New Windsor, Fishkill—the depot of supply—and the site of General Arnold's headquarters at the Beverly Robinson House, at Garrison.

In the words of Daniel Webster "It is wise for us to recur to the history of our ancestors", and we might add, to ascertain the facts and transmit accurately their gallant and glorious achievements to posterity.

As early as the 25th of May, 1775, over a year before the Declaration of Independence, the Continental Congress, at the request of the Provincial Congress of New York, adopted the following resolution: "That a post be taken in the Highlands, on each side of the

River, and batteries erected, and that experienced persons be immediately sent to examine said River, in order to discover where it will be most advisable and proper to obstruct the navigation."

In accordance with this resolution, a committee was appointed and made a report on the 13th of June, 1775, suggesting the erection of what were afterwards known as Forts Constitution, Clinton, and Montgomery, in the Highlands; the two latter situated on the same side of the river about four miles to the south of West Point, which was not then fortified.

There were also three points in the Highlands at which it was sought to obstruct navigation, through the use of heavy iron chains on booms, first between Fort Montgomery and Anthony's Nose, the second at Pollopel's Island, in Newburgh Bay, and the third between Constitution Island and West Point, the first two with not much success. Later on, April 30, 1778, a great chain was stretched from West Point to Constitution Island, This was five hundred yards long, and it is said to have weighed one hundred and eighty-six tons. It was supported on logs, so that it floated but a few feet below the surface, and remained in place until the declaration of peace, being taken up in the Autumn of 1783. The iron for this was made at Forest Dean Mine and at Ringwood, and the links were forged by Noble, Townsend Co., at the Sterling Furnace Works, about twenty-five miles to the southwest of West Point. The links weighed about 120 pounds and were taken over the mountains on muleback or by ox carts, two or three links at a time, and were finally forged together at the forges situated near New Windsor, one of which was the Brewster forge at Moodna. They were then floated down the river to West Point and put in place there. The great chain was protected a few yards below by a boom of huge short logs united at the ends by chains so as to resemble a rope ladder.

In addition to the forts already mentioned, redoubts were erected at Verplanck's Point, Peekskill (known as Fort Independence), Continental Village, and on Anthony's Nose, and later north and south redoubts opposite West Point.

Washington Comes to Highlands

General Washington's first introduction to the Highlands was after the battle of White Plains, when he went to Peekskill, on November 10, 1776, to visit General Heath, whose headquarters were there. The following is an extract from the Memoire of Maj. Gen. William Heath: "November 11, 1776. The Commander-in-Chief directed our General (Heath) to attend him in taking a view of Fort Montgomery and other works up the river. Lord Sterling, Generals

James and George Clinton, General Mifflin and others were of the company. They went as far up the river as Constitution Island, which is opposite to West Point, the latter of which was not then taken possession of; but the glance of the eye at it, without going ashore, evinced that this post was not to be neglected. There was a small work and blockhouse on Constitution Island. Fort Montgomery was in a considerable forwardness. November 12, 1776. The Commander-in-Chief directed our General (Heath) to ride early in the morning with him to reconnoitre the grounds at the gorge of the Highlands, on both sides of the River, with written instructions to secure and fortify them with all possible expedition, making a distribution of his troops to the different posts, and, at about 10 o'clock a.m., General Washington crossed over the river into the Jerseys. November 13th. Our General (Heath) made a disposition of the troops under his command to their several destinations. Col. Huntington's and Tyler's regiments to the west side of the Hudson to Sidmun's Bridge on Ramapough (Ramapo) River, to cover the passes into the Highlands, on that side; Prescott's Ward's, and Wylly's regiments, of Parson's brigade to the south entrance of the Highlands, beyond Robinson's Bridge; Gen. George Clinton's brigade to the Heights above Peekskill Landing; Gen. Scott's brigade, with the three regiments of Gen. Parson's brigade, Gen. James Clinton, with the troops under his command, were at the fort up the River (Forts Clinton, Montgomery, and Constitution)."

The actual written instructions given General Heath by George Washington, when he appointed him on November 12th, to command of the forces in the Highlands, are as follows:

"Your Division, with such troops as are now at Fort Montgomery, Independence (just north of Peekskill) and Constitution, are to be under your command, and remain in this quarter, for the security of the above posts and the passes through the Highlands, from this place, and the one on the west side of the Hudson River. Unnecessary it is for me to say anything to evince the importance of securing land and water communication through these passes or to prove the indespensable necessity of using every exertion in your power to have such works erected for the defense of them, as your own judgment assisted by that of your Brigadiers and Engineer, may show the expediency of. You will not only keep in view of the importance of securing these passes, but the necessity of doing it without delay; not only from the probability of the enemy's attempting to seize them, but from the advanced season which will not admit of any spade work after the frost sets in. Lose not a moment, therefore, in choosing the grounds on the east and west side of the River on which your intended work are to be erected. Let your men designed for each post be speedily alloted, etc."

After leaving Peekskill on November 12, 1776, Washington led his army into New Jersey to win victories at Trenton and Princeton, and later be defeated at Brandywine and Germantown, in Pennsylvania.

There was no actual fighting in the Highlands until October 6, 1777, when the British, in a half-hearted attempt to relieve Gen. Burgoyne, captured the two main forts in the Highlands, Clinton and Montgomery adjoining each other near the present west entrance to the Bear Mountain Park Bridge.

The American garrisons, under Generals George and James Clinton, were composed of untrained militia and although heavily outnumbered fought gallantly until overpowered; many, however, escaped in the darkness, including both commanding officers. The Americans gave a good account of themselves and the British losses were quite heavy, particularly among the higher officers.

Sought to Strengthen Defenses

The comparative ease with which the British expedition had passed up the Hudson River, resulting in the capture of Forts Clinton, Montgomery, Independence and Constitution, caused much anxiety to General Washington. The British had burned Kingston, where the Provincial Legislature was in session, also setting fire to Clermont* and all of its surrounding outbuildings. Washington wrote the following instructions to General Israel Putnam, then in command of the Highlands:

"Headquarters—2nd, December, 1777.

"Dear sir: The importance of the Hudson River in the present contest, and the necessity of defending it, are subjects which have been frequently and fully discussed, and are so well understood that it is unnecessary to enlarge upon them. These facts at once appear, when it is considered that it runs through the whole State; that is the only passage by which the enemy from New York or any part of our coast, can ever hope to co-operate with an army from Canada; that the possession of it is indispensably essential to preserve the communication between the Eastern, Middle and Southern States; and, further, that upon its security, in a great measure, depends our chief supplies of flour for the subsistence of such forces as we may have occasion for, in the course of the war, either in the Eastern or Northern Departments, or in the country lying high up on the West side of it. These facts are familar to you. I therefore request you, in the most urgent terms, to turn your most serious and active attention to this infinitely important object. Seize the present opportunity, and employ your whole force and all the means in your power for erecting and completing, as far as it shall be possible, such works, and obstructions as may be necessary to defend and secure the river against any further attempts of the enemy, etc."

On the recommendation of Governor Clinton and Lord Sterling,

---

*Clermont was the home of Chancellor Robert R Livingston. As the British torched the estate, the family and servants escaped. In a few years, Clermont was rebuilt and refurbished.

West Point was decided upon as the logical and strongest position to fortify. On January 20, 1778, a brigade of Continental troops, under General Parsons, were ordered to West Point and began the construction of the most formidable fortress of the Revolutionary War.

The first recorded visit of General Washington to West Point is in Thacher's Military Journal, on the date of July 16, 1778:

"His excellency, the Commander-in-Chief, visited West Point to take a view of the works, which are being constructed there. His arrival was announced by the discharge of thirteen cannons, the number of the United States."

About two months later Washington visited West Point again and wrote the following letter from there to General Duportail, the Chief Engineer of the Army:

"West Point, September 19, 1778.

"Sir: I have perused the Memorial which you delivered, relative to the defense of the North River at this place, and upon a view of it, highly approve what you have offered upon the subject. Col Kosciuszko, who was charged by Congress with the direction of the forts and batteries, has already made such progress in the construction of them as would render any alteration of them in the general plan, a work of too much time, and the favorable testimony which you have given to Colonel Kosciuszko's ability prevents any uneasiness on this head."

From July 16, 1778, the date of Washington's first visit to West Point, until the end of the war, five years later, well over half of his time was spent in the Highlands.

The storming of Stony Point, by General Anthony Wayne, on July 15, 1779, and the capture of the entire British garrison, with all the artillery, ammunition and stores, was one on the most daring and glorious feats of arms during the war. The following is the official report of General Wayne to the Commander-in-Chief:

"Stony Point — July 16, 1779
2 o'clock A.M.

"Dear General: The fort and garrison with Col. Johnston are ours. Our officers and men behaved like men who are determined to be free.
Yours most sincerely,
ANT'Y WAYNE."

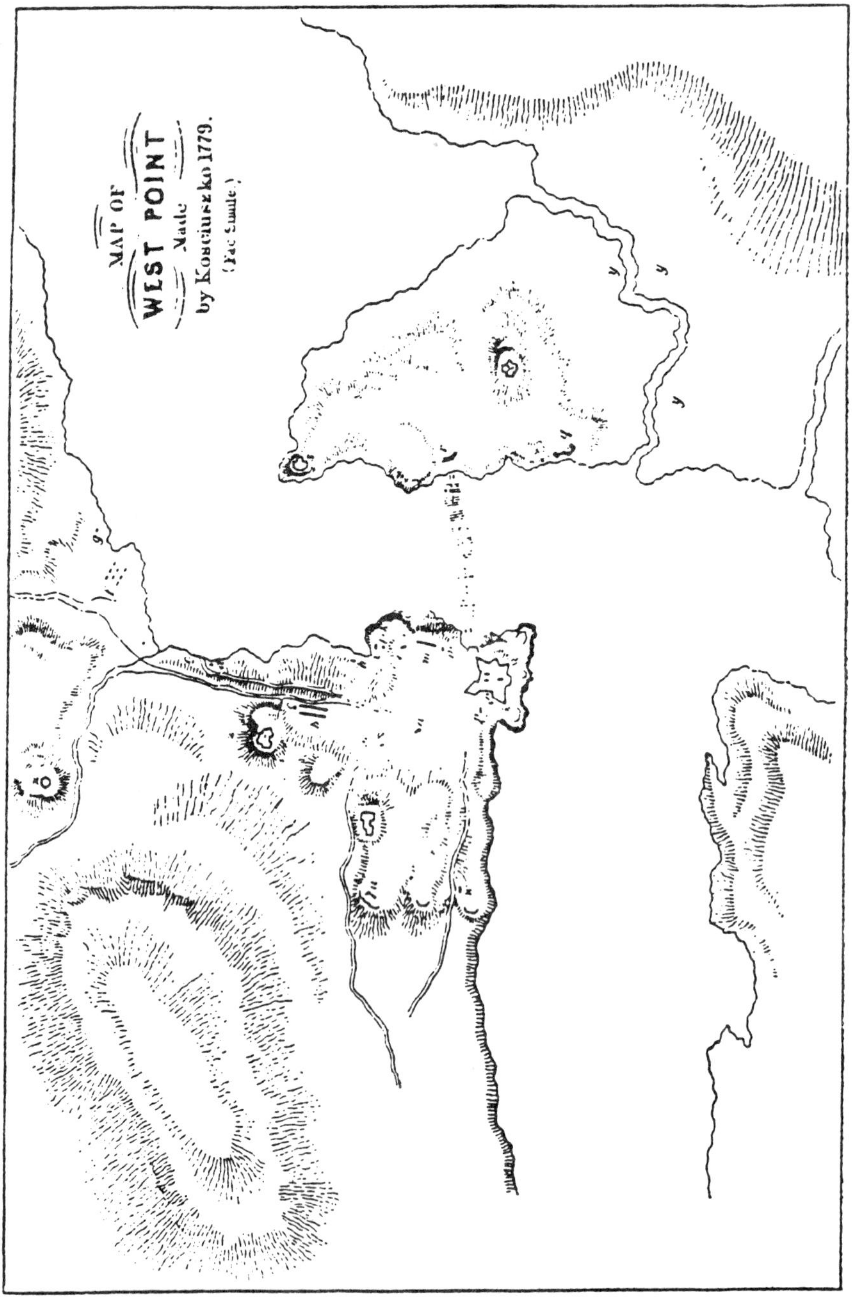
MAP OF
WEST POINT
Made
by Kosciuszko 1779.
(Fac Simile.)

The Army was immediately informed of the victory by General Washington from Headquarters at New Windsor:

> "The Commander-in-Chief is happy to congratulate the army on the success of our arms under Brig. Gen. Wayne, who last night, with corps of light infantry, surprised and took the enemy post at Stony Point, with the whole garrison, cannon, and stores, with very inconsiderable loss on our side."

Refused Crown in Newburgh

There is apparently some confusion in the minds of the present generation concerning the indignant answer made by the Commander-in-Chief of the offer of a crown from some of his disgruntled officers, in 1782. It was not delivered as is often stated in a speech from Temple Hill, near Newburgh, but was contained in a letter written to Col. Nicola, a meritorious foreign officer in the Pennsylvania line, from the Newburgh Headquarters, on May 22, 1782, rebuking the attempts of those officers, dissatisfied with the weakness of the incompetent Congress at Philadelphia, who wished to make him "King by the voice of the Army" and establish a constitutional monarchy in our country. The firm rebuke administered by Washington to those officers with monarchial proclivities was delivered ten months prior to the well known Law and Order Speech at Temple Hill, and has no connection with it, and constituted the mightiest blow struck for the formation of our republic since the Declaration of Independence was proclaimed at Philadelphia, seven years before. Washington's letter to Col. Nicola concluded with these words:

> "Let me conjure you, then if you have any regard for your country, concern for yourself or posterity, or respect for me, to banish these thoughts from your mind, and never communicate as from yourself, or anyone else a sentiment of like nature."

Later, on March 15, 1783, at Temple Hill, New Windsor, before a convention of officers, presided over by General Gates, the Commander-in-Chief answered the justifiable complaint of his officers for back pay, many of whom had expended their own means and were about to be discharged on empty promises in one of the most memorable addresses in American history and prevented his officers from open rebellion against the Congress by his wise advise and sagacious leadership. Amid the most profound attention, Washington commenced reading:

> "Gentlemen: By an annonymous summons, an attempt has been made to convene you together. Now inconsistent with the rules of propriety, how unmilitary, how subversive of all order and discipline; let the good sense of the Army decide."

Pausing a moment, he drew out his spectacles, carefully wiped and adjusted them, and while doing so, remarked:

"These eyes, my friends, have grown dim and these locks white in the service, yet I have never doubted the justice of my country."

He pointed out the dreadful consequences of following the advice of the anonymous writer, subsequently ascertained to be Major Armstrong (afterwards Secretary of War):

"Either to draw their swords against their country, or retire, if war continues, from the defense of all they hold dear.

Washington said:

"I conjure you, in the name of our common country, as you value your own sacred honor, as you respect the rights of humanity, to express your utmost horror and detestation of the man, who wishes, under any specious pretenses, to overturn the liberties of your country and who wickedly attempts to open the floodgates of civil discord, and deluge our rising empire in blood."

The convention resolved, unanimously, among other things, that the Army have unshaken confidence in Congress and view with abhorrence and reject with disdain the infamous proposition contained in a late anonymous address to officers of the Army.

This address of Washington, upholding military discipline and our existing civil government is as sublime a speech as ever delivered by any American. It was the first law and order speech which has become so common today, and had a far reaching effect on maintaining intact the fruits of victory already won after seven long years of deprivations and warfare.

The famous letter of congratulation and advice to the Governors of the Thirteen States pointing out the course he deemed it the duty and interest of the country to adopt, was written by General Washington on June 8, 1783, from his headquarters at Newburgh, and is one of the most important state papers in our history, and also stands next in general acclaim to the better known "Farewell Address". The following is an extract from this letter of advice:

"Where is the man to be found who wished to remain indebted for the defense of his own person and property at the exertions, the bravery, and the blood of others, without making one generous effort to pay the debt of honor and gratitude? In what part of the continent shall we find any man or body of men who would not blush to stand up and propose measures purposely calculated to rob the soldier of his stipend and the public creditor of his due? And were it possible that such a flagrant instance of injustice could ever happen, would it not excite the general indignation and tend to bring down upon the authors of such measures the aggravated vengence of heaven?"

Washington on Compensation

This is General Washington's view of adjusted compensation for the officers and men of the Revolutionary Army. It will be observed that the sentiment expressed, the very words used, such as "debt of honor" and the arguments set forth are almost identical with those advanced by the American Legion of today. The main difference being the extent to which General Washington urged compensation for his officers and soldiers, far beyond anything considered or proposed now in Congress. He advocated half pay for life for his officers, and land donations exemption from taxation, back pay and one full year's pay for his men.

Among other suggestions in his well known letter of congratulations and advice to the Governors, the Commander-in-Chief urged the building up of a citizen army or militia in the following words:

"The militia of this country must be considered as the palladium of our security, and the first effectual resort in case of hostility; it is essential, therefore, that the same system should pervade the whole, that the formation and discipline of the militia of the continent should be absolutely uniform; and that the same species of arms, accountrements, and military apparatus, should be introduced in every part of the United States. No one, who has not learned it from experience, can conceive the difficulty, expense, and confusion which result from a contrary system, or the vague arrangements which have hitherto prevailed."

This is practically our system of national defense today in which the reserves constitute a trained backup for our regular military forces. It is truly a democratic, American system of national defense and, besides, is voluntary and the least costly.

The letter to Col. Nicola refusing the crown, the speech on law and order at the "Temple" and the letter of congratulation and advice to the Governors, were all composed by Washington at his headquarters at Newburgh and all three are among his most important public utterances.

Students and readers may well ask why has the defense of the Highlands and Washington's Newburgh letters, and the address at Temple Hill been given so little attention by historians? My answer is that almost all the historians of the Revolutionary War hailed from New England and wrote from the point of view of Bunker Hill,

Concord, Lexington, and the Boston Tea Party. Lodge, in his life of Washington, although he mentions Washington's refusal of the crown and his speech to the dissatisfied and rebellious officers, does not even indicate that these events took place at his headquarters in Newburgh and vicinity. Most New England historians, and most of the very best, came from the Commonwealth of Massachusetts and are apparently reluctant to admit that New York State participated in the Revolutionary War, in spite of the fact that 92 out 308 skirmishes and battles fought during that war were fought within the boundaries of New York State, including the decisive battle of Saratoga.

It is also well to remember that New York State gave such leaders as the Clintons, Livingstons, Alexander Hamilton, John Jay, Gouverneur and Lewis Morris, and Generals Schuyler, McDougall, Montgomery and Herkimer, the two latter being killed in battle, to the revolutionary cause.

My object in writing this monograph is to emphasize the extremely important part played by the Highlands in the

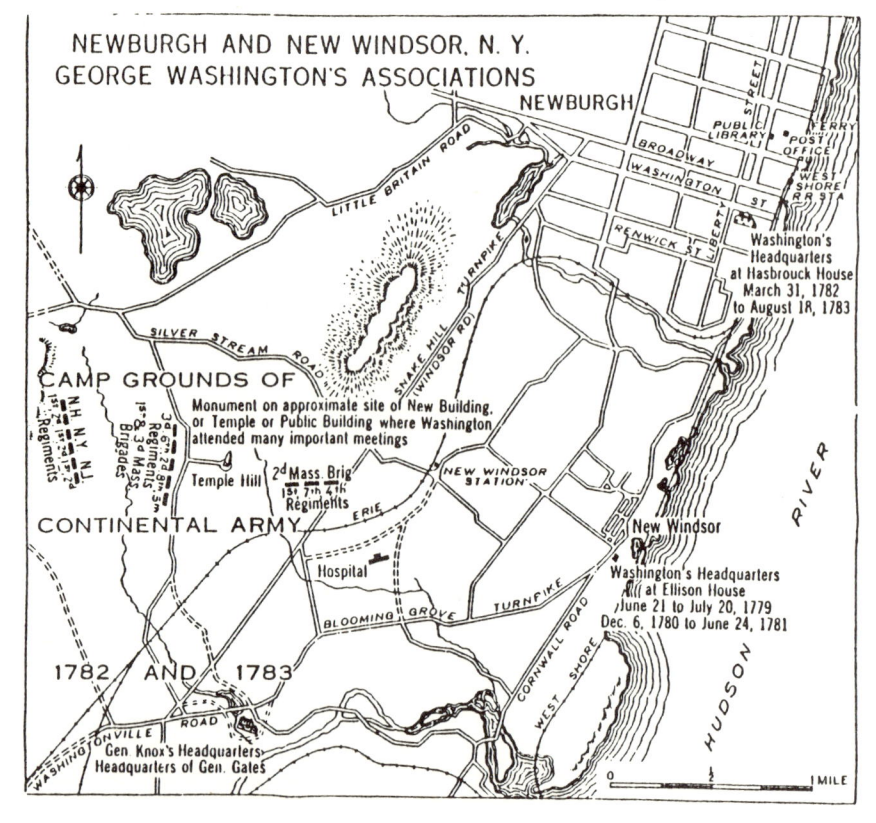

Revolutionary War, and to show that Washington had his headquarters in the Highlands for a longer period than anywhere else during the entire war, and practically right up to the time he took leave of his principal officers at Fraunce's Tavern in New York City on December 4, 1783.

I have endeavored to compute the number of days that Washington had his headquarters in the Highlands, and have reached the startling conclusion that he spent 813 days at his various headquarters there, and approximately 235 additional days within a radius of twenty-five miles. In other words, more than one-third of the eight year period of the Revolutionary War was spent by Washington in the Highlands, and more than half of the last five years.

There were three main headquarters which Washington established for a considerable length of time on the Hudson River—at New Windsor, West Point, and Newburgh—description of which, as given below, are taken from authentic historical sources:

"William Ellison House at New Windsor. Lossing refers to this house as 'a plain Dutch house long since decayed and demolished.' It was located on the hill immediately south of the Village of New Windsor, overlooking the Hudson and only a few miles from his later and more famous headquarters at Newburgh. The Ellison House served as headquarters on two different occasions, from June 24th to July 21st, 1779, and from December 6th, 1780 to June 25th, 1781."

To those skeptical people who have doubted that Independence Day was celebrated on the right or correct date, the following order of George Washington, taken from the Orderly Book, should set their minds at rest:

"Sunday, July 4th, 1779, New Windsor.

"This day being the anniversary of our glorious independence will be commemorated by firing of thirteen cannons from West Point at 10 o'clock P.M. The Commander-in-Chief thinks proper to grant a general pardon to all prisoners in the army under sentence of death. They are to be released from confinement accordingly."

The headquarters of the Commander-in-Chief was transferred to the Moore house at West Point on July 21, 1779, and remained there until November 28, 1779. The house occupied by Washington was situated in what is now called Washington Valley, about a mile to the north of West Point and near the River. It was designated in general orders as the "Moore House", and was built prior to 1749 by John Moore, a prominent merchant of New York and grandfather of the Bishop of Virginia, Richard Channing Moore. The house must have been a large costly structure, being in its day known as "Moore's folly." It was during this period that the strong works of the fortress and vicinity were constructed.

Disposition of Troops

During the autumn of 1779, when General Washington had his headquarters at West Point, the garrison consisted of two Massachusetts brigades at the Point; the Connecticut line on the east side of the River, between Garrison's House and the Robinson House; and the North Carolina brigade on Constitution Island. The light infantry and the Maryland line were encamped from Fort Montgomery northward, and Nixon's brigade occupied Continental Village. In the assignment of the Army to winter quarters, the Massachusetts line was left to garrison West Point and the Highlands, the command of which was assumed by General Heath on the 28th of November. The winter of 1779-80 was one of unexampled severity at West Point and in the Highlands. The troops, except those on garrison duty, were cantonized in huts two miles back of West Point, on the "Public Meadows", and at Budd's on the east side of the river. So intense was the cold, that for a period of forty days, no water dripped from the roofs which sheltered them. The snow was four feet deep on a level, requiring much labor to be constantly engaged in keeping open the communications with the half dozen redoubts built in the vicinity of West Point. Twice during the winter, north redoubt at Garrison's was barely saved from total destruction. Both North and South redoubts on the east side of the River were "built of stone four feet high; above the stone wood filled in with earth, very dry, no ditch, a bomb proof and three batteries outside the fort."

At his headquarters at "Moore House," West Point, on July 29, 1779, the Commander-in-Chief issued the following remarkable order against swearing:

> "Many and pointed orders have been issued against that unmeaning and abominable custom of swearing, notwithstanding which with much regret, the General observes that it prevails, if possible more than ever; his feelings are continually wounded by the oaths and imprecations of the soldiers whenever he is in hearing of them. The name of that Being from whose bountiful goodness we are permitted to exist and enjoy the comforts of life, is incessantly imprecated and profaned, in a manner as wanton as it is shocking. For the sake, therefore, of religion, decency and order, the General hopes and trusts that officers of every rank will use their influence and authority to check a vice which is as unprofitable as it is wicked and shameful. If the Officers would make it an unavoidable rule to reprimand, and if that does not do, punish soldiers for offenses of this kind, it could not fail of having the desired effect."

Hasbrouck House

The Hasbrouck House at Newburgh, which is the most important of all Washington headquarters, is still standing and justly claims to be among our few famous Revolutionary shrines. The Hasbrouck House has the distinction of being Washington's main headquarters from April 1, 1782 to August 19, 1783, which is for far longer than any other headquarters. It may properly claim to be the first White House in America.

It was from the Hasbrouck House, as referred to above, that Washington wrote his famous letter of advice to the Governors of the States, and his reply to Col. Nicola, disdaining the offer of a crown. It is probable that his law and order speech delivered at the "Temple" or new building in New Windsor was written in the Hasbrouck House.

Owing to the reputation of Congress for weakness and incapacity, General Washington, after Yorktown, was for all practical purposes not only the Commander-in-Chief of the Army, but also the real ruler of the Confederation. A steady stream of distinguished foreign officers and statesmen sought General Washington at his Newburgh headquarters.

General Knox occupied the John Ellison House, which is still standing at New Windsor, until he took command at West Point. General von Steuben occupied the Verplanck House, across the river at Fishkill, where the Society of the Cincinnati was organized on May 13, 1783. The Verplanck House is often referred to as Mount Gulian. The Marquis de Lafayette had his headquarters at the Brewster House in New Windsor, and the other generals were all near by.

The Marquis de Chastellux describes his visit, on December 5, 1782, to Washington's Headquarters at Newburgh, in the following words:

> "We passed the North River as night came on, and arrived at 6 o'clock at Newburgh, where I found Mr. and Mrs. Washington, Colonel Tilgham (Tilghman), Col. Humphreys, and Major Walker. The headquarters at Newburgh consist of a single house, neither vast nor commodious, which is built in the Dutch fashion. The largest room in it (which was the proprietor's parlour for his family, and which General Washington has converted into his dining room) is in truth tolerably spacious, but it has seven doors and only one window. The chimney, or rather the chimney back, is against the wall; so that there is in fact but one vent for the smoke, and the fire is in the room itself."

Washington's Headquarters at Hasbrouck House (Newburgh, N.Y.)

Martha Washington spent considerable time at the Newburgh Headquarters, and helped in receiving the distinguished guests and in entertaining the Generals and their wives. It is related that she maintained a flourishing flower garden in front of the Hasbrouck House.

The Order of the Purple Heart, for wounded veterans of all our wars and for those who have been awarded Meritorious Service Citations, was established by General George Washington at his headquarters at Newburgh on August 7th, 1782. The general order for the creation of the Purple Heart, issued at that time, reads as follows:

> "The General ever desirous to cherish a virtuous ambition in his soldiers, as well as to foster and encourage every species of Military merit, directs that whenever any singularly meritorious action is performed, the author of it shall be permitted to wear on his facings over the left breast, the figure of a heart in purple cloth of silk, edged with narrow lace or binding. Not only instances of unusual gallantry, but also of extraordinary fidelity and essential service in any way shall meet with a due reward. Before this favor can be conferred on any man, the particular fact, or facts, on which it is to be grounded must be set forth to the Commander-in-Chief accompanied with certificates from the Commanding officers of the regiment and brigade to which the candidate for reward belonged, or other incontestable proofs, and upon granting it, the name and regiment of the person with the action so certified are to be enrolled in the book of merit which will be kept at the orderly office. Men who have merited this last distinction to be suffered to pass all guards and sentinels which officers are permitted to do.
>
> The road to glory in a patriot army and a free country is thus open

to all — this order is also to have retrospect to the earliest stages of the war, and to be considered as a permanent one."

This was the first instance in the military history of the United States that a badge of honor was provided for enlisted men and non-commissioned officers.

Temple Hill

It was at Temple Hill, New Windsor, that General Washington made his famous law and order speech destroying "the seeds of discord and separation between the civil and military powers of the continent."

There is a small stone monument on the site of the Temple which reads:

"On this ground was erected the "Temple" or New Public Building 1782-83. The Birthplace of the Republic."

Lossing describes the building from the lips of Major Burnet:

"As a structure of rough hewn logs, oblong, square in form, one story in height, a door in the middle, many windows and a broad roof."

Lossing, writing back in 1851, says:

"It is, indeed, a hallowed spot, and if the old stone house at Newburgh, is worthy of the fostering regard of the State because it was the headquarters of the beloved Washington, surely the site of the Temple, where he achieved his most glorious victory, deserves some monument to perpetuate the memory of its place and associations."

Services in Temple

The following is a description of the Temple taken from Washington's Orderly book as of February 13, 1783:

"The new building being so far finished as to admit the troops to attend public worship therein, after tomorrow it is directed that divine service should be performed there every Sunday by several Chaplains of the New Windsor cantonment in rotation."

The New Building or Temple was a one-story structure, put up by the labor and materials furnished by the different Regiments. It stood on an eminence at New Windsor and was "handsomely finished with a spacious hall sufficient to contain a brigade of troops on Lord's Day, for public worship."

A further reference to the Temple as taken from the Military Diary of General Heath:

"Upon an eminence the troops erected a building handsomely

finished with spacious hall, sufficient to contain a brigade of troops on the Lord's Day, for public worship, with an orchestra at one end. The vault of the ceiling was arched, at each end of the hall were two sitting rooms conveniently situated for the issuing of general orders, for the sitting of Boards of Officers, Court Martials, etc., and an office and store for the quartermaster and Commissory's departments. On the top was a cupola and flag staff."

The Temple was struck by lighting on the 11th of June, 1783, and was afterwards wrecked by order of the Quartermaster General and no vestages of it remain.

No Revolutionary history of the Highlands would be complete without reference to Fishkill Village, situated about three miles back from the east side of the Hudson River opposite Newburgh. Fishkill was selected early in the war as the natural depot of supplies for its secure position at the northern end of the Highlands and for being on a direct route of communication with the New England States. Large quantities of stores from Dutchess and adjacent counties as well as from the Eastern States were accumulated there for the use of the Continental Army.

The Village of Fishkill, although only containing some fifty houses, became the principal depot of the American Army. Large barracks, magazines, hospitals and store houses were erected near the Village.

Hundreds of heroic Patriots lie buried in the soldiers burial ground, a short distance to the south of the Village.

The Dutch and Episcopal Churches served as hospitals, prisons and a meeting place for the provincial Legislature.

Washington Visits Fishkill

General Washington stopped for brief visits in October and November, 1778, at the house of Col. John Brinckerhoff, and this house is still standing, a little more than a mile from the Village. He, however, never really made his headquarters at Fishkill. When George Washington was at the Hasbrouck House at Newburgh, he often crossed over to Fishkill Landing, now Beacon, and visited his friend, Capt. Wm. Denning, at Denning's Point; and Major Schenck, at the Tuller House.

General Washington had his headquarters in Fredericksburg, between Pawling, Dutchess County, and Patterson, Putnam County, in the Autumn of 1778. His headquarters were first at the house of Reed Ferris, two miles southeast of the village of Pawling, but were moved to the John Kane house and later nearer to Patterson. The

Reed Ferris house was used for the trial and resulting exoneration of General Philip Schuyler for failure to hold the northern forts against the invading troops of General Burgoyne.

A tablet has been erected by the D.A.R., marking the site of the old John Kane house which reads as follows:

> "The residence of John Kane on this site was headquarters of Washington from September twelfth to November twenty-seventh, 1778, while the second line of the Continental Army was encamped on Quaker Hill and in the Valley nearby."

George Washington's reasons for taking the Army to Fredericksburg, almost to the Connecticut line, is best understood by reading the following excerpt from his letter to John Augustine Washington:

> "Fredericksburg, September 23, 1778.
>
> "There are two capital objects which (the enemy) can have in view except the defeat and dispersion of the Army, and those are the possession of the fortifications in the Highlands by which the Communication between Eastern and Southern States would be cut off and the destruction of the French fleet at Boston, I have therefore, in order to do the best that the nature of the case will admit, strengthened the works, and reinforced the garrison in the Highlands, and throw the Army into such positions as to move eastwards or westwards as circumstances may require."

One of the most important headquarters on the Hudson River from a Historical point of view, is the Beverly Robinson House at Garrison, opposite West Point, where General Benedict Arnold had his headquarters and from whence he escaped on September 25, 1780 to board the British ship "Vulture" when his treason was discovered. The Robinson House was burned to the ground in 1892.

Although Washington made his headquarters here for only a few days, September 25-28, 1780, they were filled with drama and suspense. It was at the Robinson House in the presence of General Knox, the Marquis de Lafayette and Alexander Hamilton that Washington, who had perfect confidence in the patriotism of General Arnold was alleged to have uttered those heart rendering words, "who can we trust now"?

While Washington was using West Point as his main headquarters in the summer of 1779, he often crossed the river and rode down a couple of miles to the Robinson House, which was part of the time used as a hospital or as headquarters for Generals Heath and McDougal.

It is stated by Sparks, that on July 24, 1779, Washington was present at the celebration of the festival of St. John the Baptist, by the "American Union Lodge of Ancient Free and Accepted Masons", at the Robinson House, a little below West Point on the opposite side of the river. Some authorities believe that this meeting was held at West Point.

Certainly, on the same day of the month, 1782, Washington celebrated with the American Union (Military) Lodge, the festival of St. John the Baptist at West Point, and later, on December 27, 1782 there is a record of Washington having visited Solomon's Lodge No. 1, at Poughkeepsie, New York, for the celebration of the festival of St. John the Evangelist. A medal was struck off in 1882 in commemoration of this visit to the Poughkeepsie Lodge, which was founded on April 18, 1777.

There are still a number of houses in the Highlands, and within a radius of twenty-five miles of it, that were visited by Washington on various occasions during the war.

The George Washington Masonic Shrine, The DeWint House, at Tappan or Orangetown, in Rockland County, is best known. It is a low, one story brick and stone dwelling. Washington had his headquarters there twice from August 8 to 23, 1780, and from September 29 to October 6, on the latter occasion during the trial and tragic execution of Major Andre.

Treason House Recalled

Washington stayed for a few days, August 20-26, 1781, when his Army was crossing the Hudson, at Stony Point on the way to Yorktown, at the house (still standing) of Joshua Hett Smith, about two miles south of Stony Point, in the town of Haverstraw. This house, sometimes referred to as treason house, possesses historical interest from being the place at which Major Andre and General Arnold had their treasonable meeting on September 22, 1780. It is beautifully situated on the ridge of a hill which commands an extensive view of the Hudson.

Washington had headquarters at White Plains on October 28, 1776, when the so-called battle was fought there, in which the Americans were worsted, but the British did not follow up their success, and retired toward New York without further fighting. He also had his headquarters at White Plains from July 20 to September 16, 1778.

Later, from July 4 to August 19, 1780, just before the Yorktown Campaign, he had his headquarters at the Joseph Appleby House (Phillipsburg) on the cross roads from Dobbs Ferry to White Plains, and about three and a half miles from the ferry. The house was destroyed many years ago; it stood on a little elevation still called "Washington's Hill."

The Van Cortlandt House, two miles to the northeast of Peekskill, erected in 1773, was occupied by Washington for a brief space, June 25-30, 1781, as his headquarters.

From August 31 to October 26, 1782, General Washington had his headquarters at Verplanck's Point, a few miles south of Peekskill, at the eastern end of Kings Ferry, the main route between New England and Philadelphia. A small fort, named after Lafayette, defended Verplanck's Point.

The American and French armies encamped together at Verplanck's Point, and took turns in presenting military manoeuvers and festivals in honor of each other. On October 22, 1782, the French Army set out for Boston in order to embark for the West Indies and the American troops returned to winter quarters at New Windsor. In addition to these various headquarters listed above, General Washington on his journeys and trips of inspection through the Highlands and vicinity, stayed at houses in Ramapo, Haverstraw, Smith Clove (about fifteen miles west of West Point, where he encamped from June 7 to 21, 1780), Warwick, Chester, Goshen, Montgomery, Blooming Grove, Cornwall, Old Hurley, Marlborough, and Kingston on the west side of the river, and at the Odell House near Hartsdale, the old Van Cortlandt Manor at Croton, Salem, Yorktown Heights, Continental Village, the Mandeville House at Garrison, Patterson, Pawling, Fishkill and Poughkeepsie on the east side.

Other nearby places, like Tarrytown, although it has no Washington headquarters, is notable in Revolutionary History because of the capture of Major Andre there on September 23, 1780, by three American militia men, John Paulding, David Williams and Isaac Van Wart.

The actual length of time spent by George Washington at his various headquarters in the Highlands are as follows:

New Windsor:
    June 24-July 21, 1779 — 27 days
    December 6-June 25, 1781. — 175 days

Total   202 days

Deduct 24 days for absence on visits to Count Rochambeau in March in Newport, and in May, 1781 at Wethersfield, Conn.

Total   178 days

West Point:
  July 21 to November 28, 1779 130 days
  November 14 to November 18, 1783. 4 days

            Total 134 days

Newburgh:
  April 1, 1782 to August 19, 1783.

            Total 505 days

  Deduct 15 days for visit to Philadelphia, July 12 to July 27, 1782, 56 days during which headquarters were at Verplanck's Point August 31 to October 26, 1782, and 16 days for tour of inspection of Northern New York, July 18 to August 4, 1783.

            Total 418 days

  To other headquarters in or adjacent to the Highlands are Verplanck's Point from August 31 to October 26, 1782.

            Total 56 days

Peekskill:
  November 10-12, 1776, November 29, 1779, August 1-6, 1780, September 18, 1780, June 24 to July 2, 1781.

            Total 18 days

Fredericksburg, Dutchess County:
  September 18 to November 28, 1778.

            Total 70 days

Robinson House:
  July 31, 1780, September 23 to 27, 1780, 4 days.
  Stony Point (Smith House) August 20-25, 1781.

            Total 5 days

The Clove (Orange County):
  July 15-23, 1777, June 7-21, 1779.

            Total 22 days

White Plains:
  October 23 to November 10, 1776, July 20 to September 16, 1778.

            Total 74 days

Dobbs Ferry (Phillipsburg):
  July 4 to August 19, 1781.

            Total 46 days

George Washington Masonic Shrine,
Tappan, Rockland County:
  August 8-23, 1780, September 28 to October 6, 1780.

            Total 23 days

The actual number of days spent by Washington in the Highlands is 813 and 235 spent within a radius of thirty miles of the Highlands, including the headquarters at Fredericksburg, which is thirty miles to the west of the Highlands, and Tappan and Dobbs Ferry, which are twenty-five miles to the south, and the Clove and White Plains, fifteen miles, all within a day's march of the fortifications in the Highlands.

Closing Days in Newburgh

The scenes and events at Washington's Newburgh Headquarters during the closing days of the Revolutionary War, prior to the evacuation of the British Army of New York, is extremely interesting and instructive; and throws considerable light on the character of the Commander-in-Chief. Much has been written, alleging that Washington was not religiously inclined and had little faith in God. The following order issued on April 18, 1783, from his Newburgh Headquarters is direct proof of his profound belief in "Almighty God":

"The Commander-in-Chief orders the cessation of hostilities, between the United States of America and the King of Great Britain to be publicly proclaimed tomorrow at 12 o'clock at the New Building, and the proclamation which will be communicated herewith to be read tomorrow evening at the head of every Regiment and Corps of the Army; after which the Chaplains with the several brigades will render thanks to Almighty God for all his mercies, particularly for His overruling the wrath of men to his own glory, and causing the rage of war to cease among nations."

After issuing this almost Pious admonition addressed to the reason and consciences of the men who had followed him so long, General Washington proclaimed a day of jubilee and ordered for every man an extra ration of grog.

The announcement of peace and victory was celebrated by the troops with general rejoicing throughout the Highlands, and by imposing military ceremonies and the singing of Billing's anthem "No King But God".

In the evening there were fireworks and military salutes and the "mountain sides resounded and echoed like tremendous peals of thunder, and the flashing from thousands of fire arms in the darkness of the evening, was like unto vivid flashings of lightning from the clouds." The last act was an illumination of a gigantic scale, the watchfires on prominent hill tops (Mount Beacon) blazing from huge stacks of timber, no longer messengers of dangers, lighted up the darkness and announced the welcome tidings of peace up and down the river and on through New England on the eighth anniversary of the Battle of Lexington and Concord, which coincided with the cessation of hostilities.

It might be interesting, while referring to the peace rejoicings, to refer to a similar festival and celebration held in honor of the birth of the Dauphin of France by the American Army at West Point, on May 31, 1782. An elaborate dinner was provided by order of the Commander-in-Chief for the officers of the Army and for a great number of ladies and gentlemen from the Counties of Orange and Dutchess. According to General Heath, at half past eleven the celebration was concluded by an exhibition of fireworks very ingeniously constructed of various figures.

General Washington attended the ball in the evening and with a dignified and graceful air, having Mrs. Knox for his partner, carried down a dance of twenty couples in the arbor on the green grass.

The occasion may well have been the first use of fireworks on a big scale in the United States. However, there are numerous references to feu de joie and celebrations by the American Army at Newburgh, New Windsor and West Point, after the Battle of Yorktown, until the end of the war.

George Washington and the Patriotic Army in the Highlands were apparently partial to military festivals and celebrations of various events, and anniversaries.

On November 16, 1783, General Washington issued an order from West Point in which he "proposes to celebrate the Peace at New York by a display of fireworks and illuminations which were intended to have been exhibited at the Post (West Point) or such of them as have not been injured by time, and can be removed."

On December 3, Washington wrote from New York City to General Knox in command at West Point:

> "The splendid display of fireworks last evening was so highly satisfactory, that I must request you to present Captain Price, under whose direction they were prepared, and to the officers who assisted him, my thanks for the great skill and attention shown in the conduct of that business."

On August 17, 1793, General Washington issued his last order from his headquarters at Newburgh, after his long and memorable residence there:

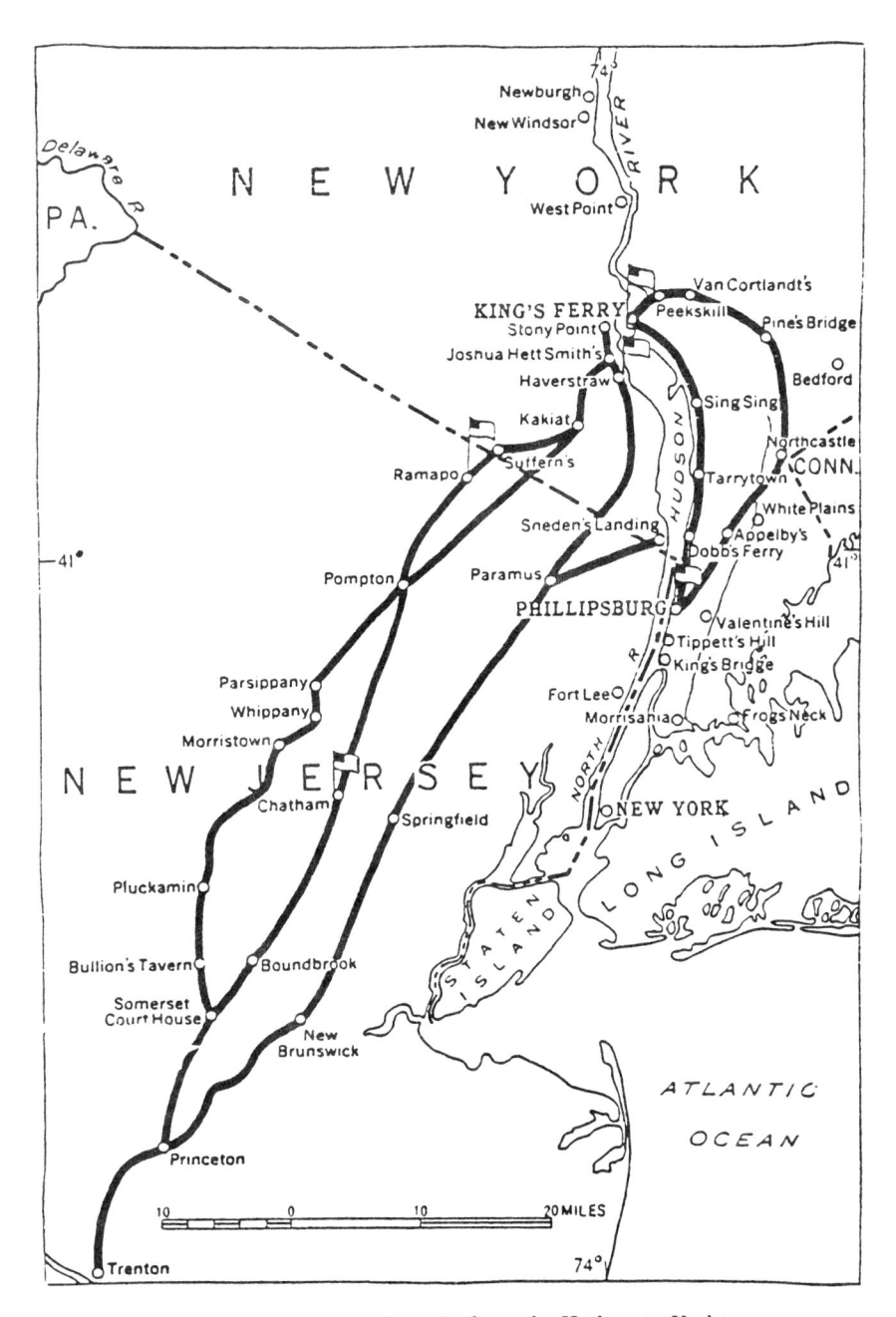

Washington's Campaign in 1781 from the Hudson to Yorktown

"The Commander-in-Chief, having been requested by Congress to give his attendance at Princeton, proposes to set out for that place tomorrow, but he expects to have the pleasure of seeing the Army again before he retires to private life."

During his absence, Major General Knox retained command of the troops, and all reports were made to him accordingly.

On the following day Washington set out for Rocky Hill, New Jersey, four miles north of Princeton, stopping at West Point on his way. An interesting incident of this visit to West Point, exists in a memorandum of the weights of several of the officers, taken on August 19, at West Point, in which General Washington is stated to be two hundred and nine pounds.

On his return from Princeton, the Commander-in-Chief stayed a few days at West Point, November 15-18, 1783, before leaving to take over the City of New York upon the evacuation of it by the British troops under Sir Guy Carlton on the 25th of November.

Receives Answer to Farewell

Before he left on November 15, he received from the officers of that part of the Army remaining on the banks of the Hudson an answer to his farewell address to the Armies of the United States.

General Knox, who had relieved General Heath in command of West Point on August 29, 1783, continued in charge there until the latter part of January, 1785, when he was appointed Secretary of War. He was succeeded by Major George Fleming, an Artillery Officer with a small detachment to look after the arsenal and ordinance stores. He remained at West Point until the establishment of an artillery school there.

On the morning of November 3, 1783, the Patriot Army encamped at Newburgh and New Windsor, assembled for the last time and listened to the farewell orders from the Commander-in-Chief issued from Princeton to the Army of the United States, invoking "the choicest of Heaven's favor upon all its members, whose efforts had secured "innumerable blessings for others", and promising his urgent recommendation to Congress on behalf of the Army.

Thacher, in his Military Journal, depicts the ensuing parting scene as painful, "no description can be adequate to the tragic exhibition. Both officers and soldiers, long unaccustomed to the affairs of private life, turned loose on the World to starve and become a prey to vulture speculators. Never can that melancholy day be forgotten when friends, companions for seven long years in joy and sorrow, were torn asunder without the hope of ever meeting again, and with the prospect of a miserable subsistance in the future".

Thus ended the occupation of the Highlands by the Continental Army after seven years of danger, hardships, and sacrifice in order to set up a new and independent nation. Verily the Highlands may justly claim to be the cradle of the Republic, in the words of the poet, Bruce:

> "No spot in all the world where Poetry and Romance are so closely blended with the heroic in history as along the bank of our Hudson."

On December 4th, General Washington took leave of his fellow officers of the Revolutionary Army, in the long room, on the second floor of Fraunce's Tavern, at Pearl and Broad Streets in New York City. This building erected in 1730 by a member of the DeLancey family is still there in good condition. The final scene of farewell was now performed by the Commander-in-Chief, who taking a glass of wine in his hand, said:

> "With a heart full of love and gratitude I now take leave of you. I most devoutly wish that your latter days may be as prosperous and happy as your former ones have been glorious and honorable."

The people living in the Highlands have a right to be proud of their historic landmarks, and none more so than the citizens of Newburgh, where Washington's Headquarters still stands, as a testimonial to the nearness of the Revolutionary War, and the far reaching events that occurred there affecting the interests and welfare of the American people, and the formation of our Republican form of Government.

Senator William M. Evarts speaking in 1883 at Newburgh at the Centennial celebration of the disbanding of the American Army, used the following eloquent and descriptive words:

> "These rolling years have shown growth, forever growth, and strength, increasing strength, and wealth and numbers ever expanding, while intelligence, freedom, art, culture and religion have pervaded and ennobled all this material greatness. Wide, however, as is our land and vast our population today, these are not the limits to the name, fame, the power of the life and the character of Washington."

and added:

> "No wonder his countrymen celebrate the transaction and scene where Washington refused a crown."

The people of the Highlands love and revere the memory of George Washington, and seek to refresh their memories and to commemorate his glorious accomplishments while serving for almost three years during the Revolutionary War along the banks of the Hudson River, in that still majestic section known as the Highlands.

Lincoln's masterful admonition and beautiful eulogy of Washington is still unsurpassed.

> "On that name no eulogy is expected. Let none attempt it. It cannot be. To add brightness to the sun or glory to the name of Washington is alike impossible. In solemn awe pronounce the name and in its naked deathless splendor leave it shining on."

Temple Hill Monument

CHAPTER III

PENNSYLVANIA AND THE GRAND LODGE OF PENNSYLVANIA

In 1777 and 1778, Washington was at Valley Forge, Pennsylvania, and on December 28, 1778, in Philadelphia at the celebration of the festival of St. John the Evangelist. The following advertisement appeared in the *Pennsylvania Packet* on December 17, 1778.

> THE Right Worshipful GRAND MASTER of the Antient and Honorable Society of Free and Accepted MASONS of the State of Pennsylvania, &c. and the Officers of the *Grand Lodge,* hereby give notice, That they have ordered a *Procession* in the *Masonic Form,* on Monday the 28th instant. All the Brethren in the City, and all distant Brethren under the grant warrant of Pennsylvania, who can conveniently attend, are earnestly requested to meet the Grand Officers at the College, precisely at Nine o'clock in the forenoon; from whence a Procession will be made to Christ Church, where a sermon will be preached by a Reverend Brother, and a Collection made; the amount of which will be laid out in the purchase of wood and the other necessaries for the relief of the poor of the city at this inclement season.
>
> There will be performances of *vocal* and *instrumental music,* suitable to the solemnity of the occasion.
>
>   *By order of the R. W. G. M.*
>   JOHN COATS, G. Sec. *Pro Tempore.*
> *Philadelphia, December 16,* A.M. 5778.

On December 21, 1778, a meeting was held at the house of Col. Thomas Proctor, of Lodge No. 2, where there were present, among others, Bro. William Ball, R. W. Grand Master; Bro. John Wood, R.W. Deputy Grand Master, and Bro. John Howard, R.W. Senior Grand Warden.

The celebration of St. John the Evangelist's Day was taken into consideration, as well as the mode of refreshment. One of the most important features of the coming pageant suggested, was to invite General George Washington, whose arrival in Philadelphia was expected, to take part in the celebration with the Brethren.

After some consideration, it was resolved that a Committee of two Brethren from Lodges 2, 3 and 4 wait upon Brother Washington upon his arrival and request his attendance.

The Brethren appointed on this Committee were:
Bro. Col. Thomas Proctor — Lodge No. 2.
Bro. Col. Isaac Melchoir — Lodge No. 2.
Bro. Col. Jacob S. Howell — Lodge No. 3.

Bro. Col. Major Scull — Lodge No. 3.
Bro. Col. Whitehead — Lodge No. 4.
Bro. Col. Alexander Boyle — Lodge No. 4.

For this purpose an address was drawn up to be presented to General Washington, who had come to Philadelphia* by order of Congress,** "in order, among other things, to confer with him on the operations of the next campaign."

Two days later, December 23, 1778, Emergency Lodges were held by both Lodges Nos. 2 and 3, at which the following action was taken:

(Minute Book, Lodge No. 2, p. 63. December 23, 1778.)

> Bro Sen. Grand Warden John Howard and Bro Kendell was deputed to wait upon Lodge No 3 in order to concur in drawing up an address to his Excellency General Washington to request his attendance with us in the procession of St John's Day. When Bros Howell and Scull of No 3 were deputed from that Lodge to agree with us, in appointing any members that might be thought proper for the Business, and it was agreed that Brother Col Proctor and Col Isaac Melchior were appointed for the purpose to meet the committee.

(Minute Book, Lodge No. 3. December 23, 1788.)

> *Lodge of Emergency* — Br Jacob S. Howell & Major Schull were appointed to wait upon No. 2 to concur in a proper mode to Address his Excellency General Washington to attend the Procession next St. John's day; who report, that The Masters Elect of the different Lodges of this City do personally wait upon Br General Washington & Inform of the time, place & mode of procession.

The result of the call of the joint committee upon General Washington, is best told in the language as recorded in the old Minute Book of Lodge No. 4:

> *December 25, 1778.* — The Committee appointed by Lodges No. 2 & 3 — to wait upon Excellency General Washington in the name of all the Lodges in the city in order to walk in Procession on St John's day, report his Excellency was pleased to express "a grateful satisfaction and consent thereto."

---

*The arrival of Gen. Washington was described in the *Pennsylvania Evening Post*, Monday, December 28, 1778, as follows: — "Last Tuesday, (December 22) George Washington, esq., commander in chief of the army of the United States arrived here (Philadelphia). Too great for pomp, and as if fond of the plain and respectable rank of a free and independent citizen, his excellency came in so late in the day as to prevent the Philadelphia troop of militia lighthorse, gentlemen, officers of the militia, and others of this city, from shewing those marks of unfeigned regard for this good and great man, which they fully intended, and especially of receiving him at his entrance into the State, and escorting him hither." (Baker, Itinerary, p. 147.)

** Baker, Itinerary, p. 147.

St. John the Evangelist's Day, December 27, 1778, falling upon a Sunday, the celebration was held upon Monday, the twenty-eighth, and is said to have surpassed any Masonic celebration in numbers and eclat ever held in America.

The following account of the celebration is copied from the *Pennsylvania Packet* or the *General Advertiser* for January 2, 1779:

PHILADELPHIA

MONDAY last, agreeable to the Constitution of the Most Ancient and Worshipful SOCIETY of FREE and ACCEPTED MASONS, was celebrated as the Anniversary of St. John the Evangelist. At nine o'clock in the morning near THREE HUNDRED of the Brethren assembled at the College, and at eleven o'clock went in regular Procession from thence to Christ Church to attend divine service. The order of Procession was as follows, viz.

1. The Sword-Bearer.

2. Two Deacons, with blue wands tipt with gold.

3. The three Orders, *Dorick, Ionick* and *Corinthian*, borne by three Brethren.

4. The Holy Bible and Book of *Constitutions*, on two crimson velvet cushions, borne by the Grand Treasurer and Grand Secretary.

5. A Reverend Brother.

6. Four Deacons, bearing wands.

7. His Excellency our illustrious Brother GEORGE WASHINGTON, Esquire, supported by the GRAND MASTER William Ball and his Deputy.

8. The two Grand Wardens, bearing the proper pillars.

9. The Past Master of the different Lodges.

10. The present masters of Lodges.

11. The Senior Wardens,
12. The Junior Wardens,
13. The Secretaries,
14. The Treasurers,

} Of the different private Lodges.

15. Brother Proctor's Band of music.

16. Visiting Brethren.

17. The Members of different Lodges, walking two and two, according to seniority.

The Procession entered the Church in the order of their march, and the Brethren took their seats in the pews of the middle (SIC) isle, which were kept empty for their reception. Prayers were read by the Reverend Mr. White, and the following Anthem was sung in its proper place by sundry of the Brethren, accompanied by the *Organ* and other instrumental music, viz.

A GRAND SYMPHONY

CHORUS

BEHOLD how good and joyful a Thing it is, Brethren, to dwell together in UNITY.

SOLO

I WILL give thanks unto Thee, O LORD! with my whole heart secretly among my Brethren, and in the Congregation will I praise Thee: I will speak the marvelous Works of thy Hands, the Sun, the Moon and the Stars, which thou hast ordained.

SOLO

THE People that walked in Darkness hath seen a great Light, and on them that dwelt in the Land of the Shadow of Death doth the glorious Light of JEHOVAH shine

SOLO

THOU hast gathered us from the East, and from the West, from the North, and from the South; Thou hast made us Companions for the Mighty upon Earth, even for Princes of Great Nations.

TRIO

O! I AM! Inspire us with Wisdom and Strength to support us in all our Troubles, that we may worship Thee in the Beauty of Holiness.

After which a most excellent and well adapted Sermon was preached by our Reverend and Worthy Brother William Smith, D. D. The text was taken from the 1st Peter 2d Chapter and 16th Verse. The Brethren have since requested the Sermon to be published, and the profits to be applied to the use of the Poor.

After divine service the Procession returned in the same order to the College; the musical bells belonging to the Church and the band of music playing proper Masonic tunes. The Brethren being all new cloathed, and the officers in the proper *Jewels* of their respective Lodges, and their other badges of dignity, made a genteel appearance.

The Brethren afterwards departed to their respective Lodges, where they dined together with their usual harmony and sociability; the sum of Four Hundred Pounds having been collected in Church among the Brethren and others their charitable Fellow citizens who honored them with their company, for the relief of the Poor.

N. B. Such Charitable Brethren and Others who have not yet had an opportunity of contributing their mite are requested to send the same to any of the following gentlemen, viz. Mess. William Ball, John Wood, John Howard, and William Shute; to whom Objects of Charity, bringing proper recommendations to the house of Mr. Ball in Market-street, after New Year's Day, between the hours of ten and twelve in the forenoon, are to apply.*

The sermon preached upon this festive occasion was published by request of the Grand Officers. A copy of this pamphlet, now exceedingly rare, is in the Library of the Grand Lodge of Pennsylvania.

The result of this great Masonic celebration in Philadelphia was two-fold — it renewed the interest of the citizens in the Craft, as it showed that most all of the Brethren were persons known to be in favor of American liberty, in direct contrast to the organization of the older Grand Lodge of "Moderns," most all of the leading members of which had left the Province on account of their adherence to the mother country, and those who remained joined the "Ancients." Thus at this time the "Moderns" had practically ceased to exist. Secondly, it brought General Washington into prominence as a Freemason, which culminated with his nomination in the year 1780 as General Grand Master of the Colonies.

The participation of General Washington in the procession in Philadelphia on St. John's Day, December 28, 1778, was the first public Masonic function in which Washington is known to have taken an active part. Henceforth, great interest was aroused among the "Ancient" Lodges of Freemasonry, both at home and in the field. The records of the various Lodges all bear evidence of the great favor in which our Fraternity was held by the officers of all grades in the Continental Army.

---

* *The Pennsylvania Packet*, or the *General Advertiser,* January 2, 1779.

TO HIS EXCELLENCY

GEORGE WASHINGTON, ESQUIRE,

GENERAL AND COMMANDER IN CHIEF

OF THE

ARMIES OF THE UNITED STATES

OF

NORTH-AMERICA;

THE FRIEND

OF HIS COUNTRY AND MANKIND,

AMBITIOUS OF NO HIGHER TITLE

IF HIGHER WAS POSSIBLE;

THE FOLLOWING SERMON,

HONOURED WITH HIS PRESENCE WHEN DELIVERED,

IS DEDICATED.

IN TESTIMONY

OF THE

SINCEREST BROTHERLY AFFECTION

AND

ESTEEM OF HIS MERIT,

BY ORDER OF THE BRETHREN,

JOHN COATS, G. Sec. pro tem.

DEDICATION OF SERMON PREACHED BY REV. BRO. WILLIAM SMITH, D.D., ST. JOHN THE EVANGELIST'S DAY, 1778.

PENNSYLVANIA AND THE GRAND LODGE OF PENNSYLVANIA

SERMON

PREACHED IN

CHRIST-CHURCH, PHILADELPHIA,

[For the Benefit of THE POOR]

BY APPOINTMENT OF AND BEFORE

THE GENERAL COMMUNICATION

OF

FREE AND ACCEPTED

MASONS

OF THE

STATE of PENNSYLVANIA,

On MONDAY December 28, 1778.

Celebrated, agreeable to their Conftitution,
as the Anniverfary of

ST. JOHN THE EVANGELIST.

By WILLIAM SMITH, D. D.
Provoft of the College and Academy of Philadelphia.

PHILADELPHIA:
PRINTED BY JOHN DUNLAP.

MDCCLXXIX.

TITLE PAGE OF SERMON PREACHED ST. JOHN THE EVANGELIST'S DAY, 1778.

—41—

Brother George Washington left Philadelphia, Tuesday morning, February 2, 1779, as shown by *The Pennsylvania Packet* of February 4, 1779:

> Tuesday Morning His Excellency General Washington set off from Philadelphia to join the army in New Jersey. During the course of his short stay (the only relief he has enjoyed from service since he first entered into it), he has been honored with every mark of esteem which his exalted qualities as a gentleman and a citizen entitle him to. His excellency's stay was rendered the more agreeable by the company of his lady, and the domestic retirement which he enjoyed at the house of the Honorable Henry Laurens, Esquire, with whom he resided.

The next Masonic function of which we have a positive knowledge of Washington's presence was at the celebration of the Festival of St. John the Baptist, June 24, 1779. The army was then encamped in Smith's Cove, Orange County, New York, about 14 miles in the rear of the Garrison at West Point.

On the 22d of June, Washington visited West Point, and on the 24th, joined with the brethren of American Union Lodge in celebrating the natal day of one of the patron saints of Freemasonry. It appears that the Lodge was opened at Nelson's Point at 8 A.M., where the officers were elected. The Lodge was then closed until 10 o'clock A.M. at West Point, where being joined by a number of Brethren from other brigades, they proceeded to the "Robinson House," slightly below West Point on the opposite side of the river. According to an old record, quoted by Brother James M. Lamberton in his address at the celebration of the Washington Sesqui-Centennial Anniversary, 1902, "After the Lodge had been opened, and after giving the names of those present, the old record continues:"

> After the usual ceremonies, the Lodge retired to a bower in front of the house, where being joined by his Excellency General Washington and family, an address was delivered to the brethren and a number of gentlemen collected on the occasion by the Rev. Dr. Hitchcock, followed by an address to the brethren in particular by Bro. Hull (General William Hull). After dinner the following toasts were drank, &c. . . His excellency Bro. Washington, having returned to the barge attended by the Wardens and Secretary of the Lodge, amidst a crowd of brethren, the music playing "God save America," embarked, his departure was announced by three cheers from the shore, answered by three from the barge, the music beating the "Grenadier's March."

Towards the close of the year 1779, the American army again took up their winter quarters at Morristown in New Jersey. At this place, various military Lodges which had been organized in the American army were at work. As St. John the Evangelist's Day drew nigh, the Brethren, having in mind the successful celebration in Philadelphia a year previous, made preparations to hold a Festal Lodge in Morristown upon that occasion, being nominally under care of the American Union Lodge, yet all "Ancient" Brethren in the encampment being invited. For this purpose, the "furniture" of St. John's Lodge, No. 1, of Newark, was borrowed. The following memorandum is taken from the old Minute Book of the Lodge, under date December 24, 1779 *(verbatim et literatim)*:

> An acct. of sundrie articles taken out of the Lodge Chest of Newark St. John's Lodge, No. 1, by consent of Bro. John Robinson, Bro. Lewis Ogden, Brother Moses Ogden and Lent unto Brother Thomas Kinney and Bro. Jerry Brewin to carry as far as Morris Town, said Bro's Kinney & Brewin promising on the word of Brothers to return the same articles as p'r Inventory below unto our Bro. John Robinson, present Secretary when called-for witness our hands Brothers as below—
>
> 24 Aprons besides one that was bound and fring'd.
>
> 3 Large Candlesticks.
>
> 2 Ebony Truntchions tipt with silver.
>
> 3 Large Candlemolds.
>
> 1 Silk Pedestal Cloth Bound with Silver Lace.
>
> 1 Damask Cutchion.
>
> 1 Silver Key with a blue Ribbon striped with black.
>
> 1 Silver Levell with a blue Ribbon striped with black.
>
> 1 Silver Square with a blue Ribbon striped with black.
>
> 1 Silver Plumb with a blue Ribbon striped with black.
>
> Newark, Dec'r 24, 1779.
>
> (Signed) THOMAS KINNEY
> JERH. BRUEN

This meeting on December 27, 1779, proved a great success, sixty-eight Brethren being present, one of whom was General Washington.

Tradition further tells us that at that meeting the question of a General Grand Master over all the States was also considered.

Washington was held in the highest esteem by his brethren in Pennsylvania, and from almost the very day of the procession to Christ Church, in Philadelphia, on St. John the Evangelist's Day, 1778, his name was suggested as a General Grand Master over all of the American Colonies. The movement continued to find favor amongst the Craft, and culminated in a motion to that effect at a

General Grand Communication of the Grand Lodge of Pennsylvania, December 20, 1779. A "Grand Lodge of Emergency" was convened on January 13, 1780, and was held in the quaint Lodge room in Videll's Alley, for the express purpose of nominating General Washington as General Grand Master.

Upon this occasion, the Deputy Grand Master, Bro. John Coats, presided. At this Grand Lodge, the following Brethren were present, all of whom approved of the choice of Washington for that exalted office:

Alex. Rutherford, D. G. M.
Jac. S. Howell, S. G. W. } pro tempore
Seph. Cronin, J. G. W.

Wm. Smith, G. Sec'y.

Bros. Jacob Bankson, Esq., W. M. } Lodge No. 2
Bros. W. C. Bradford, J. W.

Bros. Smith, J. W., No. 3 — S. G. D., pro tem.

Bros. Jno. Henderson, W. M.
Bros. _____ Croker, S. W. } Lodge No. 4
Bros. M. Hand, J. W.   } S. G. D., pro tem.
Bros. Al. Boyle, P.M.

Bros. John Bull, Esq., W. M., Lodge No. 8.

Bros. Peter Baynton, Esq., W. M., Lodge No. 13.

Bros. Benard, Past Master.

This Lodge being called by order of the Grand Master, upon the request of sundry brethren, and also in pursuance of a motion made at the last General Communication, to consider the propriety as well as the necessity of appointing a Grand Master over all the Grand Lodges formed or to be formed in these United States, as the correspondence which the rules of Masonry require cannot now be carried on with the Grand Lodge of London, under whose jurisdiction the Grand Lodges in these States were originally constituted; the ballot was put upon the question: whether it be for the benefit of Masonry that a "Grand Master of Masons throughout the United States" shall be now nominated on the part of Grand Lodge; and it was unanimously determined in the affirmative.

Sundry respectable brethren being then put in nomination, it was moved that the ballot be put for them separately, and His Excellency George Washington, Esquire, General and Commander-in-Chief of the armies of the United States being first in nomination, he was ballotted for accordingly as Grand Master, and elected by the unanimous vote of the whole lodge.

Ordered, That the minutes of this election and appointment be transmitted to the different Grand Lodges in the United States, and their concurrence therein be requested, in order that application be made to His Excellency in due form, praying that he will do the brethren and craft the honor of accepting their appointment.

A committee was appointed to expedite the business.

Resolved, That the Masters of the four Lodges, together with the Grand Secretary, be a committee to inform themselves of the number of Grand Lodges in America and the names of their officers, and to prepare the circular letters to be sent them as directed above, with all expedition.

About the same time, a petition to the above effect was presented at the meeting of the Lodge at Morristown. Fortified by the pronounced action of the Grand Lodge of Pennsylvania, a committee of the Army Lodges met at Morristown, February 7, 1780, of which Bro. Mordecai Gist, of Maryland, was chosen president, and Bro. Otho H. Williams, of Delaware, secretary.

The following address was presented by Bro. Williams:

To the RIGHT WORSHIPFUL, The GRAND MASTERS of the several Lodges in the Respective UNITED STATES OF AMERICA.

UNION — FORCE — LOVE

The subscribers, Ancient Free and Accepted Masons in convention, to you, as the patrons and protectors of the craft upon this continent, perfer their humble address. Unhappily, the distinctions of interest, the political views, and national disputes subsisting between Great Britain and these United States have involved us not only in the general calamities that disturb the tranquility which used to prevail in this once happy country, but in a peculiar manner affects our society, by separating us from the Grand Mother Lodge in Europe, by disturbing our connection with each other, impeding the progress, and preventing the perfection of Masonry in America.

We deplore the miseries of our countrymen, and particularly lament the distresses which many of our poor brethren must suffer, as well from the want of temporal relief, as for want of a source of *light* to govern their pursuits and illuminate the path of happiness. And we ardently desire to restore, if possible, that fountain of charity, from which to the unspeakable benefit of mankind, flows benevolence and love: Considering with anxiety these disputes, and the many irregularities and improprieties committed by weak or wicked brethren, which too manifestly show the present dissipated and almost abandoned condition of our lodges in general, as well as the relaxation of virtue amongst individuals.

We think it our duty Right Worshipful Brothers and Seniors in the

Craft, to solicit your immediate interposition to save us from the impending dangers of schism and apostasy. To obtain security from those fatal evils, with affectionate humility, we beg leave to recommend the adopting and pursuing the most necessary measures for establishing one Grand Lodge in America, to preside over and govern all other lodges of whatsoever degree or denomination, licensed or to be licensed upon the continent; that the ancient principles and discipline of Masonry being restored, we may mutually and universally enjoy the advantages arising from frequent communion and social intercourse.

To accomplish this beneficial and essential work, permit us to propose that you, the Right Worshipful Grand Masters or a majority of your number, may nominate as Most Worshipful Grand Master of said lodge, a brother whose merit and capacity may be adequate to a station so important and elevated, and transmitting the name and nomination of such brother, together with the name of the lodge to be established, to our Grand Mother Lodge in Europe for approbation and confirmation, and that you may adopt and execute any other ways or means most eligible for preventing impositions, correcting abuses, and for reestablishing the generous principles of Masonry; that the influence of the same in propagating morality and virtue may be far extended, and that the lives and conversation of all true Free and Accepted Masons may not only be the admiration of men on earth, but may receive the final approbation of the Grand Architect of the Universe, in the world wherein the elect enjoy eternal light and love.

Signed in convention, at Morristown, Morris County, this 7th, day of the second month in the year of our Savior, 1780. Anna Mundi 5780.

Which being repeatedly read and considered was unanimously agreed to and signed as follows viz.—

OTH. H. WILLIAMS. *Secy*

    M. GIST, *P. M., & President*

    JOHN LAWRANCE, *P. M., representing the Staff of the American Army*

    JONA. HEART, *M. M., Connecticut & American Union Lodge*

    JNO. SANTFORD, *M. M., New Jersey*

    GEORGE TUDOR, *M. M., Pennsylvania*

    JOHN PIERCE, *Junr. M. M., Massachusetts Bay and Washington Lodge No. 10*

    THOS. MACHIN, *M. M., Artillery*

    PRENTICE BOWIN, *M. M., St. John's Regimental Lodge*

    CHARLES GRAHAM, *F. C., New York*

Ordered that the foregoing address with an exact copy of these proceedings signed by the President and Secretary, be sent to the respective Provincial Grand Masters in the United States.

And the Committee adjourned with out Day.

OTH. H. WILLIAMS, *Secy.*

True Copy.

It was not until the middle of October that a reply to the Pennsylvania circular was received from the Grand Lodge of Massachusetts, and then only in response to a letter written by the Grand Secretary, Rev. Bro. Dr. William Smith. This correspondence was laid before the Grand Lodge at an Extra Communication, held October 16, 1780, viz.:

PHILADELPHIA, August 19th, 1780.

Sir:

I do myself the honor to address you, by order of the Grand Lodge of Ancient York Masons, regularly constituted in the City of Philadelphia. This Grand Lodge has under its jurisdiction in Pennsylvania and the States adjacent, thirty-one different regular Lodges, containing in the whole more than one thousand brethren. Enclosed you have a printed abstract of some of our late proceedings, and by that of January 13th last, you will observe that we have, so far as depends on us, done that honor which we think due to our illustrious Brother, George Washington, viz., electing him Grand Master over all the Grand Lodges formed or to be formed in these United States, not doubting of the concurrence of all the Grand Lodges in America to make this election effectual.

We have been informed by Col. Palfrey that there is a Grand Lodge of Ancient York Masons in the State of Massachusetts, and that you are Grand Master thereof; as such, I am, therefore, to request that you will lay our proceedings before your Grand Lodge, and request their concurrent Voice in the appointment of General Washington, as set forth in the said Minute of January the 13th, which, as far as we have been able to learn, is a Measure highly approved by all the brethren, and that will do honor to the Craft.

BOSTON, September 4th, 1780.

Sir:

Your agreeable favor of the 19th ult., I duly received the 31st, covering a printed abstract of the proceedings of your Grand Lodge. I had received one before, near three months, from the Master of a travelling Lodge of the Connecticut line, but it not coming officially, did not lay it before the Grand Lodge, but the evening after I received yours, it being Grand Lodge; I laid it before them and had some debate on it, whereupon it was agreed to adjourn the Lodge for three weeks, to the 22d instant, likewise to write to all the Lodges under this jurisdiction to attend themselves if convenient by their Master and Wardens, and if not, to give instructions to their proxies here concerning their acquiescence in the proposal.

I am well assured that no one can have any objections to so illustrious a person as General Washington to preside as Grand Master of the United States, but at the same time it will be necessary to know from you his prerogative as such: whether he is to appoint sub-grand or Provincial Grand Masters of each State; if so, I am confident that the Grand Lodge of this State will never give up their right of electing their own Grand Masters and other officers annually. This induces me to write you now, before the result of the Grand Lodge takes place, and must beg an answer by the first opportunity, that I may be enabled to lay the same before them. I have not heard of any State except yours and this that have proceeded as yet since the Independence to elect their officers, but have been hoping that they would.

I do not remember of more Grand Masters being appointed when we were under the British Government than South Carolina, North Carolina, Pennsylvania, New York, and Massachusetts, but now it may be necessary.

I have granted a Charter of Dispensation to New Hampshire till they shall appoint a Grand Master of their own, which suppose will not be very soon as there is but one Lodge in their State. Inclosed I send you a list of the officers of our Grand Lodge, and have the honor to be, with great respect and esteem,

Your affectionate Brother and humble servant,

JOSEPH WEBB.
Grand Master.

The Grand Secretary and Bro. Palfrey were appointed a committee to prepare an answer to the above letter from the Grand Master of Massachusetts, and lay the same before this Lodge tomorrow evening, to which time this Lodge is adjourned.

On the evening of October 17, 1780, the Grand Lodge was reconvened, and the draft of a lengthy letter was presented, which, after setting forth conditions in Europe, where a Grand Master General had been installed, stated the position taken by the Grand Lodge of Pennsylvania, as follows:

What the particular authorities of the Grand Master of these United States were to be, we had not taken upon us to describe, but (as before hinted) had left them to be settled by a convention of Grand Lodges or their deputies. But this is certain, that we never intended the different Provincial or State Grand Masters should be deprived of the

---

Oil painting on canvas of "GEORGE WASHINGTON" by Charles Wilson Peale. (H. 95; 61¾ in.)

The authors express their gratitude to The Metropolitan Museum of Art, Gift of Collis P. Huntington, 1896, (97.33) for permission to reproduce this photograph. (The Metropolitan Museum of Art, N.Y., N.Y. 10028)

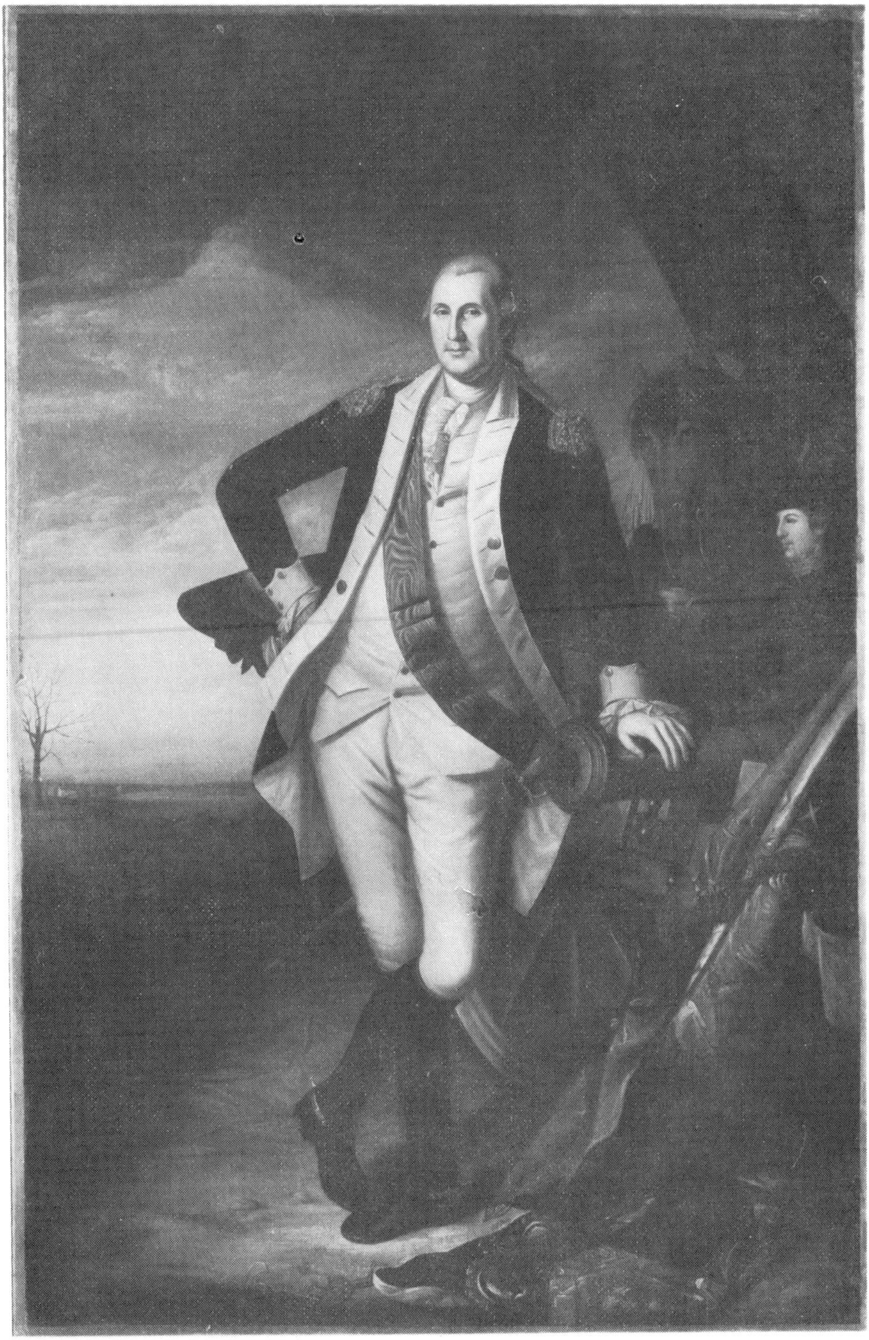

election of their own Grand Officers, or of any of their just Masonic rights and authorities over the different Lodges within the bounds of their jurisdiction.

But where new Lodges are to be erected beyond the bounds of any legal Grand Lodges now existing, such Lodges are to have their warrants from the Grand Master General, and when such Lodges become a number sufficient to be formed into one Grand Lodge the bounds of such Grand Lodge are to be described, and the warrant to be granted by the Grand Master aforesaid, who may also call and preside in a convention of Grand Lodges when any matter of great and general importance to the whole United Fraternity of these States may require it. What other powers may be given to the Grand Master General, and how such powers are to be drawn up and expressed, will be the business of the convention proposed.

For want of some general Masonic authority over all these States the Grand Lodge of Pennsylvania *ex necessitate*, have granted warrants beyond its bounds to the Delaware and Maryland States, and you have found it expedient to do the same in New Hampshire, but we know that necessity alone can be a plea for this.

By what has been said above, you will see that our idea is to have a Grand Master General over all the United States, and each Lodge under him to preserve its own rights, jurisdiction, etc., under him as formerly under the Grand Lodge of Great Britain, from whence the Grand Lodges in America had their warrants, and to have this new Masonic constitution and the powers of the Grand Master General fixed by a convention of committees aforesaid.

Others we are told have proposed that there be one Grand Master over all these States, and that the other Masters of Grand Lodges, whether nominated by him or chosen by their own Grand Lodges, should be considered as his deputies. But we have the same objections to this that you have, and never had any idea of establishing such a plan as hath been suggested before.

This letter is now swelled to a great length. We have therefore only to submit two things to your deliberation:

First. Either whether it be best to make your election of a Grand Master General immediately, and then propose to us a time and place where a committee from your body could meet a committee from ours to fix his powers and proceed to instalment; or

Second. Whether you will first appoint such a place of meeting and the powers of the proposed Grand Master, and then return home and proceed to the election, and afterwards meet anew for instalment. This last mode would seem to require too much time, and would not be so agreeable to our worthy brethren of the army, who are anxious to have this matter completed.

As you will probably choose the first mode, could not the place of our meeting be at or near the headquarters of the army, at or soon after St. John's day next? At any rate, you will not fix a place far northward on account of some brethren from Virginia who will attend, for we propose to advertise the business and the time and place of meeting in the public papers, that any regular Grand Lodges which we may not have heard of may have an opportunity of sending representatives.

Your answer as soon as possible is requested under cover to Peter _____, Esq., Postmaster in Philadelphia.

I am, etc., by order,
WILLIAM SMITH, Grand Secretary.

An answer to this communication was received from Boston, under date of January 12, 1781, and was read at the Quarterly Communication, March 26, 1781:

JOSEPH WEBB, ESQ., Grand Master of Massachusetts.

A letter was read from the Grand Master of Massachusetts enclosing the following Resolve of the Grand Lodge of Massachusetts:

As this Grand Lodge have not been acquainted with the Opinions of the various Grand Lodges in the United States respecting the choice of a Grand Master General, and the Circumstances of our public affairs making it impossible we shou'd at present obtain their sentiments upon it; Therefore: Voted, That any Determination upon the Subject cannot with the propriety and justice due to the Craft at Large, be made by this Grand Lodge until a general peace shall happily take place thro' the Continent.

From the Grand Lodge Records,

WM. HOSKING, *G. Sec.*

Boston, Jany 12th 5781.

CHAPTER IV

UPSTATE NEW YORK

In September 1780, Colonel Beverly Robinson, Washington's host during his visits to New York City in 1756, sailed up the Hudson River on the British sloop of war, Vulture, with Major John André to meet General Benedict Arnold, and arrange for the surrender of West Point. One of the unaccountable events of the American Revolution is that Major John André did not return to New York City with Arnold and Robinson. He remained ashore, removed his uniform, accepted a pass under an assumed name from Arnold, and attempted to return to New York City by land. André was captured, the plot uncovered, and West Point and the Hudson Valley saved from British military occupation. Major André was executed as a spy on October 2, 1789, near the present site of the George Washington Masonic Shrine at Tappan, New York. Arnold escaped, served during the rest of the war as a British officer, and eventually reached London where he died in 1801.

Four times during the closing years of the American Revolution, General George Washington stayed at the DeWint House. He first resided there from August 8-24, 1780. His second visit occurred September 28 to October 7, 1780, during which time the British spy, Major John Andre, was tried and executed.

When André was captured near Tarrytown on September 23, 1780, he was bearing secret American military documents which had been supplied to him by the American traitor and commandant of West Point, General Benedict Arnold. André was imprisoned in Tappan, and there on September 29, while headquartered at the DeWint House, Washington ordered a board of 14 general officers to try him as a spy. Meeting that day, the board found André guilty and recommended his execution. Washington accepted the recommendation and confirmed the sentence, but, due to the strenuous efforts of the British to save André, postponed the execution until October 2.

Washington's third visit to the house was May 4-8, 1783, when he met and conferred with the British commander-in-chief, Lt. Gen. Sir Guy Carleton, in order to discuss the British evacuation of New York City and the exchange of prisoners. Washington also accepted the hospitality of the house from November 11-14, 1783, when a snowstorm forced him to halt in Tappan while on his way from Hackensack, New Jersey, to West Point, New York.

Built about 1700 by Daniel DeClark, the DeWint House is a one-story brick-and-stone structure in the Dutch colonial style with a steep pitched gable roof and overhanging eaves. During the Revolutionary period, the dwelling was owned by Johannes DeWint. The building was acquired by the Grand Lodge of Free and Accepted Masons of the State of New York in 1931. Since that time the house has been restored and maintained as a memorial to Washington.

George Washington Masonic Shrine, Tappan, N.Y. (DeWint House)

At various times throughout the following years of conflict, Washington suggested attempts to recover New York City. In 1781, he consulted the Count de Rochambeau, and proposed a plan utilizing the French fleet, at the same time requesting estimates from his chief engineer and chief of artillery for the "intended operations against New York City." Naturally this information found its way to the British high command, and served to keep a substantial part of the British forces in New York City. In the middle of 1781, General Sir Henry Clinton, then commander of the British forces, believed Washington's attack on New York City was imminent, while Washington and his army moved through New Jersey to Yorktown to assist Lafayette in trapping Cornwallis.

After the surrender of Lord Cornwallis at Yorktown, Virginia, on October 19, 1781, the British abandoned the efforts to suppress the rebellion. On February 27, 1782, the House of Commons voted against carrying on the war in America, and a few days later, authorized the government to negotiate a peace settlement. The preliminary articles of peace were signed at Paris in November 1782.

New York City remained occupied by the British troops until November 25, 1783.

"I am at this moment on the point of setting out for Albany, on a visit to my posts in the vicinity of that place. My stay will not exceed eight or ten days, and will be shortened if any despatches should be received from you in the mean time." This was the communication from Washington to Count de Rochambeau, written at Newburgh, New York on Monday, June 24, 1782.

Albany was the only American city of consequence that had escaped enemy occupation, although strategically located, it had never been captured or looted in the wars between the French and the British. Massacres occurred nearby at Hoosic, Schenectady, Esopus, and Deerfield, but Albany was spared. During the Revolution, Albany became the target of three enemy campaigns; Burgoyne's from the north, St. Ledger's from the northwest, and Sir Henry Clinton's from the south, but all failed their objective. Albany was unmolested for more than one hundred and fifty years.

Albany as a city was unique in other ways. New York City became English soon after the occupation of 1664, and subsequently somewhat Irish. But Albany, in 1782, remained almost as Dutch as it was in 1686. Dutch architecture prevailed, and Dutch was the language of many of its people. Albany was at the head of the Hudson River navigation, and the concentration of trails and rivers in the area had enriched the city from the beginning of the fur trade, in 1614, with the opening of the west, Albany was destined to become a vital link in the access to the interior of the continent.

By his careful preparations for the Sullivan-Clinton expedition against the Iroquois indians in 1789, Washington had expressed interest in New York's western problems. The success of the Sullivan-Clinton campaign supported the United States claim to the interior of the continent of North America during the peace negotiations in Paris.

Other reasons for Washington's visit to Albany in 1782 were that in spite of the resolution of Parliament in favor of peace, military problems continued to exist, and could become serious, especially in the north where New York bordered on Canada. British troops occupied posts in the territory ceded to the United States by the Treaty of Paris, and were likely to remain there for some time. Tories and Indians might ignore the commands from London for the sake of booty or revenge, and if they continued on the warpath, it was unlikely that the British garrisons would restrain or punish their irregular allies. Even in London, the war party might succeed in driving William Shelburne from office, and renewing hostilities, especially if a substantial victory was achieved over the French. Washington's visit to Albany in 1782 had these very practical concerns in mind.

On Wednesday, June 26, 1782, Washington, accompanied by Governor George Clinton, arrived in Albany, and were received by Major Abraham Ten Broeck, Colonel of the Third Albany County Regiment in 1775 and Brigadier General in the Saratoga Campaign of 1777, members of the Common Council, Major General Philip Schuyler, Alderman Peter W. Yates who served as Master of Union Lodge No. 1 (presently Mount Vernon Lodge No. 3) in Albany, Brigadier General Peter Gansevoort, the hero of the defense of Fort Stanwix against St. Ledger in 1777 and a member of Union Lodge No. 1, and many citizens. The following address was presented to General Washington:

> To his Excellency George Washington Esquire
> General and Commander in Chief of the American Army etc.
>
> Sir.
>
> We the Mayor, Aldermen and Commonalty of the City of Albany, beg Leave to congratulate your Excellency on your Arrival in this City.
>
> Language is insufficient to convey our Ideas of the high Sense we entertain of your Abilities and Virtues—
>
> Your great and distinguished Services have justly entitled you to the Praise, the Love, and the Thanks of your Country, and Posterity will have Reason to bless you—May Victory and Glory always attend you in the Field — May Heaven prolong your Days, and bestow on you, its choicest Blessings in this Life; and a Crown of Glory in the World to come. In testimony of the grateful sense this Board entertains of your exalted Merits, permit us to present your Excellency with the Freedom of this City.
>
> Abm. Ten Broeck Mayor
>
> Albany 27th June 1782

The General replied to the Mayor and Common Council, accepting the freedom of the city, which document was presented to him in a gold box; at the same time, one of his aides passed to Mayor Ten Broeck the copy of the reply, which now rests in the archives of the Albany Institute of History and Art. The reply reads:

> *To the Worshipful the Mayor Aldermen and Commonalty of the City of Albany.*
>
> Gentlemen,
>
> Your congratulation on my arrival in this City, I receive with pleasure and gratitude.—

If in attempting to discharge those duties which every good citizen owes to his Country, I have been so fortunate as to merit your approbation, and the good wishes and benedictions of the ancient and respectable City of Albany, it will contribute not a little to my happiness.—

I accept the freedom of the City with thankfulness and shall retain a just sense of the honor done me by it.

G. Washington

Albany 27th June 1782.

Denniston's Tavern stood on the northwest corner of Beaver and Green Streets. It was removed "during the Year of the First Cholera, 1832", according to a bronze tablet placed on that site in 1886, when the city observed the 200th anniversary of the granting of its charter. The tablet also stated that there "Washington was presented with the freedom of the city in 1782 and 1783."

After this simple ceremony, General Washington and his staff were driven in coaches to the Schuyler Mansion, then known as "The Pastures," south of the city, there to dine and pass the night.

The next day began with an inspection of Fort Frederick, and a conference with that veteran soldier, Colonel Reid, a hero of the Sullivan-Clinton campaign against the western Iroquois in 1779. Later General Washington received the ministers, deacons and elders of the First Reformed Church, whose senior minister, the Reverend Dr. Westerlo, tendered him a formal address.

To His Excellency George Washington Esq. General and Commander in Chief of the American Army.

Sir:

The Auspicious visit of the Illustrious Commander in Chief fills the thankful hearts of the patriotic Inhabitants of this City with extraordinary Joy; Whilst it indicates in the most pleasing manner your Excellency's famous and justly celebrated attention to all even the remotest corners of your Extensive Command, and your friendly Intentions to faithful Citizens, who have been in former days, and Dangers and are still so Remarkably preserved, under the benign influences of a Gracious Providence, by your prosperous Direction of our Victorious Arms, from threatened and impending Ruin. We, the Minister, Elders and Deacons of the Reformed Protestant Dutch Church in this City, beg leave to address your Excellency on this Joyful occasion: Deeply impressed with Sentiments of Sincere Gratitude and respect for your exalted merits, and justly Dignified character; uniting our humble and earnest prayers to the God of all mercies and Grace, that He will be pleased Further to honor and Crown your Excellency with the choicest of his Blessings; and to prosper your Generous, Distinguished, and Disinterested attempts to restore and Establish to this injured and oppressed Land of your Nativity, that prosperity, and happiness which the Supreme possessor and Ruler of the Universe shall Judge most Subservient and conductive to the high purposes of his own Glory, and the prepetual happiness of the free and Independent United States of America.

May your Excellencies precious Health and Inestemable Life, be graciously preserved and Prolonged, and your Excellency erelong enjoy the happy era, when your unremitted zeal for the Common prosperity of this bleeding Country shall be Crowned with never fading Laurels of a Triumphant and Glorious peace.

By order of the Consistory
E. Westerlo* —
V. D. ib. Minister

Albany 28th June 1782.

On Saturday, June 29th, a mounted bodyguard of forty volunteers led by General Gansevoort, escorted Washington and his party to Saratoga — a forty-mile ride. "There he inspected", says the *Pennsylvania Gazette*, "the theatre of the glorious campaign of 1777", where the Northern Army had saved the colonies from being cut in two along the line of the Hudson by bagging Burgoyne and his entire army. Later Washington had bagged another army at Yorktown, thus making it possible for Franklin to say that the American Revolution was the only war of history in which entire armies had been captured. Here Washington reviewed the New Hampshire regiment on garrison duty, inspected the blockhouses, and conferred with the officers who flocked in to see him from a wide radius — a schedule which would have laid by the heels any but an old campaigner.

This journey on horseback reveals Washington's superb physical condition in his 51st year. From boyhood he had been inured to long journeys under wilderness conditions, and in the intervals between campaigns kept himself in training by riding to hounds and actively overseeing his large estates. Now, at the end of the Revolution, he was still hard as nails, able to go the route with horsemen years younger than himself.

The next day, Sunday June 30th, provided another test, for the party arose early and striking out for Schenectady, arrived there in time to hold an afternoon council with the Oneidas and Tuscaroras. The adherence of these two minor nations to the American cause, while the four other Iroquois tribes held to the traditional British connections, had been of vital assistance, especially in the battle of

---

* The Rev. Eilardus Westerlo was pastor of the First Reformed Dutch Church, at that time located in the center of the intersection at Broadway and State Street. This church was organized in 1642. Its first building, erected in 1656, was of wood. This was enlarged in 1715 by a stone structure being built over the wooden one. The interior building was then taken apart, so that services were but slightly interrupted. It was in this stone structure that Washington was received for the ceremony indicated here.

Oriskany. Except for their scouts, American forces would have walked blindly down many a forest path to destruction.

The story of the Schenectady meeting is briefly told by the *Pennsylvania Gazette:*

"Five miles from Schenectady, he, Washington, was received by sixty of the principal inhabitants on horseback, who attended him into town amidst the ringing of bells, the firing of cannon, and every other public demonstration of felicity. About one hundred warriors of the Oneidas and Tuscaroras completely armed and painted for war, met him without the gates. The Magistrates, military officers and respectable citizens, who had caused a public dinner to be provided, seemed anxious to give the most incontestable proofs of their gratitude and sensibility for the honor of the visit. The General viewed the town and fortifications, and returned to Albany the same evening."

The Address presented to the General at Schenectady follows:

To His Excellency George Washington Esq.
General and Commander-in-Chief of the Army of the United States —

Sir:

We the Magistrates and military officers of the Town of Schenectady, in behalf of ourselves and its other inhabitants: do most humbly congratulate your Excellency on your arrival in this Place.

Permit us also, to congratulate your Excellency on the signal success of the American Arms, during the present War. We have reason to bless and adore that providence, which has hitherto preserved your precious Life; and to offer up our fervent Prayers; for a continuance of your Health and Prosperity.

We anticipate the glorious period when the voice of war shall be at an end, when the inhabitants of our bleeding country, shall be enabled to sit under the Vines and Fig Trees, and no savage Foe to disturb their rest.

We do most humbly implore the God of all Grace, to restore Peace to these United States; and to bestow on your Excellency *that Peace which passeth all understanding.*

Schenectady 30th
June 1782

At the end of the day, which in the social routine of those days meant the middle of the afternoon, came the inevitable public dinner, held at the tavern of Abraham Clinch, who had come to America as a drum-major in Braddock's army. With his customary tact in such matters, Washington inquired particularly for Colonel Frederick Visscher (or Fisher, as he spelled it earlier in life), a colonial officer who had suffered a great deal at the hands of the Indians and Tories, and finding that for some reason he had not been invited to the dinner, asked that a messenger be sent for him. It is said that the Colonel was discovered hard at work in his barn, and consented to leave it only because his appearance was in the nature of a command performance. Washington gave him special attention when he came, at a table filled with such dignitaries as General Schuyler, Colonel Abram Wemple, Majors Abram Swits, Myndert Wemple, and Jelles Fonda, and the oldest inhabitant, Captain Peter Truax. Among this company, Visscher was given the chair next to Washington, at the General's request.

The speeches over, Washington returned to Albany that night, boarded his barge the next morning and sailed down the Hudson, in time to take part in celebrating the Fourth of July, at which "The whole army was formed on the banks of the Hudson on each side of the river. The signal of thirteen cannon being given at West Point, the troops displayed and formed in a line, when a general *feu de joie* took place throughout the whole army."

In the midst of this gaiety, Washington found time to add up carefully the detailed expenses of his first trip to the Northern frontier. They came to thirty-two pounds, eight shillings.

On August 10, 1782 Washington wrote from his Newburgh headquarters to the firm of Watson and Cassoul in Nantes, France, in which his friend, Elkanah Watson, was the chief partner, thanking the firm for the Masonic Apron and ornaments sent him from Nantes, France.

This apron is now in the possession of the Alexandria - Washington Lodge No. 22 in Alexandria, Virginia. Elkanah Watson wrote in *Men and Times of the Revolution, or Memoirs of Elkanah Watson*, "Wishing to pay some mark of respect to our beloved Washington, I employed, in conjunction with my friend M. Cassoul, nuns in one of the convents at Nantes to prepare some elegant Masonic ornaments, and gave them a plan for combining the American and French Flags on the apron designed for this use. They were executed in a superior and expensive style. We transmitted them to America, accompanied by an appropriate address."

The following letter was sent to Washington, together with the Masonic Apron and "Ornaments," by Messrs. Watson and Cassoul, from France under date "east of Nantes," 23d 1st Month, 5782.

GEORGE WASHINGTON IN NEW YORK

"To his Excellency, General Washington, America.

"*Most Illustrious and Respected Brother:*

"In the moment when all Europe admire and feel the effects of your glorious efforts in support of American liberty, we hasten to offer for your acceptance a small pledge of our homage. Zealous lovers of liberty and its institutions, we have experienced the most refined joy in seeing our chief and brother stand forth in its defence, and in defence of a newborn nation of Republicans.

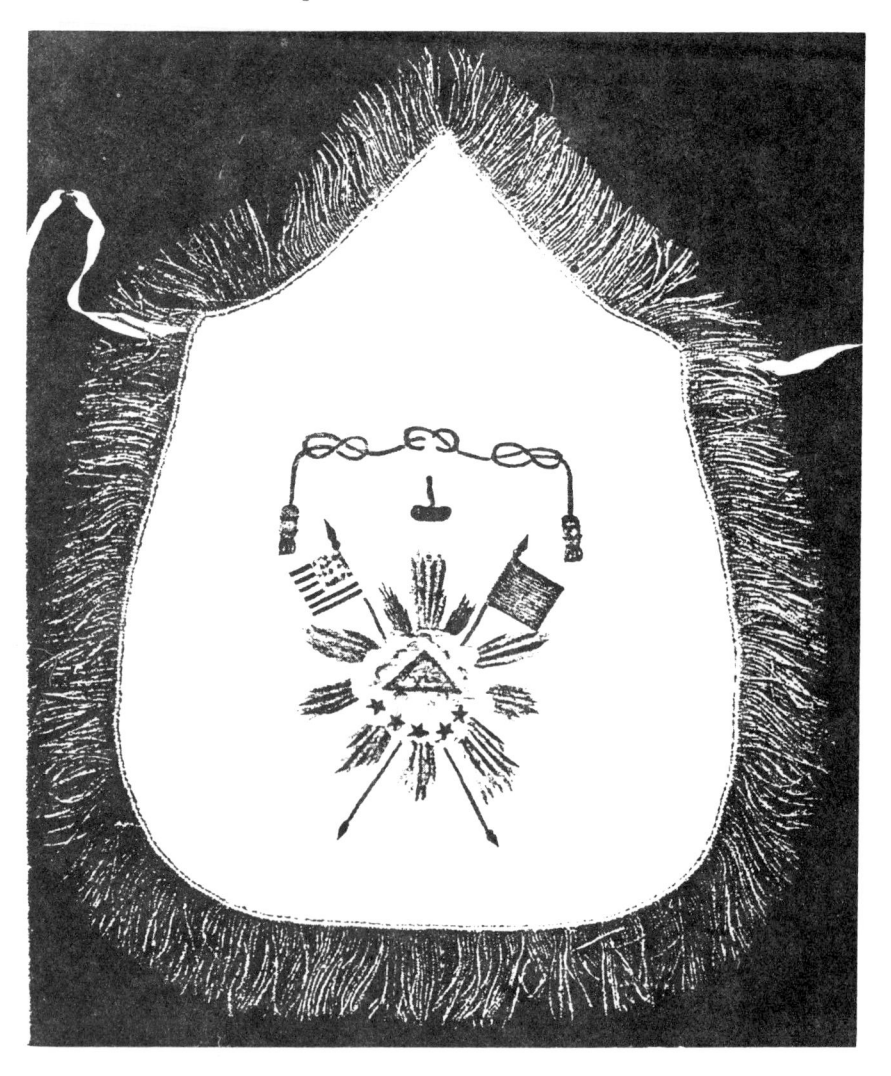

The Watson and Cassoul Apron (Alexandria-Washington Lodge, No. 22).

"Your glorious career will not be confined to the protection of American liberty, but its ultimate effect will extend to the whole human family, since Providence has evidently selected you as an instrument in his hands, to fulfill his eternal decrees.

"It is to you, therefore, the glorious orb of America, we presume to offer Masonic ornaments, as an emblem of your virtues. May the Grand Architect of the Universe be the Guardian of your precious days, for the glory of the Western Hemisphere and the entire universe. Such are the vows of those who have the favor to be by all the known numbers."
"Your affectionate brothers,
"Watson & Cassoul."

"East of Nantes, 23d 1st Month, 5782."

Owing to the uncertain intercourse between the two countries, it was almost seven months before Brother Washington received the Masonic apron, ornaments and letter from France. He at that time was in camp with the army at Newburg on the Hudson.

In reply, Washington sent the following autograph letter to the donors in Nantes, viz.:

"State of New York
"Aug. 10th 1782

"*Gent*"

"The Masonick Ornamts
"which accompanied your Bro-
"therly Address of the 23d of
"Jan last, tho' elegant in
"themselves, were rendered
"more valuable by the flattering
"sentiments, and affectionate
"manner, in which they were
"presented. —
"If my endeavours to
"avert the evil, with which this
"Country was threatned by a
"deliberate plan of Tyranny,
"should be crowned with the suc
"cess that is wished — The praise
"is due to the *Grand Architect*
"of the Universe; who did not see
"fit to suffer his superstructures
"and justice, to be subjected to the
"Ambition of the Princes of this
"World, or to the rod of oppression,
"in the hands of any power upon

"Earth. —
"For your affectionate
"Vows, permit me to be grateful;
"— and offer mine for true Brothers
"in all parts of the world; and
"to assure you of the sincerity
"with which I am
      Yrs

"Messrs
  "Watson & Cosson*
  "East of Nantes"

    This autograph letter from Washington to Messrs. Watson and Cassoul, purchased from a member of the Watson family in 1866, is now in the collections of the Chancellor Robert R Livingston Masonic Library of the Grand Lodge of New York.

    It is written upon two pages of an ordinary letter sheet, and was a copy of one written by Washington, with which he was not entirely satisfied, as shown by the changes made in the text before it was sent to France. The first copy Washington retained, and is now in the Library of Congress, and is here given for comparison, see pages 64 and 65.

    On December 27, 1782, Washington was at Solomon's Lodge in Poughkeepsie where the minutes of the Lodge state, "Brother George Washington, Comdr. in Chief, Brothers Woolsey and Graham" are recorded as visitors. The following "Address" was presented, "We the Master, Wardens, and Brethren of Solomon's Lodge No. 1 are highly sensible of the Honor done to Masonry in general by the countenance shown to it by the most Dignified characters."

    None of Washington's military headquarters during the War for Independence is of greater historical significance than the Hasbrouck House at Newburgh. Arriving at Newburgh on April 1, 1782, the commander-in-chief remained at the Hasbrouck House, save for occasional brief absences, until August 19, 1783. This was a longer period than Washington spent at any other headquarters. More importantly, Washington drafted three memorable documents at his Newburgh headquarters. In these he reaffirmed the fundamental principal of subordination of the military establishment to civilian control and helped lay the foundation for the Nation's orderly transition from war to peace.

    *It will be noted that on both the draft and letter, Washington spells the name Cassoul — "Cosson."

The first document was Washington's vehement rejection of the suggestion that the new nation become a monarchy, with Washington at its head. The second was his address to his officers in the "Temple" at the nearby New Windsor army encampment on March 15, 1783. Here he effectively quelled an incipient movement provoked by the so-called Newburgh Addresses, looking toward the coercion of Congress by the army to secure settlement of officers' claims against the government prior to demobilization. Washington's third notable act at Newburgh was drafting an oft-quoted circular letter to the governors of the States, in which he outlined his views on the future development of the Nation. These views were elaborated around four cardinal points: "An undissoluble Union of the States under one Federal Head," "A sacred regard to public justice," "The adoption of a proper peace establishment," and a "pacific and friendly disposition among the peoples of the United States which will induce them to forget their local prejudices and policies, to make mutual concessions which are requisite to the general prosperity, and in some instances, to sacrifice their individual advantages to the interest of the community."

In addition to these statements at Newburgh, an act of some interest was the establishment of the military award, the "Order of the Purple Heart," proposed by Washington, and noted in the general orders of the day, August 7, 1782. Aside from its intimate association with Washington, the Hasbrouck House has the distinction of being the first historic house preserved by a State. The State of New York obtained the property in 1850, and the building was dedicated on July 4 of that year.

The widow of Joseph Hasbrouck bought the property overlooking the Hudson River on which the headquarters building now stands, in 1749, and the next year her son, Jonathan, erected the northeast portion of the building. The southeast section was added sometime before 1770, and in that year, an addition extending the length of the west wall of both earlier sections was constructed. An initialed date stone confirms the date of this last addition. The walls of all three sections are of fieldstone. The steep-roofed house contains a large seven-doored chamber, which was used by Washington as his reception and living room, two small bedrooms, parlor and kitchen on the ground floor, another bedroom on the second floor, and a spacious attic where can be seen the maze of hand-hewn timbers that support the roof. The building is the original, except the floors in the kitchen and dining rooms. Adjacent to the headquarters building is a museum offering exhibits of local historical interest as well as material relating to General and Mrs. Washington, and the role of the Newburgh headquarters in the Revolution.

State of New York.
Aug.t 10th 1782.

Gen.n

The Masonick Ornaments which accompanied your Brotherly address of the 23d of the first Month, tho' elegant in themselves, were rendered more valuable by the flattering sentiments, and affectionate manner, in which they were offered. —

If my endeavours to avert the evil, with which this Country was threathed, by a deliberate plan of Tyranny, should be crowned with the success that is wished — the praise is due to the Grand architect

Fac-simile of The Original Draft of Washington's Letter to Watson and Cassoul, New York, August 10, 1782.

By July of the following year (1783), the General's military service was nearly at an end. He was restless and bored in his Newburgh headquarters, waiting for the word of release when he could ride to Annapolis, resign his commission and hurry to the joys of Mount Vernon which he had so long anticipated.

WEDNESDAY, JULY 16, 1783.

At Newburgh: "I have resolved to wear away a little time (while expecting the definitive treaty), in performing a tour to the northward, as far as Ticonderoga and Crown Point, and perhaps as far up the Mohawk River as Fort Schuyler. I shall leave this place on Friday next, and shall probably be gone about two weeks." — *Washington to the President of Congress.*

He set out on his "tour to the northward" July 18, crossing the Hudson at Kinder Hook, and traveling up the east bank, once more accompanied by Governor Clinton and an undetermined number of officers. At Albany, they were joined by General Philip Schuyler, and rode from there to Stillwater, where they spent the night at the home of another member of the numerous Schuyler clan, Harmonus.

Washington rode to the Saratoga battlefields, and there he had the advantage of a guided tour with General Schuyler. Today, U.S. 4 takes the traveler along the splendid plateau of Bemis Heights, with its breath-taking views to every horizon, through what has been since 1948 the Saratoga National Historical Park.

On the way northward, the General stopped to examine Fort Edward, and dined at a place which came to be known as the Red House, built by a half-pay officer named Pat Smith in 1765. The Baroness Riedesel had stayed there in 1777, and after she arrived with her husband, had given the house its name, although only the ends and the kitchen were red. The front was yellow. The building was a large two-story structure with a Dutch roof, standing between the barge canal and the Hudson River, about a quarter of a mile southeast of the fort. Washington and his party dined there, and stopped again on the way back to have breakfast.

Riding on to Lake George, they secured boats and rowed up the lake to the craggy promontory where Fort Ticonderoga, that much-fought-over guardian of the classic invasion route, stood at last in peace, contemplating the long stretches of water lying north and south. Washington inspected this fortification with more of an eye to its current military value than its exciting history, one supposes, though today thousands of tourists annually reverse this emphasis when they visit the magnificent restoration, certainly one of the finest of its kind anywhere. Then the General moved northward into the lower end of Lake Champlain, to the less celebrated fort at Crown Point, and the defenses of Putnam's Point.

That was the limit of his northern progress. Retracing their route, the party returned down the lakes, and came again to the Saratoga country, pausing at the place called High Rock Spring, where the peaceful beauty of Saratoga Springs would later rise. The place was then only a rugged pine forest sloping down to a marshy valley. Washington sampled the waters, as he had the year before, and made some shrewd observations of the territory. General Schuyler already had a tent pitched at the Springs which he used for a summer place, having cut a road through the trees from his home at the old Saratoga, now Schuylerville. Discussing the possible future of the Springs with Clinton, Washington and the Governor agreed to buy the spot and a considerable tract of land around it. Unfortunately for their prescience, Clinton discovered later that the idea had occurred to the Livingston family, who had already bought the land. It was a missed opportunity that Washington continued to regret for some time afterward, as his letters show.

From Saratoga, the General's party went on down to Schenectady, and then turned west to country that was new to Washington. The route lay down the fertile Mohawk Valley, where the river wound placidly along a plain flanked by gently rolling hills, past the manorial houses of Sir William Johnson, Provincial Grand Master in New York and founder of St. Patrick's Lodge in Johnstown, N.Y., whom Washington had met in Williamsburg, and his infamous son, John, whose bloody Tory exploits in the Cherry Valley had been one of the Revolution's dark episodes. Along this succession of lovely vistas, the party moved by horseback, although the passage would have seemed easier in boats, to Fort Schuyler. Then over the portage to Wood Creek, and a little farther to Oneida Lake, at a point somewhere northeast of the present city of Syracuse.

Apparently the trip out was made at a rather more rapid pace than the return, which included a side excursion to Otsego Lake (he may have gone as far as the southern, or Cooperstown, end of it), a place Washington particularly wanted to see because, as he explained, the headwaters of the eastern branch of the Susquehanna rose here, and he was perennially fascinated with the river systems he had spent so much time studying, surveying and traveling in his own part of the country.

Just before he made this side trip, Washington came into the vicinity of Fort Plain, in the country settled by the Palatines, and there tradition says he spent a night in the settlement of Palatine (now Palatine Bridge) at the home of Peter Wormuth. By this time, the news of his passage had spread by word of mouth up and down the valley, and those who had not been able to catch sight of him on his passage westward came flocking from miles around to see "the world's model man." It would be characteristic of Washington to feel that it was his duty to satisfy their curiosity — he did so often, even at Mount Vernon — and so the story is probably true that he came out, and walked awhile in front of the old stone house fronting the river, so that the people, at a respectful distance, could see him.

Peter Wormuth's house was small, and it is probable that most of the General's accompanying officers went that night across the river at Walrath's Ferry and found shelter in Fort Plain. Next morning, some of them came back to escort him to the fort.

At the fort, the General was introduced to the officer in command, Colonel James Clyde, a New Hampshireman, who had commanded a company of bateaumen and rangers, under Lieutenant Colonel John Bradstreet, in the war against the French. This company took part in the assault on Ticonderoga when General Howe lost his life on the slopes below the fort. Afterward, Clyde was at the capture of Fort Frontenac. As a Cherry Valley settler in 1762, he had helped develop that delightful area, and in 1770, had put up a small church for the Oneidas, equipping it with a bell brought from England which overwhelmed the Indians with joy.

The Colonel may be regarded as typical of the hardy breed of men that Washington met the length and breadth of the Mohawk's winding course. It is said the General implied to Clinton that the Governor ought to reward Clyde for his long and faithful service, which may have been the reason for his later appointment as sheriff of Montgomery County.

After dining at the fort, Washington and his party went on to spend the night in Cherry Valley, where they were the guests of Colonel Campbell, another of the Valley's heroes. His original home had been burned during the conflict, but Campbell, who had only recently returned from the wars, had put up a new log house. The accommodations were not elegant, nor were they sufficient, but the General and his suite were soldiers accustomed to rough board.

After breakfast at the Campbells', the party rode off on the excursion to Otsego Lake. That night they came back up to Fort Plain, and next morning resumed the journey to Albany. They reached there on August 4, and by the sixth, Washington was in his office at Newburgh.

WEDNESDAY, AUGUST 6, 1783.

At Newburgh: "After a tour of at least seven hundred and fif-

VAN CORTLANDT MANOR Van Cortlandt Park. An excellent example of how the landed gentry lived in the eighteenth century in and about New York is this ample stone house with its wood shutters and unpretentious exterior, contrasting strangely with its rich Georgian interior. It is interesting to note that stone was widely used for country houses but rarely in the city, where brick predominated.

ty miles, performed in nineteen days, I returned to this place yesterday afternoon, where I found your favor of the 31st ultimo, intimating a resolution of Congress for calling me to Princeton, partly, as it would seem, on my own account, and partly for the purpose of giving aid to Congress." — *Washington to James McHenry.*

On November 20, 1783, Washington was at the house of Mrs. Frederick VanCortland the beautiful stone house built by Frederick VanCortland in 1748 on the banks of Mosholu Brook. This was not New York City in 1783, but today this house is the oldest residence in Bronx County, the northernmost borough of New York City.

November 21st saw Washington at Day's Tavern in Harlem some nine miles north of New York City in 1783. Today that location is where St. Nicholas Avenue crosses 126th Street in uptown Manhattan.

Tuesday, November 25, 1783, was the day the British were to evacuate New York City. Major General Knox, in command of the American troops, marched into the city and took possession. George Washington and Governor George Clinton then made their formal

Courtesy of Fraunces Tavern Museum, New York City

entrance. The procession proceeded down Pearl Street and through Broadway to "Cape's Tavern." John Cape had been a Lieutenant in the Continental line. Before the evacuation by the British, Cape had entered the city and secured control of the old Province Arms Tavern. He removed the old sign, and replaced it with the Arms of the State of New York. From this time, the establishment was known as the State Arms, or more generally as the City Tavern.

At the City Tavern, on Friday, November 28th, 1783, an elegant entertainment was given by "the citizens lately returned from exile." On the following Tuesday, December 2nd, at the same establishment, another entertainment was given by Governor Clinton for the French Ambassador. For this event, Cape rendered a bill to the state for 120 dinners, 135 bottles of Madeira, 36 bottles of Port, 60 bottles of English beer, and 30 bowls of punch. Cape also included a charge for 60 broken wine glasses and 8 cut glass decanters.

On the morning of December 4, 1783, Washington and his officers met for the last time as soldiers of the Revolutionary Army in the Long Room of Fraunces Tavern. The room was thirty eight feet long and eighteen feet wide, just as it is today in the restored house, the Fraunces Tavern Museum. Washington bade farewell to his officers, "with a heart full of love and gratitude," and departed that same day for Annapolis, where the Continental Congress was in session. He resigned his commission on December 23, 1783, and returned to his home at Mount Vernon in Virginia.

CHAPTER V

WASHINGTON AS PRESIDENT ELECT AND HIS INAUGURATION, 1789

Washington's next, his eighth and final visit to New York City, was as President-elect of the United States of America. When the new Constitution was ratified by the necessary ninth state, New Hampshire, on June 21, 1788, Congress reported an act to implement the new government. It was decided that the presidential electors should be chosen on the first Wednesday in January 1789. The electors were to choose a President on the first Wednesday in February, and the two Houses of Congress should assemble in New York City on the first Wednesday in March.

The first Wednesday in January arrived, and electors were chosen in all the ratifying states except New York where the choice was to be made by the State legislature. The New York State Assembly was strongly anti-federalist, and led by supporters of Governor George Clinton. The New York State Senate was pro-federal and controlled, by a small majority, by followers of Alexander Hamilton.

The Assembly designed a bill wherein the Senate and Assembly would each nominate eight electors, and then meet and compare lists. Individuals on both lists would be considered elected. From the names on one but not both lists, one-half of the necessary number would be chosen by each branch of the state legislature.

The Senate changed the bill, and proposed that the two houses not meet, but exchange lists, and if the lists differed, each branch should propose names to the other for agreement, and continue to do so until all electors were chosen. The Assembly rejected this change; a conference followed; the Senate refused to alter its position and no electors were chosen. New York State did not cast a vote in the first presidential election. New York Governor George Clinton might have been the choice for vice-president under Washington, but when New York State failed to choose electors, Clinton's chances faded. Some years later, 1805 to 1812, George Clinton served as vice-president under Presidents Thomas Jefferson and James Monroe.

The Senate did not achieve a quorum until April 5, 1789, when Richard Henry Lee of Virginia arrived in New York City, and both Houses of Congress met in joint session to count the electoral votes.

Washington was aware of his election long before the official vote was counted and the formal certificate of election sent out. On

March 10, 1789, Governor George Clinton had written to Washington

". . . more than probable that, when the Result of the late Election for President of the United States shall be disclosed, your Excellency's Presence will be required in this City — Under this impression permit me Sir to solicit the Honor of your Company at my House until suitable Accomodations can be provided for you — Should Mrs. Washington accompany you, it will give additional Pleasure to my Family.

I shall be greatly gratified by being apprized seasonably of your Excellency's Approach to this City that I may be prepared to receive you in a manner which will accord as well with the high Respect due to you as the personal Attachment & Esteem I have for you.

With most respectful Compliments to Mrs. Washington in which Mrs. Clinton joins me, I have the Honor to be Dear Sir your most Obedient Servant.

Geo: Clinton

Washington replied, writing from Mount Vernon on March 25, 1789:

Dear Sir, Mount Vernon Mar. 25th 1789.

With very great sensibility I have recd the honor of your letter dated the 10th instt and consider the kind & obliging invitation to your House until suitable accomodations can be provided for the President as a testimony of your friendship & politeness; for which I shall ever retain a grateful sense — But if it should be my lot (for heaven knows it is not my wish) to appear again in a public station, I shall make it a point to take hired lodgings, or rooms in a Tavern until some house can be provided. Because it would be wrong, in my real judgement, to impose such a burden on any private family, as must unavoidably be occasioned by my company; and because I think it wd be generly expected, that, being supported by the public at large, I shd not be burdensome to Individuals.

With respect to the other part of yr let(ter,) which is expressive of a wish to be apprised of the time of my approach to the City, I can assure you, with the utmost sincerity, that no reception can be so congenial to my feelings as a quiet entry devoid of ceremony, be the manner of it what it may. With sincere good wishes, & respectful compliments to Mrs Clinton, in which I am joined by Mrs Washington I have the honr to be Dr Sir Yr most obedt Hbe Ser(vant).

Every elector had been instructed to vote for two candidates. Washington received sixty-nine votes, the entire number, and was unanimously elected president. John Adams received thirty-four votes, and was named Vice-president.

Charles Thomson, the Secretary of the Continental Congress, was chosen to carry the certificate of election to Washington. Thompson left New York City on Tuesday morning, April 7th, and

The Electoral Vote

April 5, 1789
The First Presidential Election

STATES.	Washington.	Adams.	Huntington.	Hancock.	Jay.	Clinton.	R. H. Harrison.	Rutledge.	John Milton.	James Armstrong.	Telfair.	Benjamin Lincoln.
New Hampshire	5	5										
Massachusetts	10	10										
Connecticut	7	5	2									
New Jersey	6	1			5							
Pennsylvania	10	8		2								
Delaware	3					3						
Maryland	6							6				
Virginia	10	5		1	1	3						
South Carolina	7			1					6			
Georgia	5									2	1	1	1
Total	69	34	2	4	9	3	6	6	2	1	1	1

arrived at Mount Vernon at half past twelve o'clock, Tuesday afternoon, April 14th, and presented the certificate of election to Washington.

Washington at once replied, accepting the appointment, and said:

"I am so much affected by this fresh proof of my country's esteem and confidence that silence can best explain my gratitude. Upon considering how long time some of the gentlemen of both Houses of Congress have been at New York ... I cannot find myself at liberty to delay my journey. I shall, therefore, be in readiness to set out the day after to-morrow."

Washington took his departure from home on the 16th of April. But he had not gone a mile from his door when a crowd of friends and neighbors on horseback surrounded his carriage, and rode with him to Alexandria. There the Mayor addressed him, in the fulsome manner of the time, as the first and best of citizens, as the model of youth, as the ornament of old age, and went with him to the banks of the Potomac where the people of Georgetown were waiting. With them he went on till the citizens of Baltimore met him, and led him through lines of shouting people to the best inn their city could boast. That night a public reception and a supper were given in his honor, and at sunrise the next morning he was on his way towards Philadelphia.

In size, in wealth, in population, Philadelphia then stood first among the cities of the country, and her citizens determined to receive their illustrious President in a manner worthy of her greatness and of his fame. The place selected was Gary's Ferry, where the road from Baltimore crossed the lower Schuylkill — a place well-known and often described by travelers. On the high ridge that bordered the eastern bank was Gray's Inn and gardens, renowned for the greenhouse filled with tropical fruit, the maze of walks, the grottoes, the hermitages, the Chinese bridges, the dells and groves, that made it "a prodigy of art and nature." Crossing the river was the floating bridge, made gay for the occasion with flags and bunting and festoons of cedar and laurel leaves. Along the north rail were eleven flags, typical of the eleven States of the new Union. On the south rail were two flags; one to represent the new era; the other, the State of Pennsylvania. Across the bridge at either end was a triumphal arch, from one of which a laurel crown hung by a string which passed to the hands of a boy who, dressed in white and decked with laurel, stood beneath a pine-tree hard by. On every side were banners adorned with emblems and inscribed with mottoes. One bore the words, "May commerce flourish!" On another was a sun, and under it, "Behold the rising empire." A third was the rattlesnake flag, with the threatening words, "Don't tread on me." On the hill overlooking the bridge and the river was a signal to give the people warning of the President's approach.

Toward noon on the 20th of April, the signal was suddenly dropped, and soon after, Washington, with Governor Mifflin and a host of gentlemen who had gone out to meet him at the boundary line of Delaware, was seen riding slowly down the hill toward the river. As he passed under the first triumphal archway the crown of laurel was dropped on his brow, and a salute was fired from a cannon on the opposite shore, and the people, shouting, "Long live the President!" went over the bridge with him to the eastern bank, where the troops were waiting to conduct him to Philadelphia. The whole city came out to meet him, and as he passed through dense lines of cheering men, the bells of every church rang out a merry peal, and every face, says one who saw them, seemed to say, "Long, long, long live George Washington!"

That night he slept at Philadelphia, was addressed by the Executive Council of State, by the Mayor and Aldermen, by the judges of the Supreme Court, the Faculty of the University of Pennsylvania, and the members of the Society of the Cincinnati, and early the next morning set out with a troop of horse for Trenton.

On the bridge which spanned the Assanpink Creek, over which, twelve years before, the Hessians fled in confusion, he passed under a great dome supported by thirteen columns, and adorned with a huge sunflower, inscribed "To thee alone." The women of Trenton had ordered this put up, and, just beyond the bridge were waiting, with their daughters, who, as he passed under the dome, began singing:

"Welcome, mighty chief, once more
Welcome to this grateful shore:
Now no mercenary foe
Aims again the fatal blow —
Aims at thee the fatal blow.

"Virgins fair and matrons grave,
Those thy conquering arms did save,
Build for thee triumphal bowers.
Strew ye fair his way with flowers —
Strew your hero's way with flowers."

As the last lines were sung the bevy of little girls came forward, strewing the road with flowers as they sang. Washington was greatly moved, thanked the children on the spot, and before he rode out of town the next morning wrote a few words to their mothers, as follows:

"General Washington cannot leave this place without expressing his acknowledgments to the matrons and young ladies who received him in so novel and grateful a manner at the triumphal arch in Trenton..."

Leaving Princeton at 11 a.m., Wednesday, April 22, Washington proceeded to New Brunswick, where he was met by William Livingston, the Governor of New Jersey. The next night was spent at Woodbridge. At Elizabeth Point, after crossing New Jersey, Washington was received by the committee appointed by Congress, with whom were the Chancellor of New York State, the Adjutant-General, the Recorder of the city, Mr. Jay, Secretary of Foreign Affairs; General Knox, Secretary of War; Samuel Osgood, Arthur Lee and Walter Livingston, Commissioners of the Treasury, and Ebenezer Hazard, Postmaster-General. This was early in the morning of April 23. A splendid barge, built for the purpose and manned by thirteen master pilots in white uniforms, under Commodore Nicholson, bore Washington and his suite to New York. Two other barges had been prepared for the Board of the Treasury, the Secretaries and the other dignitaries. With a favorable wind, the party glided out across Newark Bay, "the very waters seeming to rejoice in bearing the precious burden over its placid bosom." The troops that were left behind fired repeated salutes from the shore.

The landing-place was Murray's Wharf, near the foot of Wall street, where there was a ferry. Here the stairs and railings were carpeted and decorated. Governor Clinton formally received the President-elect. An enthusiastic crowd, that had been waiting expectantly at the ferry, made the air ring with tumultuous cheering as he appeared in the street. It was difficult to form a procession among the excited inhabitants, who were desperately struggling with each other in an effort to see George Washington.

The procession was headed by Colonel Morgan Lewis, aided by Majors Morton and Van Horne, all of whom were mounted. The military companies were next in line. Among them were Captain Stoke's horse-troops, accoutered in the style of Lee's famous partisan Legion; Captain Scriba's German Grenadiers, wearing blue coats, yellow waistcoats, knee-breeches, black gaiters, and towering cone-shaped hats faced with bear-skin; Captain Harrison's New York Grenadiers, composed, in imitation of the Guard of Frederick the Great, of only the tallest and finest-looking young men in the city, dressed in blue coats, with red facings and gold-lace embroideries, white waistcoats and white knee-breeches, black leggins, and wearing cocked hats trimmed with white feathers; Scotch infantry, in full Highland costume, playing bagpipes. Following the military companies were the sheriff of the county, the committee of Congress, the President-elect, Secretaries Jay and Knox, Chancellor Livingston, and distinguished men in State affairs, clergymen, and a large number of citizens. Washington was escorted to the Presidential mansion, which stood on the corner of Cherry Street and Franklin square.

Here is the formal order of the procession:

Colonel Morgan Lewis, accompanied by Majors Morton and Van Horne.
Troop of Dragoons, Captain Stokes.
German Grenadiers, Captain Scriba.
Band of Music.
Infantry of the Brigade, Captains Swartout and Stediford.
Grenadiers, Captain Harsin.
Regiment of Artillery, Colonel Bauman.
Band of Music.
General Malcom and Aid.
Officers of the Militia, two and two.
Committee of Congress.
The President-Elect; Governor Clinton.
President's Suite.
Mayor and Aldermen of New York.
The Reverend Clergy.
Their Excellencies the French and Spanish Ambassadors in their carriages.
The whole followed by an immense concourse of citizens.

Washington's house in Cherry Street. From an old print.

Every house and building along the route was decorated with flags, silk banners, floral and evergreen garlands. Men, women and children of all degrees flocked through the streets, shouting, waving hats and kerchiefs in their almost delirious enthusiasm. The name of Washington was not only upon every lip, but displayed in ornamental arches, under which the procession passed. The official residence was known as the Walter Franklin House. It had been occupied by Samuel Osgood, of the Treasury Board, who moved out to give room to Washington and family. This house was a large, three-story brick structure, with a flat roof. Shortly after arriving at his new home, Washington was called upon and congratulated by Government officials, foreign ministers, public bodies, military celebrities, and many private citizens. He dined with Governor Clinton that evening at the latter's residence in Pearl street. The city was brilliantly illuminated in the evening, when there was a Fourth-of-July display of fireworks. New York fully appreciated the importance of the occasion.

The Franklin House on Cherry Street had been acquired for the first Presidential Mansion. Built in 1770 by Walter Franklin, a prosperous merchant, it was inherited by his widow, now the wife of Samuel Osgood the new Postmaster General. Mrs. Osgood and the daughter of Lord Stirling, Kitty Duer, spent much time, labor, and expense equipping it with furniture, carpets, and china.

Martha Washington arrived in New York City on May 27th with two of her grandchildren, Eleanor and George Washington Custis. She described the house as, "a very good one . . . handsomely furnished all new for the general." Others had a different opinion. The French Ambassador reported that he "followed the President to the squalid (chetive) house provided for his residence."

The National Congress, at the time our first President was inaugurated, owed its meeting-place to the generosity of New York. After the adoption of the Constitution on September 13, 1788, it was determined that New York city should be the seat of Congress. The change occurred on December 23, 1788. The old City Hall in Wall street, in which the Continental Congress had been accustomed to meet, was placed by the corporation of the city at the disposal of Congress, and after reconstruction was known as Federal Hall. The City Hall was built about 1700. It was in the form of an L and open in the middle. The cellar contained dungeons for criminals. The first story had two wide staircases, two large and two small rooms. The middle of the second story was occupied by a court-room, with the assembly room on one side and the magistrate's room on the other. The debtor's cells were in the attic. At this time, the building was falling to decay, and the depleted treasury furnished no means with which to erect a new structure, or even to remodel the old one.

Wall Street in 1780, showing Federal Hall. From an old print.

Fortunately, in this emergency, some of the prominent and wealthy men subscribed enough money, some thirty-two thousand dollars, necessary to make the alterations. When completed, it was for that period an imposing structure. The first story was made in Tuscan style, with seven openings. There were four massive pillars in the center, supporting heavy arches, above which rose four Doric columns. Thirteen stars were ingeniously worked in the panel of the cornice. The other ornamental work consisted of an eagle and the national insignia sculptured in the entablature, while over each window were thirteen arrows surrounded by olive branches. The Hall of Representatives was an octangular room fifty-eight by sixty-one feet, with an arched ceiling forty-six feet high in the middle. This hall had two galleries, a platform for the speaker, and a separate chair and desk for each member. The windows, which were wide and high, were sixteen feet from the floor, with quaint fire-places under them. The Senate chamber was twenty feet high, with dimensions on the floor of thirty by forty feet. The arch of the ceiling represented a canopy containing thirteen stars, and a canopy of crimson damask hung over the President's chair. The chairs in the hall were arranged in semi-circular form. Three spacious windows opened out on Wall street. A balcony, twelve feet deep guarded by a massive iron railing, was over the main entrance on Wall street, where there was a lofty vestibule paved with marble.

While the Federal Hall was being transformed, building operations were active in various parts of the city. Private houses and stores were being constructed along the roads in the sparsely populated regions above Chambers street, while warehouses were springing up along the river front in the lower part of the city. All the merchants and mechanics were busy. Business of all kinds was active and vigorous under the stimulus of the new order of things in Federal affairs.

The arrangements for the inauguration proceeded rapidly. In the preliminary report of the Congressional committee of arrangements, offered on Saturday, the 25th of April, it was declared that the President should be formally received by both Houses in the Senate Chamber on Thursday, the 30th of April, and that both Houses should then move into the Representatives' Chamber, where the oath was to be administered by the Chancellor of the State of New York. Two days later the place for taking the oath was changed to the "outer gallery adjoining the Senate Chamber," and it was decided that the President, the Vice-President, and both Houses should proceed after the ceremony to St. Paul's Church to hear divine service. The idea of holding service in St. Paul's Church created considerable discussion. Senator William Maclay of Pennsylvania said in his journal, on the Monday before the inauguration:

"A new arrangement was reported from the joint committee of ceremonies. This is an endless business. Lee offered a motion to the chair that after the President was sworn (which now is to be in the gallery opposite the Senate Chamber), the Congress should accompany him to St. Paul's Church and attend divine service. This had been agitated in the joint committee, but Lee said expressly *that they would not agree to it.* I opposed it as an improper business, after it had been in the hands of the joint committee and rejected, as I thought this a certain method of creating a dissension between the Houses."

The question of holding services on the day of the inauguration had been agitated by the clergymen in town. When Bishop Provoost was applied to on the subject he replied, so Ebenezer Hazard wrote, that the Church of England "had always been used to look up to Government upon such occasions, and he thought it prudent not to do anything till they knew what Government would direct. If the good bishop never prays without an order from Government," added Hazard, "it is not probable that the kingdom of heaven will suffer much from his violence." It must have been a relief to Bishop Provoost, therefore, when Congress agreed to the service in St. Paul's Church.

Meanwhile, Washington had been waited upon by the two Houses of Congress, who offered him their congratulations. Similar congratulatory calls were made by other bodies, including the Chamber of Commerce, whose members met at the Coffee House at half-past eleven o'clock one morning, and proceeded to the presidential mansion, where they were introduced by John Broome, the president of the Chamber.

The ceremonies on April 30 were begun with a discharge of artillery at sunrise from old Fort George, near Bowling Green. At nine, the bells of the churches rang for half an hour, and the congregations gathered in their respective places of worship "to implore the blessings of heaven upon their new Government, its favor and protection to the President, and success and acceptance to his administration." The military were meanwhile preparing to parade, and at twelve o'clock marched before the President's house on Cherry street. A part of the procession came direct from Federal Hall.

Following Captain Stokes with his troop of horse were the "assistants" — General Samuel Blatchley Webb, Colonel William S. Smith, Lieutenant-Colonel Nicholas Fish, Lieutenant-Colonel Franks, Major L'Enfant, Major Leonard Bleecker, and Mr. John R. Livingston. Following the assistants were Egbert Benson, Fisher Ames and Daniel Carroll, the committee of the House of Representatives; Richard Henry Lee, Ralph Izard, and Tristram

Dalton, the committee of the Senate; John Jay, General Henry Knox, Samuel Osgood, Arthur Lee, Walter Livingston, the heads of the three great departments; and gentlemen in carriages and citizens on foot.

The full procession left the Presidential mansion at half-past twelve o'clock, and proceeded to Federal Hall via Queen Street, Great Dock and Broad Street. Colonel Morgan Lewis as Grand Marshal, attended by Majors Van Horne and Jacob Morton as aides-de-camp, led the way. Then followed the troop of horse; the artillery, the two companies of grenadiers, a company of light infantry and the battalion men; a company in the full uniform of Scotch Highlanders, with the national music of the bagpipe; the Sheriff, Robert Boyd, on horseback; the Senate committee; the President in a state-coach, drawn by four horses, and attended by the assistants and civil officers; Colonel Humphreys and Tobias Lear, in the President's own carriage; the committee of the House; Mr. Jay, General Knox, Chancellor Livingston; his Excellency the Count de Moustier, and His Excellency Don Diegode Gardoqui, the French and Spanish ambassadors; other gentlemen of distinction, and a multitude of citizens.

The two companies of grenadiers attracted much attention. One, composed of the tallest young men in the city, were dressed "in blue with red facings and gold-laced ornaments, cocked hats with white feathers, with waistcoats and breeches and white gaiters, or spatterdashes, close buttoned from the shoe to the knee and covering the shoe-buckle. The second, or German company, wore blue coats with yellow waist-coats and breeches, black gaiters similar to those already described, and towering caps, cone-shaped and faced with black bearskin."

When the military, which amounted to "not more than five hundred men," and whose "appearance was quite pretty," arrived within two hundred yards of Federal Hall, at one o'clock, they were drawn up on each side, and Washington and the assistants, and the gentlemen especially invited, marched through the lines and proceeded to the Senate Chamber of the "Federal State House."

The order in which the procession marched was as follows:

The Military.
The Sheriff of the City and County of New York.
The Committee of the Senate.
GEORGE WASHINGTON.
The Committee of the House of Representatives.
John Jay, Secretary for Foreign Affairs.
Henry Knox, Secretary of War.
Robert R Livingston, Chancellor of the State of New York.
Distinguished Citizens.

A few minutes later, he entered the room, and both Houses were formally presented.

For the occasion it is related that Washington was dressed in a dark brown cloth suit, of American manufacture (made in Hartford, Conn.), trimmed with "Eagle" metal buttons, and white silk stockings, with shoe-buckles of plain silver. He wore a steel-hilted dress sword. He had taken no part in any festivities while in New York, but had been awaiting with a solemn sense of responsibility the day which had now come.

Once inside Federal Hall, Washington climbed the stairs to the Senate Chamber where both Houses were assembled. Washington led the way to the portico overlooking Wall and Broad Streets. Beyond the balcony, he looked at streets, rooftops, and windows filled with cheering Americans. The small area of balcony was quickly filled.

Robert R Livingston, the Chancellor of the State of New York, and Grand Master of Masons in New York State since 1781, moved to the front of the balcony. Jacob Morton, the Marshall for the parade and the Master of St. John's Masonic Lodge, provided the Bible of the Lodge for the ceremony.

On the obverse and reverse covers are two inscriptions very nearly alike, the first of which is as follows:

GOD SHALL ESTABLISH
ST. JOHNS LODGE CONSTITUTED
5757
REBUILT AND OPENED
NOVEMBER 28 5770
OFFICERS THEN PRESIDING
JONATHAN HAMPTON M
WILLIAM BUTLER S W
ISAAC HERON J W

The Bible was published in London by Mark Baskett in 1767, and contains a large picture of George II., besides being handsomely illustrated with biblical scenes. The page of the Bible which Washington kissed is also indicated by the leaf being turned down. A copper-plate engraving explanatory of the forty-ninth chapter of Genesis is on the opposite page. On one of the fly-leaves is the following description of what was done on April 30, 1789 — written so indistinctly that it is almost impossible to photograph it:

| On Sacred | A picture of Stuart's Washington. | This Volume, |

On the 30th day of April, A.M. 1789,
In the City of New York,
was administered to
GEORGE WASHINGTON
The first President of the United States of America,
The Oath,
To support the Constitution of the United States.
This important ceremony was
Performed by the most worshipful Grand Master of Free
and Accepted Masons,
Of the State of New York,
The Honorable
Robert R. Livingston,
Chancellor of the State.
Fame stretched her wings and with her trumpet blew:
"Great Washington is near — what praise is due?
What title shall we have?" She paused — and said:
"Not one — his name alone strikes every title dead."

CENTRAL SECTION OF THE HISTORIC RAILING.

[*From the original in possession of the New York Historical Society.*]

WASHINGTON AS PRESIDENT ELECT AND HIS INAUGURATION, 1789

George Washington taking his oath of office as our first President on the Bible of St. John's Lodge in New York on April 30th, 1789.

The Bible is treasured by St. John's Masonic Lodge and the Masonic Fraternity, and carefully preserved in the Masonic Hall in New York City.

Washington placed his right hand on Chapters forty-nine and fifty of Genesis. "Do you solemnly swear," asked the Chancellor, "that you will faithfully execute the office of President of the United

States and will, to the best of your ability, preserve, protect, and defend the Constitution of the United States?" "I solemnly swear," Washington replied. He bent forward as he spoke, and kissed the Bible.

"It is done," Chancellor Livingston announced, and, turning to the crowd, proclaimed, "Long live George Washington, President of the United States." President Washington did not address the crowd, he bowed his acknowledgement of the cheers and, before the ovation ended, entered the Senate Chamber, and took his place at the dais specially prepared for him. When the members and guests were seated, Washington rose, and read his inaugural address.

INAUGURAL ADDRESS

"FELLOW-CITIZENS OF THE SENATE AND OF THE HOUSE OF REPRESENTATIVES: — Among the vicissitudes incident to life, no event could have filled me with greater anxieties than that of which the notification was transmitted by your order, and received on the fourteenth day of the present month. On the one hand I was summoned by my country, whose voice I can never hear but with veneration and love, from a retreat which I had chosen with the fondest predilection, and, in my flattering hopes, with an immutable decision as the asylum of my declining years — a retreat which was rendered every day more necessary as well as more dear to me, by the

Inaugural Bible, April 30, 1789

addition of habit to inclination, and of frequent interruptions in my health to the gradual waste committed on it by time. On the other hand, the magnitude and difficulty of the trust to which the voice of my country called me, being sufficient to awaken in the wisest and most experienced of her citizens a distrustful scrutiny into his qualifications could not but overwhelm with despondence one who inheriting inferior endowments from nature, and unpracticed in the duties of civil administration, ought to be peculiarly conscious of his own deficiencies. In this conflict of emotions, all I dare aver is, that it has been my faithful study to collect my duty from a just appreciation of every circumstance by which it might be affected. All I dare hope is, that if, in accepting this task, I have been too much swayed by a remembrance of former instances, or by an affectionate sensibility to this transcendent proof of the confidence of my fellow-citizens and have thence too little consulted my incapacity as well as disinclination for the weighty and untried cares before me, my error will be palliated by the motives which misled me, and its consequences be judged by my country with some share of the partiality in which they originated. Such being the impressions under which I have in obedience to the public summons repaired to the present station, it will be peculiarly improper to omit in this first official act my fervent supplications to that Almighty Being who rules over the universe, who presides in the council of nations, and whose providential aids can supply every human defect, that his benediction may consecrate to the liberties and happiness of the people of the United States, a government instituted by themselves for these essential purposes, and may enable every instrument employed in its administration, to execute with success the function allotted to its charge. In tendering this homage to the great Author of every public and private good, I assure myself that it expresses your sentiments not less than my own, nor those of my fellow-citizens at large less than either. No people can be bound to acknowledge and adore the invisible hand which conducts the affairs of men more than the people of the United States. Every step by which they have advanced to the character of an independent nation seems to have been distinguished by some token of providential agency. And the important revolution just accomplished in the system of their united government, the tranquil deliberations and voluntary consent of so many distinct communities, from which the event has resulted, cannot be compared with the means by which most governments have been established, without some return of pious gratitude, along with an humble anticipation of the future blessings which the past seems to presage. These reflections, arising out of the present crisis, have forced themselves too strongly on my mind to be suppressed. You will join with me, I trust, in thinking that there are none under the influence of which the proceedings of a new and free government can more auspiciously commence. By the article establishing the Executive Department, it is made the duty of the President to recommend to your consideration such measures as he shall judge necessary and expedient. The circumstances under which I now meet you will acquit me from entering into the subject, further than to refer to the great constitutional charter under which you are assembled, and which, in defining your powers, designates the objects to which your attention is to be given. It will be more than consistent with these circumstances and far more congenial with the feelings which actuate me, to substitute in place of a recommendation of particular measures, the tribute that is due to the talents, the rectitude, and the patriotism which adorn the characters selected to devise and adopt them. In these honorable qualifications I behold the surest pledges that as, on one side, no local prejudices or attachments, no separate views nor party animosities, will misdirect a comprehensive and equal eye which ought to watch over this great assemblage of communities and interests; so on another, that the foundations of our national policy will be laid in the pure and immutable principles of private morality, and the pre-eminence of free government be exemplified by all the attributes which can win the affections of its citizens and command the respect of the world. I dwell on this prospect with every satisfaction which an ardent love for my country can inspire. Since there is no truth more thoroughly established than that there exists in the economy and course of nature an indissoluble union between virtue and happiness; between duty and advantage; between the genuine maxims of an honest and magnanimous policy, and the solid rewards of public prosperity and felicity; since we ought to be no less persuaded that the propitious smiles of Heaven can never be expected on a nation that disregards the eternal rule of order and right, which Heaven itself has ordained; and since the preservation of the sacred fire of liberty and the destiny of the republican model of government, are justly considered as deeply, perhaps as finally staked on the experiment entrusted to the hands of the American people. Besides the ordinary objects submitted to your care, it will remain with your judgment to decide how far an exercise of the occasional power delegated by the fifth article of the Constitution, is rendered expedient at the present juncture by the nature of objections which have been urged against the system, or by the degree of inquietude which has given birth to them. Instead of undertaking particular recommendations on this subject, in which I would be guided by no lights derived from official opportunities, I shall again give way to my entire confidence in your discernment and pursuit of the public good. For I assure myself that whilst you carefully avoid every alteration which might endanger the benefits of a united and effective government, or which ought to await the future lessons of experience; a reverence for the characteristic rights of freemen, and a regard for the public harmony, will sufficiently influence your deliberations on the question, how far the former can be more impregnably fortified, or the later be safely and advantageously promoted. To the preceding observations I have one to add, which will be most properly addressed to the House of Representatives. It concerns myself, and will, therefore, be as brief as possible. When I was first honored with a call into the service of my country, then on the eve of an arduous struggle for its liberties, the light in which I contemplated my duty required that I should renounce every pecuniary compensation. From this resolution I have in no instance departed. And being still under the impressions which produced it, I must decline as inapplicable to myself any share in the personal emoluments which may be indispensably included in a permanent provision for the Executive Department, and must accordingly pray that the pecuniary estimates for the station in which I am placed may, during my continuance in it, be limited to such actual expenditures as the public good may be thought to require. Having thus imparted to you my sentiments as they have been awakened by the occasion which brings us together, I shall take my present leave, but not without resorting once more to the benign Parent of the human race in humble supplication — that since he has been pleased to favor the American people with opportunities for deliberating in perfect tranquillity and dispositions for deciding with unparalleled unanimity on a form of government, for the security of their union and the advancement of their happiness, so His divine blessings may be equally conspicuous in the enlarged views, the temperate consultations, and the wise measures on which the success of this Government must depend."

CHAPTER VI

WASHINGTON AS PRESIDENT, 1789 - 1790

After the inaugural address had been delivered, the President walked with the Senators, Representatives, New York State and City officials, friends, and guests to St. Paul's Chapel where Congress had voted to go "to hear divine service, performed by the chaplain of Congress."

Congress had authorized two chaplains of different denominations, one chosen by the House and the other by the Senate. On the 25th of April, the Senate had named the Rev. Samuel Provoost, Episcopal Bishop of New York and the Rector of Trinity Church. (The House did not act until May 1 when Rev. William Linn a minister of the Collegiate Reformed Protestan Dutch Church was named House chaplain.) The reconstruction of Trinity Church after the fire of 1775 had not been completed, St. Paul's Chapel was designated for the service.

The Bishop did not preach a sermon, and read from a "Proposed" rather than from the established *Book of Common Prayer* as the new American Protestan Episcopal Church had not yet adopted its prayers and order of service.

Washington's Pew

George Washington's pew in the north aisle is marked with the letters "G. W." and is in the location where he sat on Inauguration Day, April 30, 1789, during a special service after the inaugural ceremonies in the first capital of the United States on the site of the present Federal Hall. Over the pew is an oil painting of the Great Seal of the United States—the first such rendition in oil of the seal, which was adopted in 1782. Washington worshiped at St. Paul's for almost two years during the time that New York City was the capital of the United States of America. Directly across the chapel is the Governor's pew which George Clinton, the first Governor of the State of New York, used when he visited St. Paul's. The Arms of the State of New York are on the wall above the pew.

Each year on April 30, a special service is held here to commemorate George Washington's inauguration as America's first President. In addition, St. Paul's continues as an active part of the Parish of Trinity Church housing daily services, weekday concerts, occasional lectures and a shelter for the homeless. St. Paul's also contains exhibits of prints, photographs and artifacts.

The people meanwhile went off to their favorite taverns to drink prosperity to Washington, and wait with impatience for the

St. Paul's Chapel-New York City

coming night. As the first stars began to shine, bonfires were lighted in many of the streets, and eleven candles put up in the windows of many of the houses. The front of Federal Hall was a blaze of light. There was a fine transparency in front of the theatre, and another near the Fly Market, and a third on the Bowling Green, near the fort. But the crowd was especially attracted to the figure-pieces and moving transparencies that appeared in the windows of the house of the minister of Spain, and before the rich display of lanterns that hung round the doors and windows of the house occupied by the minister of France. The night in the city was one of enchanting beauty, the residences being brilliantly illuminated, the air filled with pyrotechnic effects and various transparencies, representing Washington amid allegorical influences, displayed at different points.

The President was taken to the house of Chancellor Livingston to view the fireworks, and it was necessary for him to return to the Executive Mansion at ten o'clock on foot, because the thronged condition of the streets made it impossible for a carriage to pass.

The Oldest Public Building In Continuous Use on the Island of Manhattan

When St. Paul's Chapel was completed in 1766, it was standing in a field outside the city. The original structure is still intact. The building is of native stone—Manhattan mica-schist with quoins of brownstone. This is the only remaining Colonial church in Manhattan. It was designed by architect Thomas McBean. St. Paul's bears a resemblance to St. Martin's-in-the-Field in London. It is an example of the Georgian-Classic Revival style. The woodwork, carving and door hinges are handmade. The ornamental design of the "Glory" over the altar is the work of Pierre L'Enfant, the French architect who laid the plans for the City of Washington. The "Glory" portrays Mt. Sinai in clouds and lightning, the Hebrew word for God in a triangle and the two Tablets of the Law with the Ten Commandments.

The pulpit is an example of 18th-century craftsmanship, surmounted by a coronet and six feathers, thought to be the only emblem of British nobility in New York surviving in its original place. Fourteen original cut-glass chandeliers handmade in Waterford, Ireland, hang in the nave and the galleries. The organ was built in 1804. The Royal Arms on the gallery are from the time of George III, the last king of the American Colonies.

On the morning after the inauguration, the President received calls from Vice-President Adams, Governor Clinton, John Jay, General Henry Knox, Ebenezer Hazard, Samuel Osgood, Arthur Lee, the French and Spanish ambassadors, "and a great many other persons of distinction."

George Washington
New York 1789

Miniature portrait by Joseph Wright, said to have been painted from observation during services at St. Paul's Chapel in New York City. The original is in the Chancellor Robert R Livingston Masonic Library in New York City.

Wright supposedly requested a sitting with Washington for the purpose of preparing a portrait, and was refused, but the opportunity was given him to sketch Washington in St. Paul's Chapel in New York City.

The scope and complexity of the task facing Washington as the first President defies description or comprehension. He was well aware that his every act would create a precedent which successors would be inclined or required to follow. Washington did not accept any salary during the revolution, accepting only his expenses and, at first, declined a salary as President. After realizing that others, especially Vice-President John Adams, could not afford to follow this precedent, Washington accepted a salary of $25,000 a year, but used it for his expenses.

The Dutch language prevailed in New York City in 1779, and many of the signs seen over business places were in Dutch. Every householder swept the street in front of his home twice a week. Oil lamps were used for lighting the streets. Coal was unknown. Hickory wood was the chief fuel. Early every morning, milkmen walked through the streets bearing yokes on their shoulders, from which dangled tin cans, and crying, "Milk ho!" Water from the "tea-water pump" was carried about in carts and retailed at a penny a gallon. The chimneys were swept by small boys, who went their rounds at daybreak shouting, "Sweep, ho! sweep, ho! from the bottom to the top without a ladder. Sweep, ho!"

The men wore long Continental coats, with brass buttons and side pockets, knee-breeches, low shoes with big buckles, and three-cornered hats. Ruffled shirts, lace sleeves, white silk stockings, powdered hair, which was combed back and tied in a queue, were conspicuous features of the men's dress. The correct thing, or full dress of gentlemen, however, was composed of cambric ruffled shirts, light-colored velvet knee-breeches, silk or satin waistcoats, silk stockings, and low shoes with brass buckles. Ladies wore low-neck dresses, flowing sleeves, hoops, and high Dutch hats. The ordinary dress of the women, was, however, more modest. It consisted of a short gown and petticoat of any color and material that suited the taste of the wearer.

Wall street presented a brilliant scene every afternoon. Ladies in showy costumes and gentlemen in silks, satins, velvets, ruffled shirts and powdered periwigs, promenaded up and down the street in front of the City Hall, and on Broadway from St. Paul's Chapel to the Battery. Broadway was also a popular thoroughfare for driving, and many stylish turnouts were seen every day rattling up and down the street. A liveried footman rode behind each carriage. Horseback riding was also popular, and gentlemen of prominence in State affairs often traveled this way, partly because it gave them exercise and because it was fashionable. The social world was in constant agitation over the arrival of statesmen and distinguished people from different parts of the Union and from Europe.

On May 4, 1789, Samuel Fraunces, a member of Holland Lodge was delegated as the President's steward.

On May 6th, Washington attended the commencement exercises of Columbia College, and endured ten orations by graduation students, the first graduate being DeWitt Clinton.

On May 7, 1789, the "New York Packet" contained an official announcement from this personage, warning all shopkeepers that to "servants and others employed to secure provisions for the household of the President of the United States moneys will be furnished for the purpose," and that no accounts were to be opened with any of them. That the first President could not claim entire immunity from the minor ills of life we find in his advertisement for a cook and a coachman, which held the columns of the "New York Packet" during at least three weeks:

> "A Cook is wanted for the Family of the President of the United States. No one need apply who is not perfect in the business, and can bring indubitable testimonials of sobriety, honesty, and attention to the duties of the station."

> "A Coachman, who can be well recommended for his skill in Driving, attention to Horses, and for his honesty, sobriety, and good disposition, would likewise find employment in the Family of the President of the United States."

"Fraunces," writes Washington to Lear, "besides being an excellent cook, knowing how to provide genteel dinners, and giving aid in dressing them, prepared the dessert and made the cake."

The Inaugural Ball was held on May 7th at the Assembly Rooms, on the east side of Broadway north of Wall Street and attended by most of Congress. The newspaper *Daily Advertiser* described in detail the gowns worn by some of the ladies.

The ball planned for the evening of Inauguration Day was postponed that the wife of the President might attend. But when it was learned that she would not arrive in New York until the last of May, it was decided to give the ball on the evening of Thursday, May 7. It was a brilliant assembly. Besides the President, Vice-President, many members of Congress, the Governor and the foreign ministers, there were present Chancellor Livingston, John Jay, General Knox, Chief-Justice Yates of New York State, James Duane (the mayor), Baron Steuben, General Hamilton, Mrs. Langdon, Mrs. Peter Van Brugh Livingston, Mrs. Livingston of Clermont, Mrs. Chancellor Livingston, Mrs. Gerry, Mrs. Thomson, Mrs. Montgomery, Mrs. Edgar, Mrs. Beekman, Mrs. Dalton, Mrs. McComb, Mrs. Lynch, the Marchioness de Brehan, Lady Stirling and her two daughters, Lady Mary Watts and Lady Kitty Duer, Lady Temple, Madame de la Forest, Mrs. Knox, Mrs. Houston, Mrs. Griffin, Mrs. Provoost, the Misses Livingston and the Misses

Bayard. About three hundred were present. It is related that the President, who had danced repeatedly while Commander-in-Chief, danced in the cotillion and the minuet at this ball. "The company retired about two o'clock, after having spent a most agreeable evening. Joy, satisfaction and vivacity were expressed in every countenance, and every pleasure seemed to be heightened by the presence of *a Washington*."

There never had been a President before, on this continent, nor any chief magistrate of the people. It was popularly supposed that he would be accessible at all times to all citizens. The throngs were self-respectful, as if under the spell of some powerful fascination, whenever Washington rode or walked in the streets. He was not followed nor his movements obstructed, as far as can be learned. The public knew when he left his house each day, which direction he took for his outing, and when he returned home—and the rush to gain admittance to an interview, the besieging of his door, was the first serious difficulty he encountered. He believed it his duty to see every caller on proper occasions and for reasonable purposes.

But he had work before him, and must secure time to accomplish it. To establish a system of special days for receptions was a delicate undertaking. John Adams, who had seen much of foreign courts, was inclined to chamberlains and masters of ceremony; John Jay was anxious to do away with the flavor of courts, and favored "republican simplicity;" Alexander Hamilton was for maintaining the dignity of the presidential office, but recommended the utmost caution lest too high a tone shock the popular notions of equality. All felt that confused theories must not be roughly jarred.

Washington finally appointed Tuesday afternoons from three o'clock until four for the reception of visits of courtesy. No invitations were extended, guests came and retired at their pleasure. A servant conducted them to the drawing-room, where Washington stood. He writes of this ceremony: "At their first entrance they salute me and I them, and as many as I can I talk to. Gentlemen often in great numbers come and go; chat with each other, and act as they please." Persons who wished to see him on business were admitted on any day of the week; and foreign ambassadors and official characters could see him at any time by appointment.

Meanwhile, he applied himself to the study of the actual condition of foreign and domestic affairs. He industriously read all the correspondence that had accumulated since the close of the war, and one notable feature of his lessons was to produce with his own hand abstracts of the reports of the secretaries, and of the treasury commissions, in order to impress facts more accurately upon his memory, and thereby enable him to master all the subjects in detail.

He also looked after his household concerns—the arrangement of furniture, the hanging of pictures, and the locating of vases, bric-à-brac, china, cut glass, silverware, and linen, which Mrs. Washington had sent by sea from Mount Vernon—with as much precision as he ever directed his farmer or steward how to plow, plant seed, buy nails, scissors, grains, gloves, buttons, shingles, hats, dishes, soap, hoes, rakes, horses, and other necessaries, all of which appears in his well-known hand-writing among the 117 folio volumes of "Washington Papers."

Mrs. Washington was setting her house in order at Mount Vernon for a protracted absence, and in the course of four weeks had made the journey to New York in her own carriage, accompanied by her two grandchildren, Nelly and George Washington Parke Custis, the latter then eight years of age.

Mrs. Washington missed the great ball on the 7th of May, but on the 29th of that month she held her first reception, or levee, as it was styled, which was attended by all the official and fashionable society. She had approached New York with a retinue of attendants, and been greeted continuously along the way.

From Philadelphia, she was accompanied by Mrs. Robert Morris, and at "Liberty Hall," the home of ex-Governor William Livingston, in Elizabeth, she was met by Mrs. John Jay. She spent the night there, and in the morning, President Washington, John Jay, and Robert Morris, and others, arrived to breakfast with her and her host and hostess, in the old historic dwelling, and then the whole party set out for New York. New York Bay presented a similar scene to that witnessed on the day of Washington's memorable reception. No foreign queen was ever welcomed by a loving people with more genuine delight.

On the evening prior to Mrs. Washington's first reception, the following gentlemen dined informally at the President's table: Vice-President John Adams, Governor George Clinton, Secretary John Jay, the French minister De Moustier, the Spanish minister Gardoqui, Governor Arthur St. Clair of the Northwest territory, Speaker Muhlenberg, and Senators John Langdon, Ralph Izard, William Few, and Paine Wingate. The latter has left a description of this dinner. He says, no clergyman being present, Washington himself said grace, on taking his seat. He dined on a boiled leg of mutton, as it was his custom to eat of only one dish. After the dessert, a single glass of wine was offered to each of the guests. When the President rose, the guests following his example, and repaired to the drawing-room, each departing at his option without ceremony.

Among the prominent ladies who grouped themselves about Mrs. Washington were Mrs. Jay, Mrs. Adams, Mrs. Hamilton, Mrs. Robert Morris, Mrs. Ralph Izard, Mrs. Knox, Lady Mary Watts, Lady Kitty Duer, Mrs Beekman, Mrs. Provoost, Mrs. Livingston, Mrs. Elbridge Gerry, and Mrs. Rufus King. Mrs. Washington, after her first grand entertainment, received every Friday evening from eight until ten o'clock. These levees were arranged on the plan of the English and French drawing-rooms, those entitled to the privilege by official station, social position, or established merit and character, coming without special invitation. But full dress was required of all.

The first Act of Congress approved by Washington was on June 1, 1789, legislation regulating the administration of oaths. On October 3, 1789, he issued a Proclamation requested by both Houses of Congress assigning Thursday, the 26th Day of November 1789, as a "day of public thanksgiving and prayer."

The most important business of the first Congress was to create the Department of State, and the Treasury and War Departments, the Constitution having left the details of administration to Congress. Troublesome questions arose on the start. The President, for instance, had been empowered to appoint the heads of departments, but the Constitution was silent as to where the powers of removal should be lodged. Equally acute thinkers and interpreters of the law stood opposed in the discussion, which was finally decided in favor of the President. That this should not be regarded as a grant of actual power by Congress, the bill was carefully worded so as to imply a constitutional power already existing in the President, thus, "Whenever the secretary shall be removed by the President of the United States," etc. . . . It is to this day a question whether our first legislators acted wisely in the matter.

It was not until September that the permanent secretaries were appointed by Washington, after which the intricate machinery of each department was to be devised, set in motion, and with much experimenting, adjusted to its purposes. Thomas Jefferson was made Secretary of State; Alexander Hamilton, Secretary of the Treasury; Henry Knox, Secretary of War; Ex-Governor Edmund Randolph of Virginia, Attorney-General; and Samuel Osgood of New York, Postmaster-General.

These officers were Washington's auxiliaries rather than his counselors, for the Cabinet as an advisory body was unknown to the Constitution and to the laws of Congress. The President called them together at intervals, but it was chiefly to give them instructions, as he was held responsible for the good conduct of the departments. He could take advice of them if he chose, but at his own option. Washington frequently asked the advice of others, but often found his own judgment proved his best guide. He chose, as he said, "the line of conduct which combined the public advantage with private convenience."

While the house was vigorously debating several knotty questions in connection with the establishment of the departments—chiefly the contemplated revenue system, and the matter of the salaries to be paid the President, Vice-President, and other officials of the government—the senate took up the subject of the national judiciary, and established the supreme court and circuit and district courts, an organization which has remained substantially the same to the present time.

John Jay, who had been the first Chief Justice of the state of New York in the most critical of all periods, became the first Chief Justice of the United States, and received the appointment although the court was not fully organized until the following April. Oliver Ellsworth was chairman of the committee that prepared the bill creating this tribunal, which was to hold two sessions annually at the seat of government. Six associate-justices were appointed— William Cushing, James Wilson, Robert H. Harrison, John Blair, John Rutledge, and Patrick Henry. Harrison declined, and James Iredell of North Carolina was appointed in his stead. These gentlemen procured homes and brought their families to reside in New York City.

There were not many good houses then to rent, and the varied experiences of the new-comers would form an amusing chapter. The salary fixed for the attorney-general was $1,500 a year; and Mr. Conway, in his work on Randolph, says that "Madison was unable to find a house in New York fit for his friend to live in for less than $250, though Randolph had begged him to get one for less. 'Frugality is my object, and therefore, a house near the town which is cheap in point of rent would suit me. An hundred and sixty-six and two-thirds dollars, ₤50 Virginia currency, is what I think I may allow per annum.' " Randolph wrote soon after to his wife: "I have a house at a mile and a half or thereabouts from Federal Hall—that is, from the most public part of the city. It is, in fact, in the country, is airy, has seven rooms, is well finished and gentlemanlike. The rent, ₤75 our money. Good water is difficult to be found in this place, and the inhabitants are obliged to receive water for tea, and other purposes which do not admit brackish water, from hogsheds brought every day in drays. At our house there is an excellent pump of fresh water, I am told . . . I am resolved against any company of form, and to live merely a private life."

Oliver Wolcott, then a young man of thirty, was appointed auditor of the treasury, and his salary was, like that of Randolph, $1,500 a year. Oliver Ellsworth furnished him with an estimate of the cost of living in New York, and remarked that he could keep his expenses within $1,000 per annum, unless he should change his style, which was wholly unnecessary. Wolcott, on reaching New York, wrote to his wife: "The example of the President and his family will render parade and expense improper and disreputable. We can live as retired or as much in the world as we choose." In December following, he wrote to his mother: "We have not been able to hire a house, and shall continue in lodgings until spring."

Washington's immense activity showed that his original endowment of nerve and brain power was magnificent. Claude Victor, Prince de Broglie, who was arrested by the revolutionary tribunal in Paris, tried, condemned, and guillotined June 27, 1794, left among the records of his visit to America the following pen-portrait of Washington: "He is tall, nobly built, and very well proportioned. His face is much more agreeable than represented in his portrait. His accost is cold though polite. His pensive eyes seem more attentive than sparkling; but their expression is benevolent, noble, and self-possessed. In his private conduct he preserves that polite and attentive good-breeding which satisfies everybody, and that dignified reserve that offends no one. He is a foe to ostentation and to vain-glory. He receives with perfect grace all the homages which are paid him, but he evades them rather than seeks them. His company is agreeable and winning. Always serious, never abstracted, always simple, always easy and affable without being familiar, the respect which he inspires is never oppressive. He speaks but little in general, and that in a subdued tone, but he is so attentive to what is said to him that, being satisfied he understands you perfectly, one is disposed to dispense with an answer. This behavior has been very useful to him on numerous occasions... At dessert he eats enormously of nuts, and when the conversation is entertaining he keeps eating through a couple of hours, from time to time giving sundry healths, according to the English and American custom. It is what they call toasting. I toasted very often with him, and among others on one occasion I proposed to drink to the Marquis de Lafayette, whom he regards as his own child. He accepted with a benevolent smile, and had the politeness to respond by proposing the health of my father and my wife."

Early in June 1789, Washington developed a "tenderness" of his left thigh and Dr. Samuel Bard was called upon to attend the President. Dr. Bard, a member of Union Lodge, had studied medicine in Edinburgh, and succeeded to the practice of his father, Dr. John Bard, a Huguenot and one of the founders of New York Hospital. Wild rumors spread that the President had a malignant tumor or was a victim of anthrax. His condition became so serious that on June 17, fifteen pounds of rope was purchased to extend across the street to prevent the passing of carriages during the President's illness.

About the 20th of June, Dr. Samuel Bard performed an operation while his father, who, according to the story, felt himself too old and shakey for the delicate work, stood over his son, constantly urging, "Cut deeper, cut deeper." Washington's recovery was slow, but by July 3, he was well enough to sign legislation, and on July 4th, 1789, the thirteenth anniversary of the Declaration of Independence, he reviewed the parade.

Medical historians suggest that Washington probably had a large carbuncle, perhaps caused by his thigh being irritated, and then infected by the rubbing of his scabbard as he wore his sword often after he came to New York City, but had not carried it previously for many months.

CHAPTER VII

WASHINGTON'S TOUR OF NEW ENGLAND

By August, Washington's health had improved to the extent that he was again taking his carriage rides over the roads on Manhattan Island, and walking from his home in Franklin Square to the Battery and elsewhere in New York City. The summer of 1789 was reported as cool and comfortable, and the Senators and Representatives in the Congress worked on throughout the summer, taking no vacation until the adjournment of Congress on the 26th of September. New York City became quiet, comparatively, as the legislators returned to their homes throughout the thirteen states.

Washington had mentioned on several occasions his desire to travel through the New England States, and began preparations for the journey, setting an example that has been followed by his successors in the office of the President.

Washington left New York City in October, when the autumn foliage was at its height of color, and was "on the road" for almost a month. He traveled in his coach, or as he called it, his "chariot", drawn by four white horses and attended by his two personal secretaries, Tobias Lear and Major William Jackson, and six servants. Washington's own account of this New England tour is a masterpiece of observation, and we include the following items taken from his diary.

"Thursday, October 15. Commenced my journey about 9 o'clock for Boston . . . The Chief Justice, Mr. Jay, and the Secretaries of the Treasury and War Departments accompanied me some distance out of the city. About 10 o'clock it began to rain, and continued to do so until 11, when we arrived at the house of one Hoyatt, who keeps a tavern at Kingsbridge, where we, that is, Major Jackson, Mr. Lear, and myself, with six servants, which composed my retinue, dined. After dinner, through frequent light showers, we proceeded to the tavern of a Mrs. Haviland at Rye; who keeps a very neat and decent Inn.

"The road for the greater part was stony but the land strong, well covered with grass and a luxuriant crop of Indian corn intermixed with pompions (which were yet ungathered) in the fields. We met four droves of beef cattle for the New York market (about 30 in a drove), some of which were very fine—also a flock of sheep for the same place. We scarcely passed a farm-house that did not abound in geese . . .

"The distance of this day's travel was 31 miles, in which we passed through (after leaving the Bridge) East Chester, New Rochelle, and Mamaroneck; but, as these places (though they have houses of worship in them) are not regularly laid out, they are scarcely to be distinguished from the intermediate farms, which are very close together—and separated, as one inclosure from another also is, by fences of stone, which

—102—

are indeed easily made, as the country is immensely stony. Upon enquiry we find their crops of wheat and rye have been abundant—though of the first they had sown rather sparingly, on account of the destruction which had of late years been made of that grain by what is called the Hessian fly.

"Friday, October 16. About 7 o'clock we left the Widow Haviland's and after passing Horse Neck, six miles distant from Rye, the road through which is hilly and immensely stony, and trying to wheels and carriages, we breakfasted at Stamford, which is six miles further (at one Webb's), a tolerably good house, but not equal in appearance or reality to Mrs. Haviland's. In this town are an Episcopal church and a meeting house. At Norwalk, which is ten miles further, we made a halt to feed our horses. To the lower end of this town sea vessels come, and at the other end are mills, stores, and an Episcopal and Presbyterian church. From hence to Fairfield, where we dined and lodged, is 12 miles; and part of it a very rough road, but not equal to that thro' Horse Neck . . . We found all the farmers busily employed in gathering, grinding, and pressing the juice of their apples; the crop of which they say is rather above mediocrity . . . The destructive evidences of British curelty are yet visible both in Norwalk and Fairfield; as there are the chimneys of many burnt houses standing in them yet. The principal export from Norwalk and Fairfield is horses and cattle—salted beef and pork—lumber and Indian corn, to the West Indies, and in a small degree wheat and flour.

"Saturday, October 17. A little after sunrise we left Fairfield, and passing through East Fairfield breakfasted at Stratford, which is ten miles from Fairfield, and is a pretty village on or near Stratford river. The road between these two places is not on the whole bad (for this country), in some places very good, especially through East Fairfield, which is in a plain and free from stone.

"There are two decent looking churches in this place, though small, viz.: an Episcopal, and Presbyterian or Congregationalist (as they call themselves). At Stratford there is the same. At this place I was received with an effort of military parade; and was attended to the ferry, which is near a mile from the centre of the town, by several gentlemen on horseback. Doctor Johnson of the Senate [William Samuel Johnson, LL.D., president of Columbia College] visited me here, being with Mrs. Johnson in this town, where he formerly resided . . . From the ferry it is almost 3 miles to Milford, which is situated in more uneven and stony ground than the last three villages through which we passed. In this place there is but one church, or in other words but one steeple—but there are grist and saw mills, and a handsome cascade over the tumbling dam . . . From Milford we took the lower road through West Haven, part of which was good and part rough, and arrived at New Haven before two o'clock; we had time to walk through several parts of the city before dinner.

"By taking the lower road we missed a committee of the Assembly, who had been appointed to wait upon and escort me into the town, to prepare an address, and to conduct me when I should leave the city as far as they should judge proper. The address was presented at 7 o'clock, and at nine I received another address from the Congregational clergy of the place. Between the receipt of the two addresses I received the compliment of a visit of the governor, Mr. Huntington, the lieutenant-governor, Mr. Wolcott, and the mayor, Mr. Roger Sherman."

The newspapers of the day give a glowing account of Washington's entertainment in New Haven, where he spent the Sabbath. In the forenoon of Sunday, he attended divine service at Trinity Church, escorted by Mr. Edwards, speaker of the Assembly; Mr. Ingersoll, and other gentlemen of prominence; and in the afternoon, went to one of the Congregational churches, escorted by the Governor, Lieutenant-Governor, the Mayor, and the Speaker of the Assembly, all of whom dined with Washington at his invitation, who notes the fact in his diary, and also that he took tea at the house of Mayor Roger Sherman.

New Haven bustled early in the morning on Monday, the 19th of October, as Washington left that city at 6 o'clock, accompanied for a considerable distance by a troop of cavalry and many of the most prominent citizens on horseback. He further wrote in his diary:

"We arrived at Wallingford (13 miles) by half after 8 o'clock, where we breakfasted, and took a walk through the town ... At this place we see the white mulberry growing, raised from the seed, to feed the silkworm. We also saw samples of lustring (exceedingly good) which had been manufactured from the cocoon raised in this town, and silk-thread very fine. This, except the weaving, is the work of private families."

At 1 o'clock in the afternoon, the Presidential chariot rolled into Middletown, on the Connecticut River, attended by a large party of mounted citizens who had gone out two or three miles to meet and do honor to the President. He dined while his horses rested, and as at many other points walked about the place "while dinner was getting ready," to observe its industrial features. At 3 o'clock, he started for Hartford, passing through Wethersfield, where he was met by an escorting party from Hartford with Colonel Wadsworth at its head, which city he reached just as the sun was setting. Turning to his diary, we read:

"Tuesday, October 20. After breakfast, accompanied by Colonel Wadsworth, Mr. Ellsworth, and Colonel Jesse Root, I viewed the woolen manufacturing at this place, which seems to be going on with spirit. Their broadcloths are not of the first quality as yet, but they are good; as are their coatings, cassimeres, serges and everlastings. Of the first, that is, broadcloth, I ordered a suit to be sent to me at New York; and of the latter a whole piece, to make breeches for my servants ... Dined and drank tea at Colonel Wadsworth's, and about 7 o'clock received from, and answered the address of, the town of Hartford.

"Wednesday, October 21. By promise I was to have breakfasted at Mr. Ellsworth's at Windsor, on my way to Springfield; but the morning proving very wet, and the rain not ceasing till past 10 o'clock, I did not set out until half after that hour. I called, however, on Mr. Ellsworth and stayed there near an hour. Reached Springfield by 4 o'clock, and while dinner was getting ready, examined the Continental stores at this place, which I found in very good order at the buildings (on the hill above the town) which belong to the United States . . . There is a great equality in the people of this state. Few or no opulent men—and no poor—great similitude in their buildings, the general fashion of which is a chimney (always of stone or brick) and door in the middle, with a staircase fronting the latter . . . two flush stories with a very good show of sash and glass windows; the size generally is from 30 to 50 feet in length, and from 20 to 30 feet in width, exclusive of a back shed, which seems to be added as the family increases."

Washington's critical observations on this first Presidential tour through the country are of enduring interest. He seems to have known how to use his eyes to the best advantage, and to have missed nothing worthy of note. He described the average farm, how it was worked "chiefly by oxen (which have no other feed than hay), with a horse and sometimes two before them, both in plow and cart," and stated the condition of the roads he passed over on each day, the style of the fences, the quality of the soil, and the exact number of the churches in the principal towns. He produced a picture of New England which brighten and deepen as the years roll on.

At Worcester, he was received with great ceremony, and with the booming of guns. To gratify the inhabitants he rode through the town on horseback, his "chariot" following in the rear. He spent the night of the 23d at Weston. Saturday, the 24th, he wrote: "Dressed by seven o'clock, and set out at eight—at ten we arrived in Cambridge, according to appointment." He called, and tarried for about an hour, at the residence of Mr. Longfellow, which was his headquarters in 1775, and then in his Continental uniform, and mounted on a white horse, he was conducted into Boston by a military escort of one thousand or more men, led by General Brooks. Lieutenant-Governor Samuel Adams, with the executive council of Massachusetts, and the officers of the city government, met, welcomed, and preceded him into Boston, while he was followed by his secretaries, Vice-President John Adams, ex-Governor James Bowdoin, Senator Tristam Dalton, distinguished citizens, committees, civil and military officers, between forty and fifty societies, and bodies of mechanics and tradesmen, carrying banners of great beauty, with appropriate devices. Washington in reference to this parade said: "It was in every degree flattering and honorable." A triumphal arch was thrown across Main Street, bearing in front the inscription, "To the man who unites all hearts," for him to pass through into the State House, and thence he proceeded to an outside gallery supported by thirteen columns, over the west door, where his appearance was greeted with prolonged shouts from the enthusiastic throng. He himself remarked: "The streets, the doors, windows and tops of the houses were crowded with well-dressed ladies and gentlemen."

Washington remained in Boston four days, until the 29th, and during this memorable Presidential visit, the ladies of Boston wore a sash of broad white ribbon, with G. W. in golden letters, encircled with a laurel wreath. At a brilliant assemblage which he attended at Concert Hall on the 28th, graced by all that was distinguished in affairs and society, the Marchioness Traversay wore in addition to the sash above described, on the bandeau of her hat, the initials G.W., and an eagle set in brilliance on a ground of black velvet. The illustrious guest of the evening observed: "There were upwards of one hundred ladies. Their appearance was elegant, and many of them very handsome."

Every moment of Washington's time was agreeably and usefully occupied during his stay in Boston, and would in itself form a chapter of marvelous interest. A "large and elegant" dinner was given him at Faneuil Hall on the 27th, by the Governor and Council, prior to which he had that morning been to an oratorio, and between noon and three o'clock, P.M., had received the addresses of the government of the state, of the town of Boston, of the president and professors of Harvard College, and of the state branch of the Society of the Cincinnati. He attended church on the Sabbath, both morning and afternoon; he visited the French squadron in the harbor, and was received with the homage offered to kings; he visited the institutions of learning, and made special note of every manufacturing establishment of public utility.

He went through Lynn on leaving Boston, and out of his way to Marblehead, because he wanted to see the place. He describes it as having "the appearance of antiquity: the houses are old; the streets dirty; and the common people not very clean." His special desire was to learn about the fishing business of its people. Of Lynn, he wrote: "It is said 175,000 pair of shoes (women's chiefly) have been made in a year by about 400 workmen. This is only a row of houses, and not very thick, on each side of the road." He was met by a committee and a handsomely uniformed military escort, who conducted him into the flourishing town of Salem, where an ode in his honor was sung, addresses presented, respect paid to him by all classes of people, and after dining he attended an assembly in the evening, where he said: "There were at least an hundred handsome and well-dressed ladies."

On Friday, the 30th, he was received in Newburyport with military honors, where he spent the night. On Saturday, the 31st, after breakfasting with Senator Tristam Dalton, he proceeded toward Portsmouth. A cavalcade came out to meet him at the state line, including the President of New Hampshire, John Sullivan and Senators John Langdon and Paine Wingate. Washington, who had thus far been riding on horseback to gratify the people who lined the road the whole distance, dismounted, and took leave of the escort which had attended him to this point. Before reaching Portsmouth, however, the clamor of the spectators along the road was such that Washington mounted his horse and rode through the ranks of men, women, and children, to their never-ending delight. He said, "With this cavalcade, we proceeded, and arrived before three o'clock at Portsmouth, where we were received with every token of respect and appearance of cordiality, under a discharge of artillery. The streets, doors, and windows were crowded here as in all other places; and, alighting at the town-house, odes were sung and played in honor of the President . . . From the town-house, I went to Colonel Brewster's tavern, the place provided for my residence; and asked the president, vice-president, the two senators, the marshal and Major Gilman to dine with me, which they did; after which I drank tea at Mr. Langdon's."

On Sunday, Washington attended religious services in two of the churches, attended by Governor Sullivan, Senator Langdon, and others; in the forenoon at the Episcopal, and in the afternoon at the Congregational, Rev. Joseph Buckminster, pastor. In both cases, he was conducted to his pew by the marshal of the district and two church wardens, with their staves. He remained in Portsmouth until Wednesday, the 4th, during which time he went in a barge to view the harbor, and landed for a few moments at Kittery, in Maine. He wrote, "Having lines we proceeded to the fishing banks a little without the harbour and fished for Cod; but it not being a proper time of tide, we caught only two, with which about one o'clock we returned to town. Dined at Mr. Langdon's, and drank tea there, with a large circle of ladies, and retired a little after seven o'clock." He said that Portsmouth contained at that time about five thousand inhabitants. "There are some good houses (among which Colonel Langdon's may be esteemed the first), but in general they are indifferent, and almost entirely of wood. On wondering at this, as the country is full of stone and good clay for bricks, I was told that on account of the fogs and damp they deemed them wholesomer, and for that reason preferred wood buildings."

On Tuesday, a public dinner was given in honor of the President, attended by the principal officers of the state government, the clergy, the members of the bar, and eminent private citizens;

and, after the first toast, Washington himself arose and offered, "The State of New Hampshire," which created the utmost enthusiasm. The same evening, he wrote, "At half after seven I went to the assembly, where there were about seventy-five well-dressed and many of them very handsome ladies—among whom (as was also the case at Salem and Boston assemblies) were a greater proportion with much blacker hair than are usually seen in the southern states. About nine I returned to my quarters."

Washington was anxious that his journey homeward to New York should be without any public receptions whatever. He had been exceedingly gratified with the evidences of respect and affection which had made this first Presidential tour, thus far, a continuous triumphal march, unparalleled in history, but he feared such ceaseless demonstrations on the part of the people would react to the disadvantage of their private occupations and business interests. He wrote in his note-book:

"Wednesday, November 4. About half after seven I left Portsmouth, quietly, and without any attendance, having earnestly entreated that all parade and ceremony might be avoided on my return. Before ten I reached Exeter, 14 miles distance. This is considered the second town in New Hampshire, and stands at the head of the tide-water of Piscataqua river . . . It is a place of some consequence, but does not contain more than 1,000 inhabitants. A jealousy subsists between this town (where the legislature alternately sits) and Portsmouth; which, had I known it in time, would have made it necessary to have accepted an invitation to a public dinner, but my arrangements having been otherwise made, I could not. From hence, passing through Kingstown (6 miles from Exeter), I arrived at Haverhill about half-past two, and stayed all night . . . The inhabitants of this small village were well disposed to welcome me to it by every demonstration which could evince their joy."

Masonic Sidelights of Washington's Visit to New Hampshire in 1789

Gerald D. Foss, Grand Historian, of the Grand Lodge of New Hampshire, devoted much time to research on President Washington's visit to New Hampshire. His work was included in Volume IX, Part 1, of the *Transactions of the American Lodge of Research* and we include it here:

Students of Masonic history search in vain for any message of a Masonic nature from President Washington to his brethren in Portsmouth, New Hampshire. This is difficult to understand because of several known factors:

1. President Washington wrote many eloquent messages to various Lodges and Grand Lodges.

2. On the dates he visited Portsmouth, October 31, 1789 to November 4, 1789, he was then Worshipful Master of Alexandria Lodge No. 22 of Alexandria, Virginia.

3. On these dates, there were two Masonic lodges in Portsmouth, St. John's Lodge, one of the oldest in the country, and St. Patrick's Lodge, which would soon forfeit its charter.

4. At least 40 members of St. John's Lodge had been in the Revolutionary War, many well known to President Washington personally.

5. The President (Governor) of New Hampshire on these dates was Major General John Sullivan, who had been elected the first Grand Master of the Grand Lodge of New Hampshire on July 8, 1789, although not installed in office at this time. His installation into office was delayed until he could be elected Worshipful Master of his lodge which the members of St. John's Lodge performed unanimously at the Annual Meeting held December 3, 1789.

Another question which arises is, why did not the Masons of Portsmouth arrange for a special meeting to greet their President fraternally?

Maybe the time element was a big factor. The town of Portsmouth had very short notice. Osborne's *New Hampshire Spy*, published in Portsmouth on Tuesdays and Thursdays, carried the first news on October 20, 1789. It was not definite. It merely reported that the President had commenced a tour of the Northeastern states and that he might come to Portsmouth, but there was not any certainty of it or any dates given if he did come. The town held a special meeting on October 23 to appoint committees and make arrangements in the event that the visit might occur. Another newspaper being published in Portsmouth at this time was the *New Hampshire Gazette*, a weekly. In its weekly edition of October 22, there is mention of the tour but the dates were not known, and it was not until the edition of October 29 that the citizens of Portsmouth learned that President Washington would arrive in Portsmouth on Saturday, October 31 about 3:00 p.m.

Even President John Sullivan must have been jittery, for on October 27, 1789 he wrote a letter to President Washington which says in part, "will you have the goodness to direct one of your aids to inform at what time you expect to leave Newbury, that your excellency may be met at the Line and escorted to whatever Town you may think it proper to honor with your presence." Thus, the President could not make any firm plans even four days before the date of arrival. By October 30, President Sullivan must have received a reply, for on that day he wrote another letter to President Washington in which he told Washington that he did not have any house in that Town (Portsmouth) and invited him to dine with him and his family in Durham on Wednesday next, an invitation which could not be accepted.

It is also a good possibility that the members of St. John's Lodge were so busily engaged in preparing, receiving and entertaining President Washington, there was none in St. John's Lodge to make preparations for a fraternal meeting. The story about to unfold will show that many of the officers and members of St. John's Lodge were engaged in numerous activities in connection with this tour. And even though there is no record of a fraternal meeting, there are adequate records available to indicate the activities of Masons in connection with this official visit of President Washington to Portsmouth, an old seaport town and the twelfth largest town by the census of 1790, population 4,720.

With this preface, let us identify a number of Masons engaged in receiving and entertaining President Washington. In his diary for October 31, he relates that he was met at the line by the President of the State of New Hampshire, the Vice President, some of the Council, Messrs. Langdon, and Wingate of the Senate, Col. Parker, Marshal of the State and many other respectable characters. One of President Washington's secretaries, Major Jackson, estimated there were 700 New Hampshire men who met President Washington that morning and escorted him to Portsmouth, about 20 miles to the north.

The three men identified by name in Washington's diary, Senators Langdon and Wingate, and Col. Parker, the United States Marshal for the District of New Hampshire, are not known to have been Masons. The President of New Hampshire, John Sullivan, had been a Mason for many years having been made in St. John's Lodge, Portsmouth, on March 9, 1767. These two men were well known to one another. There are many letters extant between them which demonstrate a strong mutual respect. It can be inferred easily from Sullivan's letters to Washington that he admired Washington. John Sullivan was one of the first two delegates to the Continental Congress from New Hampshire in 1774-75. He was commissioned by the Continental Congress one of the first Brigadier-Generals. A year later, he was promoted to the rank of Major-General. As such, he was engaged in many of the great battles of the Revolutionary War.

The papers of the period state that the "honorable Consul of France" was present at the state line. It has been implied by one author that this might have been Nicholas Rousselet, then living in Portsmouth and a member of St. John's Lodge.

The regiment of light horse at the line was commanded by Col. Amos Cogswell, a Mason and a charter member of Federal Lodge No. 5 of Dover, New Hampshire. Also in this regiment was Lt. Col. William Brewster, owner of Brewster's Tavern in Portsmouth, where President Washington would reside while in Portsmouth. Although Brewster was not a Mason on this date, he soon would be. He became a member of St. John's Lodge on April 1, 1790.

After greetings were exchanged, the trip commenced via the old Boston Post Road through the towns of Seabrook, Hampton Falls, Hampton, North Hampton and Greenland. At Greenland, the cavalcade halted, President Washington left his carriage to ride horseback to Portsmouth. The escort was increased by Col. Michael Wentworth's corps of Independent Horse. In this corps was the Worshipful Master of St. John's Lodge, Dr. Hall Jackson, serving this day as Lieutenant Colonel. Dr. Hall Jackson had probably met President Washington previously as Dr. Jackson attended the wounded at Bunker Hill; also attended the sick and wounded for some time at Cambridge, Massachusetts while President Washington was there. Dr. and Wor. Bro. Jackson would soon be appointed the first Deputy Grand Master of the Grand Lodge of New Hampshire; later elected to be its second Grand Master. Also in this same corps, is a newly-made Mason, Major Clement Storer, a physician. Later, he would be elected Worshipful Master of St. John's Lodge, 1796 and 1797, and the fifth Grand Master of the Grand Lodge of New Hampshire, 1808-09-10. He was also elected to Congress in the tenth session; to the United States Senate from 1817 to 1819.

One author writes that probably Congressman Nicholas Gilman joined the procession at Greenland. He bases his conclusion on the fact that Congressman Nicholas Gilman of Exeter, New Hampshire did in fact dine with President Washington in Portsmouth on Saturday night in Brewster's Tavern. In any event, Nicholas Gilman was made a Mason in St. John's Lodge on March 20, 1777, served in the Revolutionary War for more than six years, signed the United States Constitution as a delegate to Congress and was elected one of the first members of Congress in 1788.

From Greenland to Portsmouth Plains was a distance of three miles. The New Hampshire Militia, under the command of Major General Joseph Cilley, was waiting at Portsmouth Plains to salute the President. Major General Cilley was well known to Washington, having fought in many battles under his command, among them that miserable winter at Valley Forge. Joseph Cilley was made a Mason in St. John's Lodge on November 22, 1775, gratis for services rendered his country (probably at Bunker Hill). Soon after

Washington's visit, Bro. Cilley was a petitioner for Columbian Lodge No. 2 of Nottingham and its first Worshipful Master. At the time of his death in 1799, he was Deputy Grand Master of the Grand Lodge of New Hampshire.

It is also reported that Brother Henry Dearborn of St. John's Lodge now United States Marshal for the district of Maine was at the Plains to greet President Washington. He too, was well known to Washington having engaged in many battles of the Revolutionary War.

From Portsmouth Plains to the State House in Market Square was a distance of two miles. The route was lined with citizens to greet their President. In his diary, Washington writes that he arrived just before three o'clock where he was received with every token of respect and appearance of cordiality, under a discharge of artillery. The salute to which he referred was fired by three companies under the command of Col. Hacket. In this company, we find the then Treasurer of St. John's Lodge Col. and Bro. Thomas Thompson. He would be elected Worshipful Master of St. John's Lodge for the year 1801 and elected Grand Master of the Grand Lodge of New Hampshire in 1801 and serve as such until 1807. He was the fourth Grand Master of the Grand Lodge. He was one of the first Navy Captains to be commissioned by the Continental Congress. He was placed in command of the frigate "Raleigh."

The town had appointed a committee to make arrangements. Here we find three more members of St. John's Lodge, namely Jonathan Warner moderator of the special town meeting, Col. Joshua Wentworth, a merchant of iron and anchors, who had been most helpful in securing supplies during the Revolutionary War, and Brother Woodbury Langdon Second Selectman of the town of Portsmouth and brother of Senator John Langdon.

Major and Bro. Joseph Bass, who had served as Junior and Senior Warden of St. John's Lodge for many years was occupied with other constables in maintaining law and order. He had served at West Point during the war. He would soon be appointed the first Junior Grand Warden of the Grand Lodge of New Hampshire and was the second Senior Grand Warden, serving as such for five years.

It was Washington's custom to attend church each Sunday. On Sunday, November 1, 1789, in the morning, he attended Queen's Chapel, later renamed St. John's Church (Episcopal) where the Rector, Rev. and Bro. John C. Ogden preached an excellent sermon. Bro. Ogden was a member of St. John's Lodge, was then its chaplain and was appointed the first Grand Chaplain of the Grand Lodge of New Hampshire. President Washington was met at the door by the church wardens, Captain George Turner, a mariner, and Col. Thomas Thompson. They escorted him with his party to the warden's pew, formerly the pew of the Royal Governors. Captain Turner served St. John's Lodge for many years as an officer and was soon to be appointed as the first Senior Grand Warden of the Grand Lodge of New Hampshire. Col. and Bro. Thompson, the other church warden, was the same person, who on the Saturday before was in the company which fired a thirteen gun salute for President Washington.

It is well documented that one of the Royal Governors, Benning Wentworth, used this pew in Queen's Chapel many times during his 25 years as Governor of the Province. He was also considered by the brethren of St. John's Lodge to be a Mason, though the minute books do not show that he received his degrees in this old lodge. The minute book of the period show a special meeting to attend the funeral of our late brother at Queen's Chapel on October 18, 1770, which is the day on which his funeral services were conducted by the Rev. and Bro. Arthur Brown, long time Rector of Queen's Chapel (1736-73).

In the afternoon, President Washington and his party attended divine service at the North Congregational Church in Market Square. He was seated in the pew of the widow of our late brother, William Whipple, Signer of the Declaration of Independence, a member of St. John's Lodge.

On Monday morning, the committee arranged a trip down the harbor. The coxswain of the President's barge was Bro. Hopley Yeaton, who became a member of St. John's Lodge during the year 1770. He had been active in the lodge ever since. Bro. Yeaton served first in the Continental Army but switched to the Navy with the rank of Lieutenant on the frigate "Raleigh" under Captain Thomas Thompson. Bro. Yeaton was appointed by President Washington as Captain of the "Scammell," in the Revenue Cutter Service (1791) the forerunner of the United States Coast Guard. He served in this capacity until 1809 when he retired. In spite of the many days patrolling the coasts of Maine and New Hampshire, the records of St. John's Lodge and the Grand Lodge show that he attended frequently while in the Revenue Cutter Service.

On Tuesday, November 3, formality required the President of the United States to call upon the President of the State. For this visit, the headquarters of the state government was the Stavers Tavern, owned and operated by Bro. John Stavers, a long time member of St. John's Lodge. Bro. Stavers had built this tavern in 1767 and had one room on the third floor constructed and insulated for use as a Masonic Lodge room. It was occupied by St. John's

Lodge from early 1768 until 1792. This tavern was also the birthplace of the Grand Lodge of New Hampshire, for it was here that the deputies met on July 8, 1789 to form the Grand Lodge and to elect its officers. After the official exchange of greetings were passed, we wonder if the Grand Master-elect, President John Sullivan invited President Washington to visit the old lodge room on the third floor. This building is still standing although deteriorated by the passage of time. It is soon to be restored as a part of the Strawberry Banke historical project, now under way in Portsmouth.

When this visit was concluded, President Washington walked to the home of one of his secretaries, Tobias Lear, not yet a Mason, but who would be made a Mason in Washington's lodge at Alexandria, Virginia in 1803.

On Tuesday evening, a dinner was held at the Assembly Room with about 100 in attendance. If the list were available, we would probably find the names of many Masons. The papers report that it was an elegant ball, but we know not how the guests were chosen or who attended. This was the finale of a busy four days. On Wednesday morning early, President Washington departed from Portsmouth, without fanfare, as he requested. On his return trip, he traveled via the way of Exeter, New Hampshire. He made a brief stop at the Folsom Tavern where he was greeted by many citizens, among whom was Major and Bro. Nicholas Gilman, then serving in the first Congress.

Although there is no record that another congressman in that first Congress was in Portsmouth to greet President Washington, yet it should be mentioned that Samuel Livermore, Past Master of St. John's Lodge during 1772-73 was serving in the first Congress. His absence might be explained, if it was indeed a fact, that his home was now in Holderness, New Hampshire, about 100 miles north of Portsmouth.

The last regular meeting of St. John's Lodge prior to the visit of the President was held on October 8, 1789. The minutes for this evening show that Worshipful Master, Dr. Hall Jackson, was in the East. Moses Woodward, Senior Warden and Daniel Rogers, Junior Warden were present. Nicholas Rousellet was acting Treasurer in the absence of Col. Thomas Thompson and Nathaniel Folsom was secretary. Bro. Nathaniel Folsom was the son of Nathaniel Folsom, who with Bro. John Sullivan, was appointed a delegate to the first Continental Congress. Also present were Bros. Clement Storer, Elijah Hall, Lieutenant on the Ranger under Capt. John Paul Jones, Hopley Yeaton and John Stavers. On this night, it is most unlikely that any of them had any idea that they would soon be host to the President of the United States. The only business recorded was a proposal to ballot on John Melcher, owner of the *New Hampshire Gazette*, at the next lodge night. Normally, there would have been a lodge meeting on November 5, 1789, but if one were held on this date, the day after the departure of the President, no minutes were recorded. The next meeting for which the minutes are in usual order was for the annual meeting on Thursday, December 3, 1789. At this meeting, it is recorded that Bro. John Sullivan was unanimously chosen as Worshipful Master for the ensuing year. This was done to make it possible for him to be installed as Grand Master of the Grand Lodge of New Hampshire.

Bro. Thomas Thompson was reelected to serve as Treasurer and Bro. Nathaniel Folsom was reelected Secretary. At this time, these were the only elective offices. All other offices were filled by appointment by the Worshipful Master. In the minutes for this night, there is no mention of a visit by their beloved President of the United States. Yet, only ten years later, when the death of President Washington occurred, the lodge voted to sing an ode, composed for the occasion, for the following three months as a mourning period. It also formed a procession and marched to St. John's Church for a memorial service together with other citizens of this community.

Although there is no record of any fraternal visit as such, one can see from comparing the officers of St. John's Lodge and of the Grand Lodge of New Hampshire for this period, that most of them were engaged in one way or another with receiving and entertaining the President on his visit to New Hampshire. Undoubtedly other Masons were involved, but if so, their names do not appear in any of the old records or newspapers now available for writing this story.

President Washington returned to New York City by a different route from that taken for the trip to Boston and Portsmouth. He continued to be interested in the many details of every-day life he encountered, frequently stopping to converse with the farmers along the way, questioning them about their crops.

He stopped over the Sabbath on November 8th, giving his reasons as follows:

> "It being contrary to law and disagreeable to the people of this State (Connecticut) to travel on the Sabbath day—and my horses after passing through such intolerable roads wanting rest, I stayed at Perkins' tavern (which, by the way, is not a good one) all day—and a meeting-house being within a few rods of the door, I attended morning and evening service, and heard very lame discourses from a Mr. Pond."

Washington passed through Mansfield, which was even then making a larger quantity of silk than any other town in the state. He spent the night of November 9 in Hartford, and at seven the next morning, took the middle road to New Haven, which city he reached just before sundown. Here he met Mr. Elbridge Gerry, just in from New York, who gave him the first certain account of the health of Mrs. Washington since he parted from her. He reached his own house in Franklin Square between two and three o'clock on Friday, November 13, his horses looking as fresh and spirited as if they had not been traveling continuously for a month; and he was just in time to be present at Mrs. Washington's reception, of which he said: "A pretty large company of ladies and gentlemen were present."

CHAPTER VIII

WASHINGTON'S TOUR OF LONG ISLAND

The winter of 1790 was superlatively mild and pleasant until February, and New York was indeed the gayest and most charming city on the continent. The presence of so much dignity of character, statesmanship, legal lore, culture, and social elegance inspired all manner of ambitions. John Trumbull wrote to Oliver Wolcott early in December:

"I see the President has returned all fragrant with the odour of insence. It must have given him satisfaction to find that the hearts of the people are united in his favor; but the blunt and acknowledged adulation of our addresses must often have wounded his feelings. We have gone through all the popish grades of worship, at least up to the *Hyperdoulia.* This tour has answered a good political purpose, and in a great measure stilled those who were clamoring about the wages of Congress and the salaries of officers."

The President was each day in consultation with the new secretaries in shaping the conduct of their departments, and the most complex and important subjects that came before the legislators in Wall Street were constantly being brought to his notice. But, notwithstanding the weighty affairs of state, he found time for loyalty to social duty.

The city was astir with all manner of festivities, public and private—the balls and dinners were far more numerous than the evenings—and statesmen were constantly meeting in polite circles and everywhere discussing the great topics of the hour, such as the trouble the Indians were giving on the Ohio river, and in the Carolinas, Georgia, and Alabama, the disturbed condition of foreign affairs, Hamilton's bill for funding the public debt, and the location of the permanent seat of government. The President continued his Thursday dinner parties, inviting members of Congress, foreign ministers, and other eminent persons. On the 18th of February, the guests were Mr. and Mrs. Elbridge Gerry, Elias Boudinot, the New Jersey philanthropist, and Mrs. Boudinot, Isaac Coles and Mrs. Coles from Virginia, the brilliant Alexander White and Mrs. White, Samuel Griffin and Mrs. Griffin, Judge Cushing and his lady, and Postmaster-General Osgood and Mrs. Osgood.

On Tuesday afternoons, Washington was ready to receive visitors at three o'clock, usually dressed in coat and breeches of rich black velvet, with a white or pearl-colored satin vest, his hair powdered and gathered into a silk bag, silver knee-buckles and shoe-buckles, a cocked hat in his hand, and an elegant sword in its scabbard of polished white leather at his side.

At Mrs. Washington's Friday levees, he appeared as a private gentleman, without hat or sword. Mrs. Jay, Mrs. Hamilton, and Mrs. Knox each had a special evening aside from giving dinners every week. Chancellor Livingston's home in Broadway below Trinity Church was open to all that was notable in the world of politics and letters. Livingston was a great lover of art treasures, and the walls of his mansion were adorned with beautiful paintings and Gobelin tapestry of unique design, while costly ornaments greeted the eye in every apartment. His table service was of solid silver, valued, it is said, at upwards of thirty thousand dollars; four side-dishes each weighed twelve and one-half pounds.

The McComb Mansion.

[Washington's Residence in Broadway]

On the anniversary of his fifty-eighth birthday, February 22, 1790, Washington was in the turmoil of removal from the Franklin house, which was not adequate for the expanding needs of the President of the United States. When Washington learned that the Macomb house was to be vacated by the French Minister, he arranged to lease it. On February 23-24, 1790, before some of the improvements were completed, Washington moved in, and had his first reception there on February 23, 1790.

The house was erected in 1787 by Alexander Macomb, "four story and an attic high, with a width of fifty six feet." From the rear of the main floor glass doors opened on a balcony with a direct view of the Hudson River. The entrance hall led to a continuous flight of stairs to the top of the house. On each side of the hall were spacious, high-ceiling rooms, used for levees and receptions, and always referred to by Washington as "public rooms." This house was later converted to a hotel known as "Bunkers Mansion House", and in 1928, a 36 story office building was erected on the site. Today a plaque on the building marks this site of the second Presidential Mansion.

The Tammany Society or Columbian Order, then recently instituted in New York, held a meeting at their wigwam, and resolved that forever after it would "commemorate the birthday of the illustrious George Washington." Some extracts from Washington's diary are of special interest in this connection.

"Tuesday, February 23. Few or no visitors at the Levee to-day, from the idea of my being on the move. After dinner, Mrs. Washington and myself and children removed, and lodged at our new habitation.

Wednesday 24 Employed in arranging matters about the house and fixing matters.

Thursday 25 Engaged as yesterday. In the afternoon a committee of Congress presented an Act for enumerating the inhabitants of the United States.

Friday 26 A numerous company of ladies and gentlemen here this afternoon. Exercised on horseback this forenoon.

Saturday 27 Sat for Mr. Trumbull this forenoon; after which exercised in the coach with Mrs. Washington and the children.

Sunday 28 Went to St. Paul's Chapel in the forenoon. Wrote letters on private business afterwards.

Monday, March 1. Exercised on horseback this forenoon, attended by Mr. John Trumbull, who wanted to see me mounted. Informed the House of Representatives (where the bill originated) that I had given my assent to the act of taking a census of the people . . .

Tuesday 2 Much and respectable company at the Levee to-day. Caused a letter to be written to the Gov'r of St. Iago respecting the imprisonment of a Captain Hammond.

Wednesday 3 Exercised on horseback between 9 and 11 o'clock.

Thursday 4 Sat from 9 until half after 10 o'clock for Mr. Trumbull. The following gentlemen dined here to-day, viz; the vice President (John Adams) Messers (John) Langdon, (Paine) Wingate, (Tristam) Dalton, (Caleb) Strong, (Oliver) Ellsworth, (Philip) Schuyler, (Rufus) King, (William) Patterson, (Robert) Morris, (William) Maclay, (Richard) Bassett, (John) Henry, (William Samuel) Johnson, (Benjamin) Hawkins, (Ralph) Izard, (Pierce) Butler, and (William) Few, all of the Senate.

Friday 5 A very numerous company of ladies and gentlemen here this evening.

Saturday 6 Exercised in the coach with Mrs. Washington and the children, and in the afternoon walked around the Battery."

Washington also visited Long Island, driving through many of the towns, and carefully jotting observations into his note-book. Mrs. Jay wrote to her husband, who was in Boston, of the President's absence on this trip, and remarks: "On Wednesday Mrs. Washington called upon me to go with her to wait upon Miss Van Berckel, and on Thursday morning, agreeable to invitation, myself and the little girls took an early breakfast with her, and then went with her and her little grandchildren to breakfast at General Morris's, at Morrisania. We passed together a very agreeable day, and on our return dined with her, as she would not take a refusal. After which I came home to dress, and she was so polite as to take coffee with me in the evening." In another letter Mrs. Jay mentions, "Mr. and Mrs. Hamilton dined with me on Sunday and on Tuesday." She also refers to having entertained informally Mrs. Iredell and her daughter, and Mr. and Mrs. Munro. Stephen Van Rensselaer, of Albany, known as the patroon, was the newly elected Senator whose bride was Mrs. Hamilton's sister, Margaret. Later became Grand Master of the Grand Lodge of New York (1825-29), and laid the cornerstone of the first Masonic Hall in New York City in 1828.

Washington noted in his diary on Monday, April 19, 1790 "Prevented from beginning my tour upon Long Island to day from the wet of yesterday and the unfavorableness of the Morning." The next day he was off on the journey and his own notes tell the tale far better than any interpretation.

Tuesday 20th. About 8 Oclock (having previously sent over my Servants, Horses and Carriage I crossed to Brooklin and proceeded to Flat Bush—thence to Utrich—thence to Gravesend thence through Jamaica where we lodged at a Tavern kept by one Warne—a pretty good and decent house. At the House of a Mr. Barre, at Utrich, we dined. The Man was obliging but little else to recommend it. He told me that their average Crop of Oats did not exceed 25 bushels, to the Acre but of Indian Corn they commonly made from 25 to 30 and often more bushels to the Acre but this was the effect of Dung from New York (about 10 Cart load to the Acre)—That of Wheat they sometimes got 30 bushels and often more of Rye.

The land after crossing the Hills between Brooklyn & flat Bush is perfectly level, and from the latter to Utrich, Gravesend and in short all that end of the Island is a rich black loam. Afterwards, between [ ] and the Jamaica Road it is more Sandy and appears to have less strength, but is still good & productive. The grain in general had suffered but little by the openess, and Rains of the Winter and the grass (clover &ca.) appeared to be coming on well. The Inclosures are small & under open Post & Rail fencing. The timber is chiefly Hiccoey & Oak, mixed here and there with locust & Sasafras trees and in places with a good deal of Cedar. The Road until I came within a mile or two of the Jamaica Road, called the middle road kept within sight of the Sea but the weather was so dull & at times Rainy that we lost much of the pleasure of the ride.

From Brooklyn to Flat bush is called 5 miles—thence to Utrich 6—to Gravesend 2 and from thence to Jamaica 14—in all this day 27 miles.

Before I left New York this Morning I signed Commissions appointing Mr. Carmichael Chargé des Affaires at the Court of Versailles, & Mr. Short Chargé des Affaires at the Court of Versailles which though not usually given to Diplomatic characters of their Grades was yet made necessary in the opinion of the Secretary of State by an Act of Congress.

Wednesday 21st. The Morning being clear & pleasant we left Jamaica about Eight o'clock, & pursued the Road to South Hempstead passing along the South edge of the plain of that name—a plain said to be 14 miles in length by 3 or 4 in breadth without, a Tree or a Shrub growing on it except fruit trees (which do not thrive well) at the few settlements, thereon. The Soil of this plain is said to be thin & cold and of course not productive, even in Grass. We baited in South Hemstead (10 Miles from Jamaica) at the House of one Simmonds, formerly a Tavern, now of private entertainment for Money. From hence turning off to the right we fell into the South Rd. at the distance of about five miles where we came in view of the Sea & continued to be so the remaining part of the days ride, and as near it as the road could run for the small bays, Marshes and guts, into which the tide flows at all times rendering it impassible from the height of it by the Easterly Winds. We dined at one Ketchums wch. had also been a public House but now a private one receivg. pay for what it furnished. This House was about 14 Miles from South Hemstead & very neat & decent one. After dinner we proceeded to a Squire Thompsons such a House as the last, that is, one that is not public but will receive pay for everything it furnishes in the same manner as if it was.

The Road in which I passed today, and the Country were more mixed with sand than yesterday and the Soil of inferior quality: Yet with dung wch. all the Corn ground receives the land yields on an average 30 bushels to the Acre often more. Of Wheat they do not grow much on acct. of the Fly but the Crops of Rye are good.

Thursday 22d. About 8 Oclock we left Mr. Thompson's—halted a while at one Greens distant 11 Miles and dined Harts Tavern in Brookhaven town ship five miles farther. To this place we travelled on what is called the South road described yesterday but the Country through which it passed grew more and more Sandy and barren as we travelled Eastward, so as to become exceedingly poor indeed but a few miles further Eastward the lands took a different complexion we were informed. From Harts we struck across the Island for the No. side, passing the East end of the Brushey Plains and Koram 8 Miles—thence to Setakit 7 Mi. more to the House of a Captn. Roe which is tolerably dect. with obliging people in it. The first five Miles of the Road is too poor to admit Inhabitants or cultivation being a low scrubby Oak, not more than 2 feet high intermixed with small and ill thriven Pines. Within two miles of Koram there are farms but the land is of an indifferent quality much mixed with Sand. Koram contains but few houses. From thence to Setalket the Soil improves, especially as you approach the Sound; but is far from being of the first quality, still a good deal mixed with Sand. The road across from the So. to the No. Side is level, except a small part So. of Koram but the hills there are trifling.

Friday 23d. About 8 Oclock we left Roes, and baited the Horses at Smiths Town, at a Widow Blidenbergs—a decent House 10 Miles from Setalkat— thence 15 Miles to Huntington where we dined and afterwards proceeded Seven Miles to Oyster-bay, to the House of a Mr. Young (private & very neat and decent) where we lodged. The house we dined at in Huntington was kept by a Widow Platt and was tolerably good. The whole of this days ride was over uneven ground and none of it of the first quality but intermixed in places with pebble-stone. After passing Smithstown & for near five Miles it was a mere bed of white Sand, unable to produce trees 25 feet high; but a change for the better took place between that & Huntington, which is a sml. village at the head of the Harbour of that name and continued to improve to Oyster-bay about which the Lands are good and in the Necks between these bays are said to be fine. It is here the Lloyds own a large & valuable tract, or Neck of Land from whence the British whilst they possessed New York drew large supplies of Wood and where, at present, it is said large flocks of Sheep are kept.

Saturday 24th. Left Mr. Youngs before 6 Oclock, and passing Musqueto Cove, breakfasted at a Mr. Underduncks at the head of a little bay; where we were kindly received and well entertained. This Gentleman works a Grist & two Paper Mills, the last of which he seems to carry on with Spirit, and to profit—distc. trom Oyster bay 12 Miles. From hence to Flushing where we dined is 12 more & from thence to Brooklyne through Newton (the way we travelled and which is a mile further than to pass through Jamaica) is 18 miles more. The land I passed over to day is generally very good, but leveller and better as we approached New York. The soil in places is intermixed with pebble, and towards the Westend with other kind of stone which they apply to the purposes of fencing which is not to be seen on the South side of the Island nor towards the Eastern parts of it. From Flushing to New Town

8 miles, & thence to Brooklyn, the Road is very fine, and the Country in a higher State of Cultivation & vegitation of Grass & grain forwarded than any place else I had seen—occasioned in a great degree by the Manure drawn from the City of New York. Before Sundown we had crossed the Ferry and was at home.

Observations

This land (as far as I went) from West to East seems to be equally divided between flat, & Hilly land—the former on the South next the Sea board & the latter on the No. next the Sound. The high land they say is best and most productive but the other is the pleasantest to work except in wet seasons when from the levelness of them they are sometimes (but not frequently having a considerable portion of Sand) incommoded by heavy & continual rains. From a comparative view of their Crops they may be averaged as follow. Indian Corn 25 bushels—Wheat 15—Rye 12—Oats 15 bushels to the Acre. According to their accts. from Lands highly manured they sometimes get 50 of the first, 25 of the 2d. & 3d. and more of the latter. Their general mode of Cropping is—first Indian Corn upon a lay, manured in the hill, half a shovel full in each hole (some scatter the dung over the field equally)—2d. Oats & flax—3d. Wheat with what Manure they can spare from the Indian Corn land. With the wheat, or on it, towards close of the snows, they sow Clover from 4 to 6 lb; & a quart of Timothy seed. This lays from 3 to 6 years, according as the grass remains, or as the condition of the ground is, for so soon as they find it beginning to bind they plow. Their first plowing (with the Patent, tho' they call it the Dutch plough) is well executed at the depth of about 3 or at most 4 Inches—the cut being 9 or 10 inches & the sod neatly & very evenly turned. With Oxen they plough mostly. They do no more than turn the ground in this manner for Indian Corn before it is planted; making the holes in which it is placed with hoes the rows being marked off by a stick. Two or three workings afterwards with the Harrows or Plough is all the cultivation it receives *generally.* Their fences, where there is no stone, are very indifferent; frequently of plashed trees of *any & every* kind which have grown by chance; but it exhibits an evidence that very good fences may be made in this manner either of white Oak or Dogwood which from this mode of treatment grows thickest, and most stubborn. This, however would be no defense against Hogs.

Sunday 25th. Went to Trinity Church, and wrote letters home after dinner.

The general upheaval of society in France at this juncture, as described from time to time by Gouverneur Morris, caused much uneasiness. After spending an evening with De Moustier, the French minister, who had returned to Paris, Morris wrote: "I find that, notwithstanding public professions as to the public proceedings of America, both De Moustier and Madame de Brehan have a thorough dislike to the country and its inhabitants. The society of New York is not sociable, the provisions of America are not good, the climate is very damp, the wines are abominable, the people are excessively indolent." Thomas Jefferson, coming home from his mission to France, was overflowing with sympathy for the French revolutionists. He spent a few weeks at his Virginia country seat, and then traveled to New York to assume his duties of Secretary of State. He arrived on Sunday. Washington had just returned from church when Jefferson was announced. "Show him in," was the quick and pleased response, and then the President, without waiting, stepped forward and greeted his guest with special warmth and cordiality in the entrance hall. Jefferson's coming on that day was particularly opportune. Washington and Jay were earnestly considering the course to be pursued in relation to some captives of Algiers—and also about the sending of *charges d'affaires* to the courts of Europe. Jefferson was fresh from the old world, and brought the latest exact intelligence touching upon its affairs. But he did not find things in America as he expected. He was disappointed with the Constitution; and, he thought the leaning was toward a kingly instead of a republican government. Hamilton's project of a national bank shocked him—he regarded it as a fountain of demoralization.

It was at Hamilton's dinner-table that he first advocated aiding France to throw off her monarchical yoke. Hamilton declared himself in favor of maintaining a strict neutrality. This question presently assumed vital importance. Jefferson opposed Hamilton's funding system, and seemed to distrust all his measures. Stormy discussions were of daily occurrence, trifles were magnified, and political excitement spread through the country.

Thus developed that division in politics, which, gradually rising to the dignity of party organization, was known as Federalism and Republicanism.

The Assumption Bill brought to the front all the local prejudices of a century, and created such feuds that when it was lost in the house by a vote taken one hot July afternoon, the whole business of the nation was in a deadlock. The northern members threatened secession and dissolution of the union. Congress actually adjourned from day to day because opposing parties were too much out of temper to do business together. Washington was seriously alarmed.

For some weeks the controversy over the location of the permanent seat of government had been almost as heated as that concerning the Assumption Bill. "The question of residence is constantly entangling every measure proposed," wrote Wolcott. New York city was preferred by the majority; the gentlemen from the New England states could reach it with ease, and it was accessible by sea from the south. A house, intended for a Presidential residence, was already in process of erection near the Battery, on the site of the old fort, overlooking the Bowling Green. But neither the state nor the city authorities were ready to cede the territory and the jurisdiction of the ten miles square which it must include, even if such a tract could be found appropriately situated. Harlem Heights was suggested as suitable for the proposed district, as was also Westchester and the heights of Brooklyn. Washington was incessantly active and observant. His morning exercise on horseback was frequently extended to the site of the Harlem Heights battlefield, where he won his first absolute victory in an open field encounter with the British; and this picturesque elevation between Manhattanville and Kingsbridge might have been his choice for the site of a capitol and public buildings, if the question had been decided in favor of New York.

One charming summer day a party was formed for a drive over Harlem Heights, and a visit to the remains of Fort Washington. The party consisted of the President and Mrs. Washington, the two children, Mrs. Lear, the gentlemen of the President's household, Vice-President John Adams and Mrs. Adams, their son and Miss Smith, Secretary and Mrs. Hamilton, Secretary Thomas Jefferson, and Secretary and Mrs. Knox. Returning, they alighted at the old Roger Morris mansion, with which Washington, as we all know, was thoroughly familiar, where a dinner had been provided for the entire party by Mr. Mariner, the farmer who occupied the premises. This fine house with its extensive grounds had been confiscated, and was at the time in the care of a man employed by the government. Towards evening the party descended Breakneck Hill and drove back to the city. The "fourteen mile round," Washington's favorite drive, was over the old Bloomingdale road to the high bluff where Grant now sleeps, thence across to the Kingsbridge and old Boston roads in returning.

Pennsylvania made great efforts to secure the establishment of the future capital on the banks of the Delaware; and Maryland, Delaware, and Virginia were anxious that it should be located on the Potomac. The South Carolinians objected decidedly to Philadelphia because her Quakers "were eternally dogging southern members with their schemes of emancipation." The subject of slavery had indeed been introduced into congress by a petition from the Quakers that negroes should receive their freedom. The Philadelphians resented any mention of New York as the ultimate choice. Dr. Rush wrote to Muhlenberg: "Do as you please, but tear congress away from New York in any way; do not rise until you have effected this business."

Jefferson was on his way to see the President one morning when he met Hamilton on the street, and the two walked arm in arm backward and forward in front of the President's house in Broadway for half an hour, Hamilton explaining with the utmost earnestness the anger and disgust of the creditor states, and the immediate danger of disunion, unless the excitement was calmed through the sacrifice of some subordinate principle. Hamilton appealed with such persuasive eloquence and so directly to Jefferson for aid in silencing the clamor which menaced the very existence of government that the latter yielded, and afterwards said he "was most innocently made to hold the candle" to Hamilton's "fiscal manoeuvre" for assuming the state debts. He proposed that Hamilton should dine with him the next day, inviting two or three other gentlemen; and at the dinner-table the situation was discussed in all its bearings. It was finally agreed that two of the Virginia members should support the Assumption Bill, and that Hamilton and Robert Morris should command the northern influence sufficient to locate the seat of government on the Potomac. The result was the adoption of Hamilton's funding system by a small majority in both houses, and the final decision which founded the city of Washington on its present site.

Congress determined that Philadelphia was to be the seat of government until 1800, and after that year, the Capital was to be near Georgetown, on the Potomac River. However, the first filibuster occurred during the debate on this legislation when Elbridge Gerry of Massachusetts spoke at length in opposition. Those who favored New York City as the permanent capital were furious, and the New York City newspapers presented an argument that the proposal was unconstitutional.

The bill for establishing the temporary and permanent seat of government was passed and presented to the President on July 12, 1790. Washington, after conferring with his advisors, signed the legislation on July 16, 1790.

Congress adjourned on August 12, 1790, and planned to convene in December, expressing thanks to the corporation of the City of New York "for the elegant and convenient accomodations furnished the Congress of the United States."

On August 30, 1790, in spite of Washington's request for "an unceremonious leave taking, the Governor of New York, the Chief Justice of the United States, the heads of Federal departments, and other State and City officers escorted Washington to the wharf at Elizabeth Town Point. The crowd was not large, because the exact hour of departure had not been announced. New York was losing both George Washington and the seat of government. "All was quietness, save the report of the cannon that were fired on his embarkation . . . the heart was full—the tear dropped from the eye; it was not to be restrained; it was seen; and the President appeared sensibly moved by this last mark of esteem.

George Washington never returned to New York.

CHAPTER IX

WASHINGTON'S TOUR OF RHODE ISLAND

On August 14th, Washington sailed for Newport, Rhode Island, arriving there on Tuesday morning, August 17, 1790.

FREEMASONRY in Rhode Island, at the close of the War of the Revolution, was represented by St. John's Lodge in Providence and King David's Lodge in Newport. The first Lodge (St. John's) in Newport was inactive, as it had been for a long time. The Lodge in Providence, after its revival, had greatly prospered under the efficient leadership of Bro. Jabez Bowen, its Wor. Master from 1778 to 1790, and had received among its new members a large accession of influential citizens. One of these, William Barton, initiated in 1779, is deservedly remembered and honored for his heroic exploit in making prisoner of the British General, William Prescott, on the island of Rhode Island, and for other patriotic services. Another, John Carlile, initiated in 1783, served the Craft with exceptional skill in many important offices for a long term of years.

The membership of King David's Lodge, at this same period, included a goodly number of intelligent and zealous brethren. Its prosperity was retarded by some unfavorable conditions. As pointing to some of these conditions affecting itself and the dormant first Lodge in Newport, and also as showing the general condition of Freemasonry in Rhode Island, the following paper is presented. It was prepared by a Committee of the Lodge in reply to a communication from the Grand Lodge of Virginia, making enquiry as to the "standing of Masonry" in Rhode Island and the grounds on which its Grand Lodge was established. The reply was sent in December, 1787.

BRETHREN—The annexed copy of the proceedings of King David's Lodge, No. 1, will apprize you of the receipt of your polite and Brotherly letter, under date of 30th October last, which would not have fell immediately under our view had there been any Grand Lodge within

---

Full-length 1790 canvas of John Trumbull's "George Washington" (credit and gratitude is expressed for this photograpic reproduction to and by courtesy of the Art Commission of the City of New York - City Hall, N. Y. 10007).

The original canvas painting is now in the Council Chamber of the City Hall of New York.

Full uniform of Commander-in-Chief of the Army, standing in front of his horse which rubs its nose against its left front leg. In the background is seen the bay of New York and river scene, the Narrows with men-of-war in full sail.

Praised by Custis, who wrote, "For correct figure we must in all cases turn to the work of Trumbull." According to Hart, p. 63, the painting was altered by Trumbull in 1804. Engraved in Mezzotint by A. Edwards. Ordered by the Council of the City of New York, July 19, 1790. Trumbull's own descriptions, "in the background view of Broadway in ruins," cannot be made out clearly in the present darkened state of the painting. See Plate CLVII, p. 679.

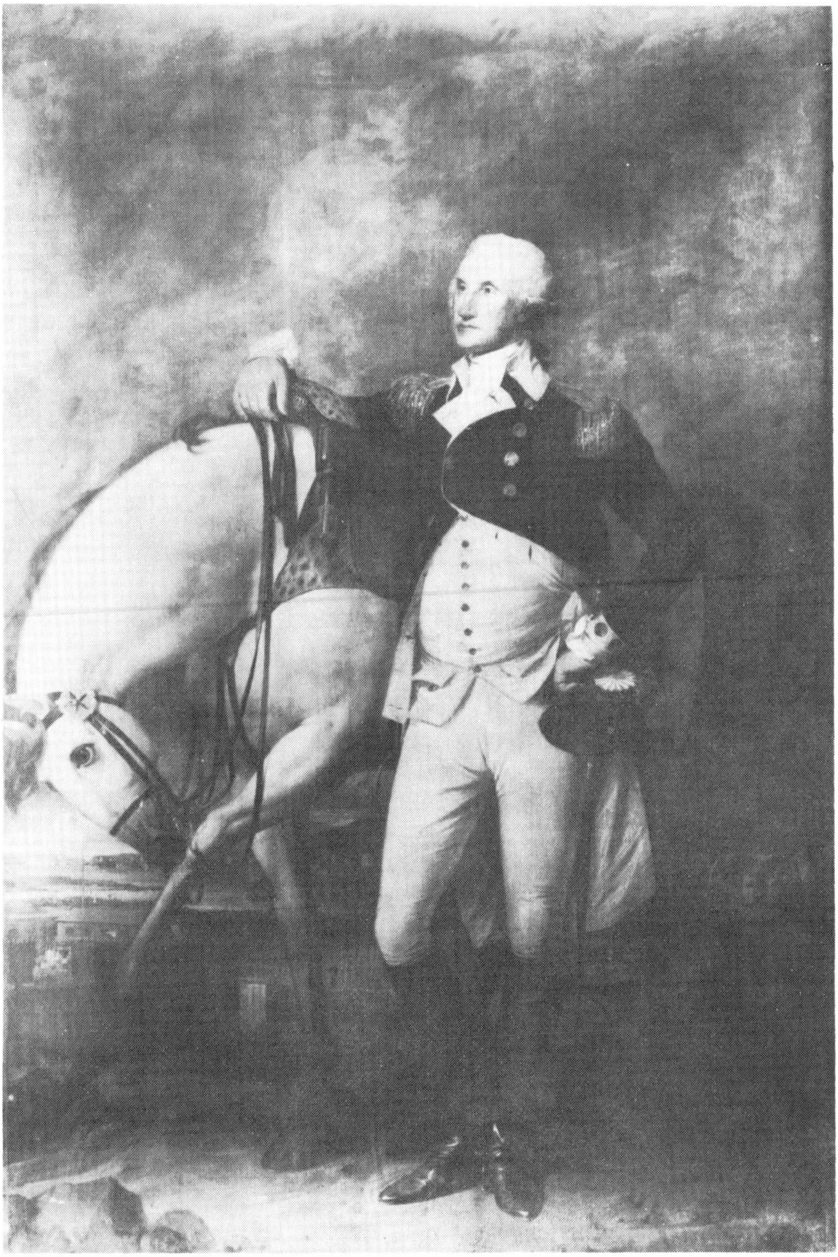

this State; neither should we have arrogated to ourselves the right of opening it could we have supposed it would not have been perfectly agreeable to our Worthy Brethren of St. John's Lodge, No. 1, at Providence, to whom we have transmitted a copy thereof. By the tenor of your letter you only require to know upon what ground any Grand Lodge which may be within this State is established, but we deem it necessary to communicate to you the standing of Masonry within this State and therefore shall proceed to a detail thereof.

By the records of the first Lodge in Newport, which we have in our possession, we find that there had been a Lodge here previous thereto, but by the caprice of the Master he with-held from them the Deputation with which he was clothed by Thomas Oxnard, Esq., Provincial Grand Master, as also the records of the said Lodge, whereupon the petition from several members of the aforesaid Lodge, the aforesaid R. W. Thomas Oxnard, Esq., under his hand and seal at Boston, May 14, 1753, appointed Robert Jenkins Master of the Lodge here, and at which period its records commence.

On the eve 24th of January, 1760, the Right Worshipful Jeremy Gridley, Esq., Grand Master of all Free and Accepted Masons in North America, where no other Grand Master is appointed, by virtue of the authority delegated to him by the Rt. Hon. Worshipful James Bridges, Marquis of Carnavan, Grand Master of Masons, appointed him, the aforesaid Robert Jenkins, Deputy Grand Master of Masons in the then Colony of Rhode Island and Providence Plantations, with full power and authority to constitute and regulate Lodges and transact and execute all the duties of and appertaining to the office of Provincial Grand Master.

On the 11th of November, 1756, we find that the Rt. Worshipful Robert Jenkins convened the Lodge of this place to meet at Providence, for the express purpose of initiating several inhabitants of that town into our Ancient arts and mysteries, and then, if our memory serves us right, was constituted and established the present Lodge of Providence.*

At the commencement of the Revolution an absolute decay took place in the first Lodge in Newport, and it has never been revived under that description, and we are of the opinion it never will, as most of its members compose the body of our Lodge, which was instituted and established June 7th, 1780, by the Rt. Worshipful Moses M. Hayes, by authority which he obtained 23 of February, 1769, from the Rt. Worshipful George Harrison, Esq., Provincial Grand Master of New York, he then being a resident of New York, but at the institution of King David's Lodge an inhabitant of this place. He now resides in Boston and is a respectable character there, and is clothed with a warrent of Masonry, the most sublime that ever came under our observation, a copy of which from our records we inclose for your perusal.

---

*Evidently this is a mistake. The Lodge of Providence was not constituted at that time, but at a later date. The Newport Lodge did, however, make some eight Masons at that meeting in Providence, having made two previously in Newport, who were the first members of the Providence Lodge.

On the 13th day of June, 1759, the Legislature granted a partial Charter to the Fraternity, incorporating them under the name in law of the Master, Wardens and Society of Free and Accepted Masons in the Town of Newport. The advantages of which we think we can at any time avail ourselves of. Several of our members are dignified with the higher orders of Masonry, and we, the under-writers, have attained from the 16th to the 29th Degree of its Sublimity. We strictly enjoin you to be cautious of Masons appearing from these parts as there is a certain J—N—whose private character is such as that we have denied him admittance into our Lodge for several years past. . . .He has also assumed to himself the right of making Masons, and, as we are informed, he yet continues so to do, refusing none that present themselves, let what will be their character. This information we entreat you to communicate to all within the circle of your correspondence. We shall at times feel ourselves happy to communicate with you as Brethren touching any subject that may be for the wellfare of Masonry and for the furtherance and good of the craft, holding it as worthy the attention of all men who have entered into the principles and taken the obligations of Masonry, to be conscientious by attendance and scrupulously exact in its duties, which are founded on Benevolence, Brotherly Love and the happiness of mankind in general.

We salute you with cordial and Brotherly wishes, and are very respectfully,

Your very humble servants,

MOSES SEIXAS,
HENRY DAYTON,   } *Committee*
HENRY GOODWIN,

Moses Seixas, who undoubtedly composed this response sent to the Grand Lodge of Virginia, was a prominent merchant of Newport. His residence was on Washington Square, later the property of Commodore O. H. Perry. He was Cashier of the Bank of Rhode Island (of which Christopher Champlin, Grand Master of Masons in Rhode Island, was President), a position which he held until his death in 1809. He was a devoted Craftsman, and often represented the Fraternity in matters requiring Masonic and general knowledge. He presented the address of the members of King David's Lodge to President Washington when he visited Newport.

The body of Seixas was laid to rest in the Parish Cemetery, Newport, and a monument erected to his memory, on which the following inscription can be read:

MATESBETH
MONUMENT OF
MOSES SEIXAS,
DIED 4TH CHISLEN, 5570,
BEING Nov. 29, 1809,
AGED 66.

He was Grand Master of the
Grand Lodge of the Masonic
Order of this State and Cashier of
The Bank of Rhode Island From Its
Commencement to His Death.

The minutes of King David's Lodge disclose the following entry on the very day George Washington arrived in Newport, Rhode Island.

"At a Lodge, called by request of several Brethren on Tuesday evening, August 17, 1790, an Entered Apprentice Lodge being opened in due form proceeded to business, when it was proposed to address the President of the United States. The R. W. Master (Moses Seixas) Henry Sherburne, and the Secretary, [William Littlefield] were appointed a committee for that purpose, after which the Lodge closed."*

The following address was prepared and according to local tradition was publicly presented, by the Committee to President Washington, in the Venerable Sanctuary of the Jewish Congregation at Newport; the Brethren of King David's Lodge being present:

"TO GEORGE WASHINGTON, *President of the United States of America.*

"We the Master, Wardens, and Brethren of
"King David's Lodge in New Port Rhode Island
"with joyful hearts embrace this opportunity to
"greet you as a Brother, and to hail you welcome
"to Rhode Island. We exult in the thought that
"as Masonry has always been patronized by the
"wise, the good, and the great, so that it stood
"and ever will stand, as its fixtures are on the
"immutable pillars of faith, hope, and charity.
"With unspeakable pleasure we gratulate
"you as filling the presidential chair with the

---

*A copy of the Extracts from the Records of King David's Lodge No. 1, as made by Ara Hildreth, Esq., is in the Archives of the Grand Lodge of Pennsylvania, Mss. Volume Q, R.I. 7.

Cf. also a verified copy of the Minute in "Proceedings of the Antimasonic Republican Convention of Massachusetts, Boston, 1832," p. 22.

"applause of a numerous and enlightened people
"Whilst at the same time we felicitate ourselves
"in the honor done the brotherhood by your many
"exemplary virtues and emanations of goodness
"proceeding from a heart worthy of possessing
"the ancient mysteries of our craft; being persuaded
"that the wisdom and grace with which heaven
"has endowed you, will square all your thoughts,
"words, and actions by the eternal laws of honor,
"equity, and truth, so as to promote the advancement
"of all good works, your own happiness, and that
"of mankind.
   "Permit us then, illustrious Brother,
"cordially to salute you with three times three
"and to add our fervent supplications that the
"sovereign architect of the universe may always
"encompass you with his holy protection.

"New Port Aug 17, 1790
"By order
   "Wm LITTLEFIELD, *Sec.*"

                    "Moses Seixas *Master*
                            Committee.
                    "Hy SHERBURNE

Touro Synagogue (1763) was the first synagogue to be built in America. It is named for Isaac Touro, the spiritual leader of the congregation at the time. It was designed by Peter Harrison after the eighteenth-century Spanish and Portuguese Sephardic synagogues of London and Amsterdam.

Brother Moses Seixas was born in New York, March 28, 1744; died in New York City, November 29, 1809. He was a merchant in Newport, Rhode Island, and one of the founders of the Newport Bank of Rhode Island, of which he was cashier until his death. He succeeded Brother Moses M. Hays as Worshipful Master of King David's Lodge at Newport. He was also Grand Master of the Grand Lodge of Rhode Island. It was Moses Seixas who addressed a letter of welcome in the name of the Jewish congregation to George Washington when the latter visited Newport, and it was to him that Washington's answer was addressed.

The Town Hall at Newport being out of repair at that time the ancient Jewish Synagogue on the main street was used, upon that and several other public occasions. It is an interesting fact that this sacred edifice is still preserved in the same condition as it was during the Colonial period.

So far as known this address was the first of Masonic import made to Washington as President. Unfortunately, the exact date of presentation and receipt of his answer is not known to a certainty, as there does not appear to be any date upon either the original documents or the copies in Washington's letter book.

The original address and Washington's reply to the Master, Wardens and Brethren of King David's Lodge in Newport, the latter signed in autograph by Washington, are in the Athenaeum collection at Boston, Massachusetts.

The copy of the President's answer is on page 134 and is taken from his letter book. Both address and answer in the letter book are in the handwriting of Major William Jackson, secretary to the President.

President Washington arrived at Newport, R.I., at eight o'clock on Tuesday morning, August 17, 1790. On the next day, Wednesday, the President and his suite left on the Packet "Hancock" at nine o'clock in the morning for Providence.

His company consisted of Governor Clinton of New York, Thomas Jefferson, Secretary of State, Senator Theodore Foster, Judge Blair, Mr. Smith of South Carolina and Mr. Gorman of New Hampshire; members of Congress.*

Washington left Providence, Saturday, August 21, and arrived in New York upon the following day, Sunday, August 22, 1790,** and sent the following reply to the Newport Brethren: It will be noted that there is neither place nor date given on the manuscript letter.

---

*Cf. "Washington after the Revolution," W. S. Baker, Philadelphia, 1898, p. 192.
**Cf. Pennsylvania Packet, August 30-31 1790.

WASHINGTON'S TOUR OF RHODE ISLAND

To the Master, Wardens, and Brethren of King David's Lodge in Newport Rhode Island.

Gentlemen

I receive the welcome which you give me to Rhode-Island with pleasure, and I acknowledge my obligations for the flattering expressions of regard, contained in your address, with grateful sincerity.

Being persuaded that a just application of the principles, on which the masonic fraternity is founded, must be promotive of private virtue and public prosperity, I shall always be happy to advance the interests of the society, and to be considered by them as a deserving brother.

My best wishes, Gentlemen, are offered for your individual happiness.

G Washington

Fac-simile of Reply to King David's Lodge No. 1, Newport, R. I.
Letter Book II, pp. 27-28.

"TO THE MASTER, WARDENS, AND BRETHREN OF "KING DAVIDS LODGE IN NEWPORT RHODE ISLAND."

"*Gentlemen,*

"I receive the welcome which you "give me to Rhode Island with pleasure, and I "acknowledge my obligations for the flattering "expressions of regard, contained in your address, "with grateful sincerity.

"Being persuaded that a just "application of the principles, on which the Masonic "Fraternity is founded, must be promotive of "private virtue and public prosperity, I shall "always be happy to advance the interests of "the Society, and to be considered by them as "a deserving brother.

"My best wishes, Gentlemen, are offered "for your individual happiness."*

---

*Copy of Address in Letter Book II, pp 27-28, Photostat of same in Archives of Grand Lodge of Pennsylvania.

CHAPTER X

BRIEF MASONIC HISTORY

Washington resigned his commission as Commander-in-Chief of the Armies of the United States, on December 23, 1783, and returned to Mt. Vernon. Alexandria Lodge wrote him a fraternal letter of felicitation, and carrying an invitation to join the brethren on Masonic occasions. To this Washington replied:

Gentlemen: Mount Vernon, 28th Dec. 1783.

With pleasing sensibility I received your favor of the 26th, and beg leave to offer you my sincere thanks for the favorable sentiments with which it abounds.—

I shall always feel pleasure when it may be in my power to render service to Lodge N° 39, and in every act of brotherly kindness to the Members of it; being with great truth.
Your affect Brother and Obed Servant
G. WASHINGTON

Washington was invited to join the brethren of Alexandria Lodge in the celebration of St. John's Day, June 24, 1784. He answered thus:

Dear Sir: Mount Vernon, June 19, 1784.

With pleasure, I received the invitation of the master and members of Lodge No. 39, to dine with them on the approaching anniversary of St. John the Baptist. If nothing unforeseen at present interferes, I will have the honor of doing it. For the polite and flattering terms in which you have expressed their wishes, you will please accept my thanks.
With esteem and respect, I am, dear sir,
Your most Ob't serv't
G. WASHINGTON

It was upon this occasion that Washington was elected an honorary member of the Lodge.

The Layfayette Apron at Philadelphia

Lafayette visited Washington at Mount Vernon in August, 1784, and presented him with a white satin Masonic apron which had been embroidered by the Marquise de Lafayette in colored silks. This apron, depicted herewith, shows the conventional emblems of the Craft, but is particularly noteworthy because of the emblem on the flap depicting the Mark Degree. The apron is embordered with red, white and blue bands. It measures 23 inches in length and 16 1/2 and 18 inches in breadth at top and bottom, respectively. The flap is semi-circular, rather than triangular, and the corners of the apron itself are rounded, rather than square, thus conforming to the earlier type of Masonic apron depicted in old engravings.

—137—

This interesting apron was presented October 26, 1816, to the Washington Benevolent Society of Philadelphia by the legatees, and upon the dissolution of that society, the apron was in turn presented on July 3, 1829, to the Grand Lodge of Pennsylvania, where it can now be seen among other valuable treasures in its Library and Museum.

THE APRON PRESENTED TO WASHINGTON BY LAFAYETTE

The apron here depicted is now owned by the Right Worshipful Grand Lodge of the Most Ancient and Honorable Fraternity of Free and Accepted Masons of Pennsylvania, and can be seen in the Library of the Grand Lodge in Philadelphia.

February 12, 1785 George Washington attended the Masonic funeral of Bro. William Ramsay at Alexandria, and made the following entry in his diary:

> "Received an Invitation to the Funeral of Willm. Ramsay, Esqr. of Alexandria, the oldest Inhabitt. of the Town; and went up. Walked in a procession as a free mason, Mr. Ramsay in his life being one, and now buried with the ceremonies and honors due to one."

The Pennsylvania "Ahiman Rezon," 1783, was authorized by the Grand Lodge of Pennsylvania November 22, 1781, and bears this dedication:

> To His Excellency GEORGE WASHINGTON, Esq., General and Commander in Chief of the Armies of the United States of America: In *Testimony*, as well of his exalted Services to his Country, as of that noble Philanthropy which distinguishes Him among Masons, the following Constitutions of the most ancient and honorable Fraternity of *Free and Accepted Masons*, by Order and in Behalf of the Grand Lodge of *Pennsylvania*, &c. is dedicated, By his Excellency's Most humble Servant, and faithful Brother, William Smith, G. Secretary.

The book is a 16mo., of 166 pages, with an engraved frontispiece showing the arms of the Operative Stone Masons. Its title is *Ahiman Rezon Abridged and Digested: Help to all that are, or would be Free and Accepted Masons*. Added thereto is a sermon preached in Christ-Church, Philadelphia, December 28, 1778, by William Smith, D.D. The volume was printed at Philadelphia, by Hall and Sellers, in 1783. It was item No. 140 in the inventory of Washington's property. Upon passing out of the possession of Judge Bushrod Washington and Lawrence Washington, it was sold at auction in Philadelphia for $8.00. It was resold for $50; in 1891, it was acquired by John Nicholas Brown, of Providence, and is now in the John Carter Brown Library, Providence, Rhode Island. The book does not have Washington's signature, but contains what is believed to be a restrike bookplate. The red morocco label on the inside front cover has the following wording stamped upon it: "His Excellency George Washington, Esq. late Commander in Chief of the American Army." The book itself is bound in red morocco, with gold tooling and gilt edges, there are no Masonic emblems on the covers.

Several of the early editions of *The Constitutions of the Antient & Honourable Fraternity of Free and Accepted Masons: Containing all the particular Ordinances and Regulations of the Grand Lodge of the State of New-York* were dedicated to Washington. The edition of 1785, as well as those of 1789, 1801, 1805, 1815, 1820, 1827 and 1832 has the following dedication:

> To His Excellency, GEORGE WASHINGTON, Esq. In testimony, as well of his exalted Services to his Country, as of his distinquished Character as a MASON, the following BOOK of CONSTITUTIONS of the most antient and honourable Fraternity of *Free and*

Accepted Masons, by order and in behalf of the GRAND LODGE of the State of New-York, is dedicated, By his most Humble Servant. JAMES GILES, G. Secretary. A. L. 5785.

George Washington's Honorary Membership In The Holland Lodge

An extract from the minutes of a Communication held early in 1789, over which W. Reinier Jan Vanden Broek presided as Master, reads as follows:

The Worshipful Master proposed his Excellency George Washington, Esq., for a member of this Lodge, which was properly seconded and, the ballots being taken, he was unanimously elected.

And this resolution was then passed:

Resolved, that the Worshipful Master Vanden Broek, Senior Warden Stagg and Junior Warden Willcocks be a Committee to communicate to his Excellency, in any mode they may deem most proper, this proceeding of the Lodge.

The Certificate was duly forwarded, accompanied by a letter of which the original draft survives; this was undoubtedly prepared by the Committee referred to in the resolution above mentioned. It reads as follows:

Holland Lodge, New York, 7th March, 1789

Sir:

As a Committee appointed for this purpose, we have the honor of transmitting to Your Excellency the enclosed Certificate from the Holland Lodge.

We are directed, Sir, to express a hope that the earnest wishes of our Constituents on the Subject may not be disappointed,—that the name of Washington may adorn as well the Archives of our Lodge as the Annals of our Country and that we may salute as a Masonic Brother him whom we honor as the Political Father of our Country.

We have the honor, &C,—

This diploma, together with the envelope addressed to Bro. Washington at Mount Vernon, is now in the Manuscript Room of the Library of Congress. It is unique in that such diplomas of honorary membership are rare in the 18th Century and, of course, its association with Washington gives it priceless value. As will be seen from the reproduction, Bro. Vanden Broek signed it as Master of Holland Lodge.

The diploma reads:

"In the East a Place of Light And the Darkness
Where Peace and Silence Reign Comprehendeth it not

To all men enlightened and spread abroad on the Face of the Earth

BRIEF MASONIC HISTORY

Greeting We the Master, Wardens and Brethren of Holland Lodge, ancient Masons, held in the City and State of New York in North America, DO hereby certify, that, in consideration of the masonic Virtues which distinguish our worthy Brother HIS EXCELLENCY GEORGE WASHINGTON ESQUIRE, he was unanimously elected an honorary Member of our said Lodge.

In Testimony whereof We the Master and Wardens have hereunto set our Hands and caused the Seal of the Lodge to be affixed this Seventh Day of March A: D: 1789 & A: M: 5789.
F. J. vanden Broek Master
J: Stagg Junr. Sen. Warden
Wm Willcocks Junr. Warden
Attest Henry Remsen Junr. Secretary"

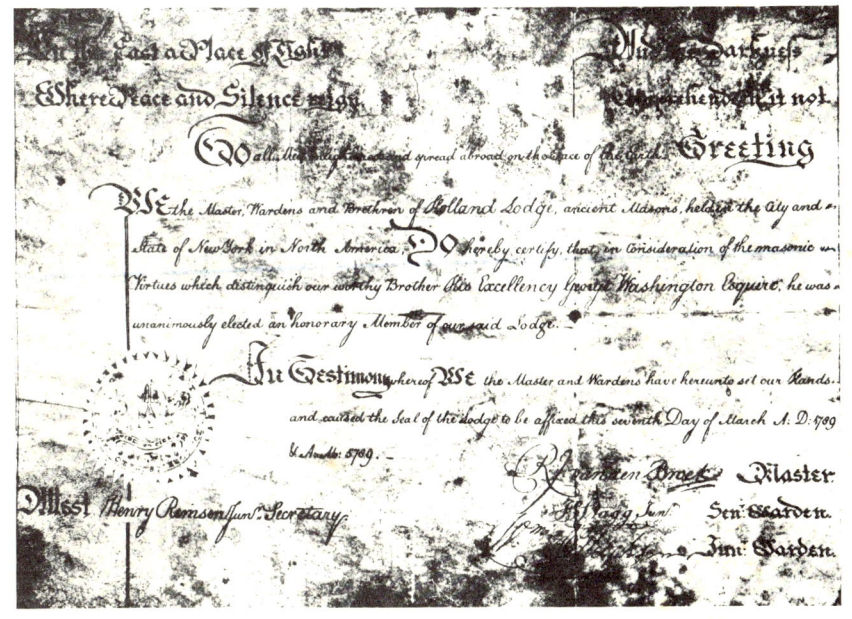

Certificate of honorary membership in Holland Lodge No. 8 granted to George Washington on March 7, 1789, and signed by Reinier Jan Vanden Broek as Master. From the Library of Congress.

The Grand Lodge Of Free And Accepted Masons Of The State Of New York During Washington's Presence In New York 1789 And 1790

In March of 1789, the Masonic Lodges in New York City began preparations for a procession on St. John's Day, June 24, 1789. The Grand Secretary was directed to give notice to the respective Lodges in the State of the observance of the day, and to have notice published in the public newspapers.

Precedence of Lodges

Worshipful Brother Vandenbroeck observed, in Grand Lodge, that as a procession had been agreed upon for the next St. John's Day, it appeared to him highly necessary that the rank of the several Lodges should be settled previous to that day. Accordingly it was

"*Resolved*, That a Committee consisting of one member from each of the Lodges in this city meet in Holland Lodge Room, on the first Saturday in April next, at six o'clock in the evening, for the purpose of settling the rank of the respective Lodges in this city, and that they make report of their proceedings to the next Grand Lodge."

The Committee on this important subject was appointed, and of it, R. J. Vandenbroeck was made Chairman, and Jacob Morton, Grand Secretary, verified the report of June 3, 1789. The report was to ascertain and determine the rank of the several Lodges, and was in the following language:

"The Committee for ascertaining the rank of the several Lodges in New York City, consisting of one member from each Lodge appointed in pursuance of a resolve of the Grand Lodge, met at Holland Lodge Room, on Saturday evening, April 4, 1789.

Worshipful Bro. Vanderbroeck presiding.
Present:
Right Worshipful Bro. Cock, from No. 212.
Worshipful Bro. Malcom, from St. John's No. 2.
" Bro. Scott, from St. Andrew's No. 169.
" Bro. Adams, from No. 5.
" Bro. Cannon, from St. John's No. 4.
" Bro. John Harrison, from No. 210.
" Bro. Welsh, from No. 8.
" Bro. Vandenbroeck, Chairman, from Holland Lodge.

The Right Worshipful, the Grand Secretary, having by desire attended, ordered that he take minutes of the proceedings of the Committee this evening.

The Chairman having called the Committee to order, and having stated the business for which they had been called together, Worshipful Bro. Malcom moved as the first step necessary to be taken, that the Warrants of the several Lodges be read, and that the Grand Secretary be directed to note down their several *dates*, the *places* where the Lodges were to be *held*, and under what *jurisdiction*. The question being put, was carried in the affirmative, and the Warrants being read, their dates, etc., were as follows:

BRIEF MASONIC HISTORY

Styles of Lodges.	Places where to be held.	Jurisdiction	Dates Of Warrant.
No. 211,	City of New York,	Gr. = of England,	Nov. 1, 1780
St. Patrick's, 212,	" "	Gr. = of State, N.Y.,	Oct. 21, 1788
St. John's No.4,	" "	Prov. G = of N.Y.,	Feb. 5, 1783
" " 210,	" "	Gr. = of England,	Feb. 20, 1779
Ind. Royal Arch 8,	" "	Pro. = of N.Y.,	Dec. 15, 1760
St. Andrew's, 169,	City of Boston in the Pro. of MASS.	Gr. = of England	July 13, 1771
St. John's, No. 2,	City of New York,	Pro. Gr. = of N.Y.,	Dec. 7, 1757
" " " 5,	" " "	" " "	March 10, 1783
Holland Lodge	" " "	Gr. = of State N.Y.,	Sep. 20, 1787

Worshipful Bro. Malcom then moved that the Committee so proceed, to ascertain the ranks of the several Lodges from the dates of their respective Warrants. The question being put was carried in the affirmative. He then moved that St. John's Lodge No. 2 be considered as the oldest Lodge in this city, and take rank as the first, which was seconded by Bro. Harrison, and the question being put was carried in the affirmative, as follows:

Affirmative.   *Negative.*
No. 169   No. 210   No. 4   No. 212   No. 5
     2   8
Holland Lodge.

Worshipful Bro. Welsh then moved that No. 8 be considered the second in rank, which being seconded by Bro. Malcom was carried in the affirmative, as follows:

Affirmative.   *Negative.*
No. 169   No. 210   No. 4   No. 212   No. 5
     2   8
Holland Lodge.

Worshipful Bro. Scott then moved that St. Andrew's Lodge No. 169 be considered as the third in rank, which was seconded by Bro. Welsh. Right Worshipful Bro. Cock moved as an amendment that No. 169 be considered as the first in rank. Bro. Malcom objected to the amendment as being out of order, and moved that the sense of the Committee be taken whether the amendment of Bro. Cock be in order. On the question being put it was carried in the negative as follows:

Negative.   *Affirmative.*
No. 2   No. 8   No. 4   No. 210   No. 212   No. 5   No. 169

Bro. Scott's motion was then put and carried in the affirmative, as follows:

—143—

Affirmative.   *Negative.*
No. 169   No. 2   No. 210   No. 4   No. 8   No. 5   No. 212
Holland Lodge.

    Worshipful Bro. Harrison moved that No. 210 be considered as the fourth in rank. Seconded by Bro. Malcom, and carried in the affirmative, as follows:

Affirmative.   *Negative.*
No. 2   No. 169   No. 8   No. 4   No. 210   No. 212
Holland Lodge.

    Worshipful Bro. Cannon then moved that No. 212 be considered as the fifth in rank, which being seconded, was carried in the affirmative, as follows:

Affirmative.   *Negative.*
No. 169   No. 2   No. 210   No. 4   No. 5   No. 8   No. 212
Holland Lodge.

    Worshipful Bro. Cannon then moved that St. John's Lodge No. 4 be considered as the sixth in rank, which being put was carried in the affirmative as before. Bro. Malcom, seconded by Bro. Harrison, moved that No. 5 be considered as the seventh, and carried in the affirmative, as follows:

Affirmative.   *Negative.*
No. 2   No. 8   No. 168   No. 4   No. 210   No. 212   No. 5
Holland Lodge.

    Bro. Malcom then moved that Holland Lodge be considered as the eighth in rank, which being seconded, was carried in the affirmative, as before.

    The foregoing minutes being read and confirmed, it was resolved unanimously that a copy thereof should be transmitted to every Lodge, signed by the Chairman; and also a copy signed by the Chairman and Grand Secretary to the Right Worshipful Grand Lodge."

    The report having been read, Worshipful Brother Malcom moved that the Grand Lodge approve of said report, and that the same stand confirmed. The question being taken, it was carried in the affirmative, Worshipful Brother Adams, Past Master of No. 5, being the only dissentient.

The Old Warrants To Be Surrendered

    It was then ordered, that the several Lodges surrender their old Warrants agreeably to a former resolution of the Grand Lodge, and that the Grand Secretary issue new Warrants under the jurisdiction of this Grand Lodge.

At the request of Worshipful Brother Thomas, of Lodge No. 210, the new Warrant to be granted to that Lodge was to state that the Lodge shall be styled "Temple Lodge," in addition to the number which by rank it was entitled to.

In due order the Grand Lodge then proceeded to the election of officers for the ensuing year, as prescribed by the Constitution, with the following result:

The Honorable Robert R Livingston was unanimously re-elected Grand Master.

Peter McDougall was elected Senior Grand Warden.
John Myer, Junior Grand Warden.
White Matlack, Grand Treasurer.
George Hopkins, Grand Pursuivant.
Duncan McDougall, Grand Tyler.

It was

Resolved, That the Grand Stewards' Lodge appoint the Stewards and Deacons for the Grand Lodge.

The Right Worshipful Brother McDougall having, by request of the Grand Lodge, withdrawn from the Hall, it was unanimously resolved, that the thanks of this Lodge be presented to said brother, for the fidelity and unremitted attention with which he discharged the duties of his office as Junior Grand Warden; and resolved, further, that the Grand Secretary be directed to present the thanks of this Lodge in writing to said brother.

Festival Of St. John The Baptist

On the following June 18, the Grand Lodge opened in Extra Session for the purpose of installing the officers elect, five Lodges being represented.

Right Worshipful Brother Malcom produced a letter from the Most Worshipful, the Grand Master, appointing him Deputy Grand Master, which was read, and was as follows:

"New York, June 8, 1789.

Brother,—Our worthy Bro. Richard Harrison, Esquire, having resigned the place of Deputy Grand Master of Masons for this State, I have turned my eyes to you as most capable of supplying his loss, and by your zeal, knowledge, and diligence of continuing to the Lodges under my care, the advantages they derived from his attention; I must, therefore, pray you to take upon you the office of Deputy Grand Master; to consider this as your Warrant for so doing, and to cause it to be entered, accordingly, on the records of the Grand Lodge.

I am, Brother, with the sincerest wishes for your happiness and prosperity,

Your affectionate Brother,
R.R. LIVINGSTON.

To Right Worshipful William Malcom, Esquire.

It appeared from this letter that the said brother was duly appointed Deputy Grand Master of this State, the Right Worshipful Brother McDougall proceeded in due form, and with the accustomed ceremonies, to install him into that important office. The Right Worshipful, the Deputy Grand Master, then took the chair, and in like form installed the Right Worshipful Brother McDougall to the office of Senior Grand Warden, Brother Myer to that of Junior Grand Warden, Brother White Matlack to that of Grand Treasurer, Right Worshipful Brother Jacob Morton signifying his continuance in the office of Grand Secretary.

The officers then received from the brethren present the accustomed Masonic honors and congratulations.

It was decided by the Grand Lodge that a sermon should be preached on the ensuing festival of St. John the Baptist, and further resolved, that a Committee wait upon the Rev. Dr. Beach, and request that he preach a sermon for them on the 24th June, in St. Paul's Chapel.

Arrangements for the procession were left to the Grand Steward's Lodge.

Permission was granted to Steuben Lodge to celebrate the festival at Newburgh, in consequence of the inconvenience of attending at New York.

The Grand Stewards' Lodge on June 10, decided that the Grand Lodge on St. John's Day, would assemble at the Coffee House at eleven in the morning, the Lodges at contiguous convenient places, that all should move in line through Queen and Beekman streets to St. Paul's Chapel, and after service, return through Broadway and Wall Street to the Grand Lodge Room in the Coffee House.

That the collection at the church be given to the Society instituted for the relief of distressed debtors confined in prison, to be applied by it to the benevolent purposes of the Institution.

And furthermore, that it be recommended that the different Lodges dine together.

On St. John's Day, June 24, 1789, the Grand Lodge was opened in ample form by Grand Master Robert R Livingston; William Malcom, Deputy Grand Master; Peter McDougall, Senior Grand Warden; John Myer, Junior Grand Warden; White Matlack, Grand Treasurer; Jacob Morton, Grand Secretary.

ORDER OF PROCESSION.

Knights Templars.
Holland Lodge, in the following order:
Tyler.

Steward.   Steward.
Members, two and two.
Treasurer.   Secretary.
Junior Warden.   Senior Warden.
Past Masters.
A Master Mason bearing the Warrant of the Lodge,
supported by two Brethen.
Deacon. Master. Deacon.
Jamaica Lodge.
Hiram No. 5.
St. John's No. 4.
Band of Music.
St. Patrick's No. 212.
Lodge No. 210.
St. Andrew's No. 169.
Independent Royal Arch No. 8.
St. John's No. 2.
Band of Music.
Grand Lodge.
Grand Tyler.
Visiting Brethren of Distinction.
Past Grand Officers, two and two.
Grand Treasurer.   Grand Secretary.
Junior Grand Warden.   Senior Grand Warden.
Chaplain.

Grand Deacons.   { Grand Pursuivant bearing the Bible. }   Grand Deacons.

Knights Templars.   { Deputy Grand Master. Grand Master. Grand Master of Georgia. Grand Deacon. Grand Deacon. Knights Templars. }   Knights Templars.

There were also present the Rev. Brother Beach and a number of brethren of distinction. The Right Wor., the Hon. Brother James Jackson, Representative in Congress of the United States from the

—147—

State of Georgia, and Grand Master of Masons in said State, was introduced by the Grand Secretary and received with Masonic honors. At twelve o'clock the Grand Lodge, attended by the other Lodges, went in procession to St. Paul's Chapel, in the order previously mentioned, where an excellent sermon was delivered by Bro. Beach, and a handsome collection made, which was applied, by the direction of the Grand Lodge, to the Humane Society of New York City, instituted for the relief of distressed debtors. After Divine services, the brethen returned in like order to the Coffee House, and were dismissed.

The officers of the Grand Lodge, the Grand Master of Georgia, and many brethren of distinction, together with the officers and brethren of Lodges Nos. 2, 169, 210, and Holland Lodge, dined at the City Tavern. The day was spent with festivity and harmony. The several Lodges dined separately from the Grand Lodge, and congratulations were offered by the Grand Lodge to them.

The collections at the Church amounted to fifty pounds, "exclusive of coppers," and were so reported in August. Forty pounds were directed to be forwarded to the Society for the Relief of Distressed Debtors, the balance to pay the expenses of the festival, and if insufficient, the funds of the Grand Lodge were to be drawn upon. Futhermore, six pounds were voted for charity, and in the succeeding month a larger sum.

The services of Rev. Brother Beach had been called upon on several occasions, and it therefore behooved Grand Lodge, not only to acknowledge the same with thanks, but the reverend brother was appointed the Grand Lodge Chaplain.

Tobias Lear, Secretary to the President, recorded in his cash book for July 6, 1789,

> "By Contingent Exps ret'd Mrs Washington 2 Guineas wh she gave the children for the contribution at Church at the Mason's Sermon 3 14 8"

The entry is in pounds, shillings, and pence as the decimal system adopted by Congress in 1787 was not in general use and each state was still using its own currency, based on the English system. While Washington was in New York the entries were made in New York currency. During Washington's Presidency the value of a New York Pound was two and one half dollars, or eight shillings to the dollar.

The Financial Situation

Brother R.J. Vandenbroeck, Chairman of the Committee on Accounts, reported in December, that there was due the Grand Secretary two shillings and six pence, which when paid would leave a balance of twenty-eight pounds, sixteen shillings and six pence. Further, that the city Lodges owed the Grand Body about fifty pounds, which was exclusive of amounts due from country Lodges.

It was during this period that the difficulties of Lodge No. 210 exacted so much of the time of the Grand Lodge, and finally resulted in dissolving the Lodge, from which a new Warrant and a new Lodge evolved.

Efficiency Of A Master

Brother Vanderbroeck urged the passage of a resolution of efficiency, on the part of "every Master Mason being or having been a Master, Past Master, or Warden, elected or re-elected to preside in any Lodge, requiring that he shall hereafter, previous to his installation into office, be examined by the Grand officers, or by some skillful person or persons appointed by them, as to his being sufficiently acquainted with Masonry, and if he is possessed of the required abilities to fill the chair, and that on his producing a certificate of his having passed a regular and strict examination, and found to be qualified, he then shall be installed into his office, and not before." The resolution was defeated, but nevertheless Bro. Vandenbroeck insisted on its being placed in full upon the record.

A Grand Lodge of Emergency was held December 23. R. W. Brother William Malcom, Deputy Grand Master, in the Chair, and representatives of seven Lodges present. The Deputy Grand Master moved the following Regulation, which was established.

> That at all future meetings of the Grand Lodge, previous to the opening, none but the members of the Grand Lodge shall be admitted, but that the Tyler may report the names of such as shall come as visitors, after the Grand Lodge is opened, that the Grand Lodge may have an opportunity of knowing, either by examination or by the vouchers of Brethren, who are proper Brethren to be admitted as visitors."

1790

In 1790, June 2, the Grand Lodge held its annual election, with the following result: The Hon. Robert R Livingston was unanimously re-elected Grand Master; Peter McDougall was re-elected Senior Grand Warden; John Myer was re-elected Junior Grand Warden. White Matlack declined re-election as Grand Treasurer, and John Pintard, of Holland Lodge, was elected to that office; Rev. Dr. Abraham Beach was re-elected Grand Chaplain; George Hopkins was re-elected Grand Pursuivant, and Duncan McDougall was re-elected Grand Tyler.

The following official Communication and resolutions were received from James Jackson, Past Grand Master of Masons of the State of Georgia, and read:

"New York, May 1, A. L. 1790.
RIGHT WORSHIPFUL BROTHER:

Enclosed I have the honor to transmit you copies of two resolutions of the Grand Lodge of Georgia. It is needless for me to point out the propriety of the step on which they are founded. Our being members of the same political community, and the benefits which would result to our Society from a general controlling power, will, of themselves, evince its necessity. I cannot, however, forbear mentioning that the frequent innovation in the mode of work, and the authorities set up in some States under Warrants from other States, demand the serious attention of the Brotherhood.

I authorized Bros. Stevens and Lloyd to communicate with the Grand Lodges of the more northern States, and to assent to a convention at such time and place as may be generally convenient.

Requesting that I may be favored with an answer, as early as the opinion of your Grand Lodge can be obtained,

I am, Right Worshipful,
Your very obed't servant and brother,

JAS. JACKSON, Past G. Master, State of Georgia.
Right Worshipful Grand Master, New York."

"Grand Lodge of Georgia,
December 28, 5789.

PRESENT.
The Right Worshipful James Jackson, G. M.

Resolved, As the sense of this Grand Lodge, that there ought to be a Federal or Supreme Grand Lodge constituted, to have jurisdiction over the respective Grand and other Lodges throughout the continent, and that . . . have authority to communicate with the Grand Lodges to the northward, to pledge the faith of this Grand Lodge in support of such an undertaking, and to assent to a Masonic Convention for that purpose.

Extract from the minutes.

U. Tobler, Gr. Sec'y"

"Grand Lodge of Georgia,
March 5, 5790.

PRESENT.
The Right Worshipful Sir George Houston, Bart., G. M.
On motion,

Resolved, That Right Worshipful Bros. Jackson and Stevens, and Worshipful Bro. Edward Lloyd, be a committee to carry into effect the resolution entered into at last meeting, for the purpose of establishing a Federal Grand Lodge in America.

Extract for the minutes.

U. Tobler, Gr. Sec'y"

Whereupon, it was *Resolved*, That the said resolutions be referred to a committee, consisting of the officers of the Grand Lodge, and that they be requested to report, as early as possible, their ideas of the proposed measures, as also of the mode in which they should be carried into effect, if approved.

On June 22 a Warrant was authorized to be issued to Isaac T. Tallman as Master, Willian Terry as Senior Warden, and Oliver Kellogg as Junior Warden, of a Lodge to be known as Lafayette, in the vicinity of Dover, Duchess County.

August 13.—A Grand Lodge of Emergency was specially summoned for the purpose of taking into consideration the resolutions adopted by the Grand Lodge of Georgia, in the matter of a

Supreme Federal Grand Lodge

Debate having been had thereon, the following was

"*Resolved*, That this Grand Lodge do concur with the Grand Lodge of Georgia, in the proposed measure of calling a convention, for the purpose of establishing a Supreme Federal Grand Lodge, to have jurisdiction over the respective Grand Lodges of the United States, and the Most Worshipful, the Grand Master of this State, is hereby requested to assure the Grand Lodge of Georgia, that this Grand Lodge will meet by its delegates the other Grand Lodges by their delegates, for the purpose above mentioned at such time and place as shall be agreed on."

On September 20, a Warrant was authorized for Washington Lodge at Clermont, Columbia County, of which Philip Hoffman was to be Master, William Wheeler, Senior Warden, and John A. Fonda, Junior Warden.

On December 1, authority was given to establish a Lodge in Kingston, Ulster County, by the name of Livingston Lodge.

At this meeting Brother John Myer resigned as Junior Grand Warden.

March 2, the Grand Lodge accepted the offer of Wor. Brother Pintard, of Holland Lodge, to hold the Grand Communications at Holland Lodge Room.

CHAPTER XI

WASHINGTON'S MASONIC CORRESPONDENCE

Washington's Masonic Correspondence is presented here in chronological order to show the esteem in which Washington held the Masonic Fraternity, and as Julius F. Sachse stated in his book, *Washington's Correspondence as found among the Washington Papers in the Library of Congress*, the entente cordiale which existed between Washington and his Masonic Brothers.

On April 30, 1789, Washington was inaugurated as the first President of the United States in Federal Hall on Wall Street in New York City. Washington was Master of his Lodge at the time, and for many years this was the only instance where one of our Masonic Presidents was a Master of a Lodge during their term as President.

President Harry Truman was Grand Master of Masons in Missouri while serving as a United States Senator from Missouri, and although Congress was in session much of the time, took an active part in the affairs of his jurisdiction. The Missouri Lodge of Research was established in 1950, and Truman served as Master while President of the United States, becoming the second President to serve as Master of a Lodge during his term as the President.

Washington's interest in the Craft is best shown by his own expressions in the letters which he wrote. Space limitations do not permit a complete presentation of all the circumstances leading up to his own letters; Julius F. Sachse, for many years Librarian of the Grand Lodge of Pennsylvania, has gone into this rather thoroughly in his *Washington's Masonic Correspondence as Found Among the Washington Papers in the Library of Congress*, (Philadelphia, 1915).

1. *Letter to Watson & Cassoul, 1782*

The firm of Watson & Cassoul, Nantes, France, presented a Masonic apron to Washington, which was accompanied by a letter of transmittal dated "23rd 1st Month, 5782," which was *March* 23, not January, as usually supposed, and an error which Washington himself fell into when replying. His reply reads:

>   State of New York,
>   Augt. 10th, 1782.
> Gent.
> The Masonic Ornam which accompanied your Brotherly Address of the 23rd of Jan. last, tho' elegant in themselves, were rendered more valuable by the flattering sentiments, and affectionate manner, in which they were presented.—
> If my endeavours to avert the evil, with which this Country was threatened by a deliberate plan of Tyranny, should be crowned with the

success that is wished—The praise is due to the Grand Architect of the Universe; who did not see fit to suffer his superstructures and justice, to be subjected to the Ambition of the Princes of this World, or to the rod of oppression, in the hands of any power upon Earth.—

For your affectionate Vows, permit me to be grateful;—and offer mine for true Brothers in all parts of the World; and to assure you of the sincerity with which I am

Yrs

G. WASHINGTON

This letter has been in the Library of the Grand Lodge of New York since 1866

2. Letter to Alexandria Lodge No. 39, Alexandria, Va.

Washington resigned his first commission as Commander-in-Chief of the Armies of the United States, received June 17, 1775, on December 23, 1783, and returned to Mt. Vernon Christmas Eve. Alexandria Lodge wrote him a fraternal letter of felicitation and carrying an invitation to join the brethren on Masonic occasions. To this Washington replied:

Mount Vernon, 28th Dec. 1783.

Gentlemen:

With pleasing sensibility I received your favor of the 26th, and beg leave to offer you my sincere thanks for the favorable sentiments with which it abounds.—

I shall always feel pleasure when it may be in my power to render service to Lodge No. 39, and in every act of brotherly kindness to the Members of it; being with great truth.

Your Affect Brother and Obed Servant

G. WASHINGTON

3. Second Letter to Alexandria Lodge No. 39

Washington was invited to join the brethren of Alexandria Lodge in the celebration of St. John's Day, June 24, 1784. He answered thus:

Mount Vernon, June 19, 1784.

Dear Sir:

With pleasure, I received the invitation of the master and members of Lodge No. 39, to dine with them on the approaching anniversary of St. John the Baptist. If nothing unforeseen at present interferes, I will have the honor of doing it. For the polite and flattering terms in which you have expressed their wishes, you will please accept my thanks.

With esteem and respect, I am, dear sir,

Your most Ob't serv't

G. WASHINGTON

It was upon this occasion that Washington was elected an honorary member of the Lodge.

4. *Letter to King David's Lodge No. 1, Newport, R. I.*

To the Master, Wardens and Brethren of King Davids Lodge in Newport, Rhode Island.

Gentlemen,

I receive the welcome which you give me to Rhode Island with pleasure, and I acknowledge my obligations for the flattering expressions of regard, contained in your address, with grateful sincerity.

Being persuaded that a just application of the principles, on which the Masonic Fraternity is founded, must be promotive of private virtue and public prosperity, I shall always be happy to advance the interests of the Society, and to be considered by them as a deserving brother.

My best wishes, Gentlemen, are offered for your individual happiness.

G. WASHINGTON

The letter, while not dated, was written at New York, Sunday, August 22, 1790.

5. *Letter to St. John's Lodge No. 2, Newburn, N. C.*

Washington made a trip to the South in 1791. Upon his arrival in Newburn, N. C., he was presented with an address which had been authorized at a meeting of the Lodge April 1, 1791. The opening paragraph begged leave to hail him welcome "with three times three." This letter was answered in this fraternal spirit:

To the Master, Wardens, and Members of St. John's Lodge No. 2 of Newbern.

Gentlemen,

I receive the cordial welcome which you are pleased to give me with sincere gratitude.

My best ambition having ever aimed at the unbiassed approbation of my fellow-citizens, it is peculiarly pleasing to find my conduct so affectionately approved by a fraternity whose association is founded in justice and benevolence.

In reciprocating the wishes contained in your address, be persuaded that I offer a sincere prayer for your present and future happiness.

G. WASHINGTON

6. *Letter to Prince George's Lodge No. 16, Georgetown, S. C.*

Continuing his journey southward, Washington reached Georgetown, South Carolina, on Saturday, April 30, 1791. Here he was presented with an address of the same date by a committee from Prince George's Lodge No. 16, Georgetown, S. C. The reply made by Washington is undated, and the text given is to be found in Washington's Letter Book No. II, folio 60-61. Copies of the correspondence in the "United States Chronicle," Vol. VIII, No. 388, Providence, R. I., issue of Thursday, June 9, 1791. The text of Washington's reply as given in the copybook reads:

To the Brethren of Prince George's Lodge No. 16.
Gentlemen:

The cordial welcome which you give me to George Town, and the congratulations, you are pleased to offer on my election to the chief magistracy receive my greatful thanks.

I am much obligated by your good wishes and reciprocate them sincerity assuring the fraternity of my esteem, I request them to believe that I shall always be ambitious of being considered a deserving Brother.

G. WASHINGTON

7. Mordecai Gist's Letter and Washington's Reply

To The President of the United States
Sir

Induc'd by respect for your public and private character as well as the relation in which you stand with the Brethren of this Society, We The Grand Lodge of the State of South Carolina, Ancient York Masons beg leave to offer our sincere congratulations on your arrival in this state.

We felicitate you upon the establishment and exercise of a permanent Government, whose foundation was laid under your auspices, by military achievements; upon which has been progressively rear'd the Pillars of the free Republic over which you Preside, supported by Wisdom, Strength and Beauty, unrival'd amongst the Nations of the World.

The fabric thus rais'd and committed to your superintendence, we earnestly wish may continue to produce order & harmony to succeeding ages, and be the Asylum of virtue to the oppress'd of all parts of the universe.

When we contemplate the distresses of War, The instances of humanity display'd by the Craft afford some relief to the feeling mind; and it gives us the most pleasing sensations to recollect that amidst the difficulties attendant on your late military Station, you will associate with, and patronized the Ancient Fraternity.

Distinguish'd always by your virtues more than the exalted stations, in which you have mov'd, we exult in the opportunity you now give us of hailing you Brother of our Order; and trust from your knowledge of our Institution to meet your countenance and support.

With fervent zeal for your happiness, we pray that a life so dear to the bosom of this Society and to mankind in general, may be long, very long preserv'd; and when you leave the temporal Symbolic Lodges of this world, you may be receiv'd into that Celestial Lodge of Perfection where the Grand Master Architect of the Universe Presides
done in behalf of the Grand Lodge.

Charleston 2nd. May 1791   M. GIST. G.M.

Washington responded in this manner:

Gentlemen:—I am much obliged by the respect which you are so good as to declare for my public and private character. I recognize with pleasure my relation to the brethren of your Society, and I accept with gratitude your congratulations on my arrival in South Carolina.

Your sentiments, on the establishment and exercise of our equal government, are worthy of an association, whose principles lead to purity of morals, and are beneficial of action.

The fabric of our freedom is placed on the enduring basis of public virtue, and will, I fondly hope, long continue to protect the prosperity of the architects who raised it. I shall be happy, on every occasion, to evince my regard for the Fraternity. For your prosperity individually, I offer my best wishes.

G. WASHINGTON

8. *Washington and the Grand Lodge of Georgia*

Washington continued his journey, and reached Savannah, Georgia, Thursday, May 12, 1791. The following Saturday he was greeted by the Georgia brethren and given a letter signed by Geo. Houston, Grand Master. It was thus acknowledged:

> To the Grand Master, Officers and Members of the Grand Lodge of Georgia.
> Gentlemen,
> I am much obliged by your congratulations on my arrival in this city, and I am highly indebted to your favorable opinions.
> Every circumstance contributes to render my stay in Savannah agreeable, and it is cause of regret to me that it must be so short.
> My best wishes are offered for the welfare of the fraternity, and for your particular happiness.
>
> G. WASHINGTON

9. *Washington and the Pennsylvania Craft, 1792*

Pennsylvania Masons, in common with the Craft elsewhere in the new-born nation, honored Washington as one of their own brethren. On December 27, 1791, formal resolutions were passed for the preparation of an address to Washington. It is a model of brevity and clarity, written by the Rev. Bro. Dr. William Smith, tendering the congratulations of the Grand Master upon Washington's election as President in terms which are Masonic in form and spirit. It was formally presented to Washington by a deputation whom he received in the presidential dining room. Written acknowledgment was subsequently made:

> To the Ancient YORK Masons of the Jurisdiction of Pennsylvania.
> Gentlemen and Brothers,
> I receive your kind Congratulations with the purest sensations of fraternal affection:—and from a heart deeply impressed with your generous wishes for my present and future happiness, I beg you to accept my thanks.
> At the same time I request you will be assured of my best wishes and earnest prayers for your happiness while you remain in this terrestrial Mansion, and that we may thereafter meet as brethren in the Eternal Temple of the Supreme Architect.
>
> G. WASHINGTON

10. *Washington and the Massachusetts Dedication*

Elsewhere herein reference is made to Masonic books dedicated to Washington; the courtesy of Massachusetts in dedicating its first *Constitution* to Washington in 1792 was acknowledged by Washington in this manner:

> To the Grand Lodge of Free & Accepted Masons, for the Commonwealth of Massachusetts.
>
> Flattering as it may be to the human mind, & truly honorable as it is to receive from our fellow citizens testimonies of approbation for exertions to promote the public welfare, it is not less pleasing to know, that the milder virtues of the heart are highly respected by a Society whose liberal principles must be founded in the immutable laws of truth and justice.—
>
> To enlarge the sphere of social happiness is worthy the benevolent design of a masonic institution; and it is most fervently to be wished, that the conduct of every member of the fraternity, as well as those publications that discover the principles which actuate them; may tend to convince mankind that the grand object of Masonry is to promote the happiness of the human race.
>
> While I beg your acceptance of my thanks for the "Book of Constitutions" which you have sent me, & the honor you have done me in the dedication, permit me to assure you that I feel those emotions of gratitude which your affectionate address & cordial wishes are calculated to inspire; and I sincerely pray that the Great Architect of the Universe may bless you here, and receive you hereafter into his immortal Temple.
>
> G. WASHINTON

11. *Washington's Second Letter to the Pennsylvania Craft, 1796*

The responsibilities of the Presidency did not interfere with Washington's interest in Freemasonry, for he laid the cornerstone of the Capitol at Federal City September 18, 1793, and on St. John's Day the following December, he attended services at St. Paul's Episcopal Church in Philadelphia.

Upon Washington's declining a third term of office, the Grand Lodge of Pennsylvania drafted another letter "to the Great Master Workman, our Illustrious Br. Washington," and being authorized at its sessions of December 27, 1796, the communication was received by the President at noon the following day. Contrary to some of the other letters, which were in the handwriting of his secretary, Washington's response was written by himself:

> Fellow-Citizens and Brothers, of the Grand Lodge of Pennsylvania.
>
> I have received your address with all the feelings of brotherly affection, mingled with those sentiments, for the Society, which it was calculated to excite.
>
> I have been, in any degree, an instrument in the hands of Providence, to promote order and union, and erect upon a solid foundation the true principles of government, is only to have shared with many

others in a labour, the result of which let us hope, will prove through all ages, a sanctuary for brothers and a lodge for the virtues.—

Permit me to reciprocate your prayers for my temporal happiness, and to supplicate that we may all meet thereafter in that eternal temple, whose builder is the great Architect of the Universe.

G. WASHINGTON

12. *Third Letter to Alexandria Lodge No. 22*

Upon Washington's retirement from the Presidency, he returned to Mount Vernon, arriving home March 15th, 1797. His brethren of Alexandria Lodge did not neglect the opportunity to greet him, and he not only received a formal letter of felicitation but was sent another, dated the 28th, inviting him to dine with the brethren, on an occasion most convenient to him. He attended Lodge April 1st, and his reply was read at that time:

> Brothers of the Ancient York Masons of Lodge No. 22.
>
> While my heart acknowledges with Brotherly Love, your affectionate congratulations on my retirement from the arduous toils of past years, my gratitude is no less excited by your kind wishes for my future happiness.—
>
> If it has pleased the supreme architect of the universe to make me an humble instrument to promote the welfare and happiness of my fellow men, my exertions have been abundantly recompensed by the kind partiality with which they have been received; and the assurance you give me of your belief that I have acted upon the square in my public capacity, will be among my principal enjoyments in this Terrestrial Lodge.
>
> G. WASHINGTON

13. *Letter to Massachusetts 1797*

The Proceedings of the Grand Lodge of Massachusetts (Reprint, Vol. II, 1792-1815, page 97) show that on March 13, 1797, it was

> On motion, VOTED, That a committee be appointed to draft an Address, to be presented to our Illustrious Brother, George Washington, Esq'r, when the M. W. Paul Revere, Grand Master, R. W. John Warren, Rev. Bro. Thaddeus M. Harris, R. W. Josiah Bartlett, Bro. Thomas Edwards, were appointed a committee for that purpose.

The Proceedings of the next Quarterly Communication, June 12, 1797, carry the draft of the address:

> The East, the West and the South, of the Grand Lodge of Free and Accepted Masons of the Commonwealth of Massachusetts.
> To Their Most Worthy George Washington:
> Wishing ever to be foremost in testimonials of respect and admiration for those virtues and services with which you have so long adorned and benefited our common country; and not the last nor least, to regret the cessation of them, in the public councils of the Union; your Brethren of the Grand Lodge embrace the earliest opportunity of greeting you in the calm retirement you have contemplated to yourself. Though as citizens

they lost you in the active labors of political life, they hope, as Masons, to find you in the pleasing sphere of Fraternal engagement.

From the cares of state and the fatigues of public business our institution opens a recess affording all the relief of tranquillity, the harmony of peace and the refreshment of pleasure. Of these may you partake in all their purity and satisfaction; and we will assure ourselves that your attachment to this social plan will increase; and that under the auspices of your encouragement, assistance and patronage, the Craft will attain its highest ornament, perfection, and praise. And it is our ardent prayer, that when your Light shall be no more visible in this earthly temple, you may be raised to the ALL Perfect Lodge above; be seated on the right of the Supreme Architect of the Universe, and there receive the refreshment your labors have merited.

In behalf of the Grand Lodge, we subscribe ourselves with the highest esteem,

Your affectionate Brethren,
PAUL REVERE, Grand Master.
ISAIAH THOMAS, S. Grand Warden.
JOSEPH LAUGHTON, J. Grand Warden.

DANIEL OLIVER, Grand Secretary,
Boston, 21st March, 5797.

Some delay occured in getting this to Washington, as is shown by his acknowledgment:

To Paul Revere Grand Master, Isaiah Thomas Senior Grand Warden and Joseph Laughton Jun. Grand Warden.
Brothers,

I am sorry that the enclosed answer to the affectionate address of the Grand Lodge of Ancient, Free and Accepted Masons, of the Commonwealth of Massachusetts transmitted under your signatures, should appear so much out of season; but from the lapse of time between the date & reception of the address (from what cause I know not) it was not to be avoided, and is offered as an apology, for the delay. With brotherly affection

I am always yours,
G. WASHINGTON

His formal reply to the address reads:

To the Grand Lodge of Ancient, Free & Accepted Masons of the Commonwealth of Massachusetts.
Brothers,

It was not until within these few days that I have been favoured by the receipt of your affectionate Address dated in Boston the 21st of March.

For the favorable sentiments you have been pleased to express on the occasion of my past services, and for the regrets with which they are accompanied for the cessation of my public functions, I pray you to accept my best acknowledgments and gratitude.—

No pleasure, except that which results from a consciousness of having, to the utmost of my abilities, discharged, the trusts which have been reposed in me by my Country, can equal the satisfaction I feel from the unequivocal proofs I continually receive of its approbation of my public conduct, and I beg you to be assured that the evidence thereof which is exhibited by the Grand Lodge of Massachusetts is not among the least pleasing, or grateful to my feelings.—

In that retirement which declining years induced me to seek, and which repose, to a mind long employed in public concerns, rendered necessary, my wishes that bounteous Providence will continue to bless & preserve our country in Peace & in the prosperity it has enjoyed, will be warm & sincere; and my attachment to the Society of which we are members will dispose me always, to contribute my best endeavours to promote the honor & interest of the Craft.—

For the prayer you offer in my behalf I entreat you to accept the thanks of a grateful heart; with the assurance of fraternal regard and best wishes for honor, happiness & prosperity of all the members of the Grand Lodge of Massachusetts.

G. WASHINGTON

14. *Maryland Letter 1798*

Freemasonry cannot be studied as a thing separate and apart from the times in which it grew. In similar fashion, it is generally unwise to consider Washington's Masonic correspondence without regard for the time and occasions upon which it was written. This is especially true of his letter to the Grand Lodge of Maryland in November, 1798. It must be remembered that the relations between the United States and France were severely strained at the time because of aggressive acts by the French revolutionists. Washington had been tendered command of the provisional army raised by Congress, and was on his way to Trenton to take command when waited on in Baltimore November 7th by William Belton, Grand Master of Maryland, who presented him with a copy of the book of Constitutions, the *Maryland Ahiman Rezon* of 1797.

Washington drafted a reply, but revised it before dispatching it. In its final form it appears thus:

To the Right Worshipful Grand Lodge of Free Masons for the State of Maryland.
Gentlemen and Brothers:

Your obliging and affectionate letter, together with a copy of the Constitution of Masonry, has been put into my hands by your Grand Master, for which I pray you to accept my best thanks. So far as I am acquainted with the principles and doctrines of Freemasonry, I conceive them to be founded on benevolence, and to be exercised for the good of mankind; I cannot, therefore, upon this ground withdraw my approbation from it.

While I offer my grateful acknowledgements for your congratulations on my late appointment, and for the favorable sentiments you are pleased to express of my conduct, permit me to observe, that, at this important and critical moment, when high and repeated indignities have been offered to the Government of our country, and when the property of our citizens is plundered without a prospect of redress, I conceive it to be the indispensable duty of every American, let his station and circumstances in life be what they may, to come forward in support of the Government of his choice and to give all the aid in his power towards maintaining that independence which we have so dearly purchased; and under this impression, I did not hesitate to lay aside all personal considerations and accept my appointment. I pray you to be assured that I receive with gratitude your kind wishes for my health and happiness and reciprocate them with sincerity.

    I am, Gentlemen and Brothers,
Very Respectfully,
Your most Ob's Servant,

G. WASHINGTON

CHAPTER XII

WASHINGTON AND THE SOCIETY OF THE CINCINNATI

One of the generally unknown associations in American history is that of George Washington's connection and significant relationship with the Society of the Cincinnati.

On June 19, 1783, Washington was elected the first President-General of the Society, the office which he held until his death.

The SOCIETY OF THE CINCINNATI was formed on May 10, 1783, by the officers of the victorious American army at the cantonment near Newburgh, New York.

The principal purposes were to "render permanent the cordial affection subsisting among the officers of our army" who had taken part in the war; and, to be prepared to render assistance to the members of their families who might be in need.

The constitution of the Order, THE INSTITUTION, expressed the purposes thus, and are read at every meeting:

"An incessant attention to preserve inviolate those exalted rights and liberties of human nature for which they have fought and bled, and without which the high rank of a rational being is a curse instead of a blessing.

"An unalterable determination to promote and cherish, between the respective states, that union and national honor so essentially necessary to their happiness and the future dignity of the American Empire.

"To render permanent the cordial affection subsisting among the officers. This spirit will dictate brotherly kindness in all things, and particularly extend to the most substantial acts of beneficence, according to the ability of the Society, towards those officers and their families who unfortunately may be under the necessity of receiving it."

Andre de Maricourt, in the magazine, "France—Etats-Unis", also expressed one of the objects of its formation by saying that it "sealed in a solemn manner, and in an hereditary way, the friendships of two peoples."

One of the first acts of the meeting of May 13, 1783, was to extend membership to certain grades of French officers, declaring that the "Society, deeply impressed with a sense of the generous assistance this country has received from France, and desirous of perpetuating the friendships which have been formed, and so happily subsisted, between the officers of the allied forces, in the prosecution of the War, direct that the President-General transmit, as soon as may be, to each of the characters hereafter named, a medal containing the Order of the Society, viz: His Excellency the Chevalier de la Luzerne Minister Plenipotentiary, His Excellency the Sieur Gerard, late Minister Plenipotentiary, Their Excellencies the Count d'Estaing, the Count de Grasse, the Count de Barras, the Chevalier des Touches, Admirals and Commanders in the Navy, His Excellency the Count de Rochambeau, Commander-in-Chief, and the Generals and Colonels of his army, and acquaint them, that the Society does itself the honor to consider them members."

After the French military left this country, the Society of the Cincinnati was organized. General Washington, who as previously mentioned, was elected the first President of the Society, wrote Rochambeau this letter:

TO THE COUNT DE ROCHAMBEAU

Rocky hill in New Jersey, 29 October 1783

Sir

The Officers of the American Army, in order to perpetuate that mutual friendships which they contracted in the hour of common danger and distress, and for other purposes which are mentioned in the instrument of their association have united together in a society of Friends under the name *Cincinnati;* and, having honored me with the office of president, it becomes a very agreeable part of my duty to inform you that the Society have done themselves the honor to consider you and the generals and officers of the army which you commanded in America as members of the Society.

Major L'Enfant, who will have the honor to deliver this letter to you, will execute the Order of the Society in France, amongst which he is directed to present you with one of the first Orders that are made, and likewise with Orders for the other gentlemen of your army, which I take the liberty to request you would present to them in the name of the Society. As soon as the diploma is made out, I will have the honor to transmit it to you.

[Archives of the General Society]

The letter was then transmitted through the Minister of War to King Louis XVI, who promptly on December 18th signified his approval, and the French Order of the Cincinnati was organized on July 4, 1784. Up to that time, the King of France had not allowed his officers to wear any foreign decorations. He immediately, however, made an exception in favor of the insignia of the Society of the Cincinnati. Membership in the Order was so eagerly sought that it soon became one of the most coveted in Europe.

Of the geographic branches of the Order, the Society in France has a most interesting history.

Its members, said Baron de Contenson, included "the very elite of the French nobility, "such as the Marquis de Lafayette, the Count Jean Baptiste de Rochambeau, the Count de Grasse, The Prince de Broglie, the Viscount de Noailles, The Bailli de Sufferen, de Wagram (Berthier), the Count de Fersen, of Sweden, and La Motte-Picquet. The Society's first President was the Count d' Estaing. The members were scattered during the French Revolution, many of them perishing on the guillotine.

The first French list prepared by the General-in-Chief comprised seven General officers, eight Brigadiers, and eighteen Colonels. It is said that just after the war they made a subscription of sixty thousand livres, in aid of the impoverished officers of the American Army, but Washington, in the name of his associates, courteously declined to accept the gift.

Some of the descendants of the original members started a movement in 1887 to revive the French Society, which had been dormant for many years. The Marquis de Rochambeau, Comte d'Ollone, Vicomte de Noailles and others were chiefly behind the attempt just before the coup d'etat of Louis Napoleon, but were not successful, and the French Society remained inactive again.

In 1922, a visiting American committee, with the help of the Duc de Broglie, reorganized the Society, and was formally recognized by the general society in the United States in 1925. It functions well to this day.

Among the French members whose names are well known, owing to the fact that their ancestors participated in the American Revolution, are the Duc de Broglie, Marquis de Chambrun, a descendant of Lafayette, Baron de Montesquieu, Comte D'Aboville, Ethis de Corny, Comte de Guichen, Comte Louis de Segur, Duc de Noailles, and the Marquis de Rochambeau (although the present Rochambeaus are not descendents in blood, but by adoption).

To General Henry Knox belongs the title of founder of the Cincinnati, for it appears from Thomas Jefferson's diary that in a conversation with John Adams as early as 1776, General Knox expressed a "wish for some ribbon to wear in his hat or in his button-hole, to be transmitted to his descendants as a badge and proof that he fought in defense of their liberties."

The original copy of the "Proposals" to form such an Order is in Knox's handwriting, and is now among the papers left in the care of the New England Historic Genealogical Society of Boston, by his grandson, Admiral Henry Knox Thatcher, who served as president of the Massachusetts branch of the Cincinnati.

The State Societies of the Cincinnati were formed on different dates. The General Society of the Cincinnati was established on May 13, 1783, at Newburgh, N.Y., the cantonment of the American Military Forces, by the officers of the victorious American Army.

THE MOUNT GULIAN SOCIETY also establishes that the Society was instituted on May 13, 1783, at the Dutch Colonial homestead known as "Mount Gulian", Fishkill, N.Y.

By April 15, 1783, Knox had produced draft proposals (now in the Knox Papers). On May 10, there was a preliminary meeting at which the draft was considered, and it was decided to prepare a more finished and formal copy on May 13, 1783, the formal copy was adopted and signed, and the Society then came into existence.

Mount Gulian is also known as the Verplanck House, which was built between 1730 and 1740 by Gulian Verplanck, on land that had been purchased by his grandfather, also known as Gulian, and Francis Rombout from the Wappinger Indians in 1683. The second Gulian named the house for his grandfather. The term "Mount" was often used in the naming of country homes, whether or not they stood upon a hill. In case of "Mount Gulian," the house is set upon high ground which gradually slopes downward to the Hudson River, affording a fine view.

The Verplanck House served as the headquarters of General (Baron) Fredrich Wilhelm von Steuben during the final period of the Revolutionary War. It was here in 1783 that General von Steuben, at the suggestion of Washington, drew up the "Plan for the disbanding of the Army," which was adopted and carried out at Newburgh, N.Y., where General Washington also had his headquarters.

Of particular architectural interest is the gambrel roof, considered one of the best examples of its kind to be found anywhere. It slopes down and outward in a graceful bell-like curve to become the roof of the verandah. Also of special interest is the orginal basement kitchen with large cooking fireplace and beehive oven.

Adjacent to the house is the restored 18th century barn, originally owned by Phillip Verplanck. It is considered unique for a new World Dutch barn because of its overhanging gable ends.

Still to be restored are the extensive gardens which were laid out in 1804 and which still contain rare old plants and shrubs.

Mount Gulian has always remained in the Verplanck family, although the house was largely destroyed by fire in 1931. The Mount Gulian Society was formed in 1966 by descendants of Gulian Verplanck in order to restore the house and preserve it as a site of historic interest.

The name of the Society was selected from that of the illustrious Roman General, Lucius Quinctius Cincinnatus, who, at the call of country, left his home to lead the armies of Rome to Victory, and when that victory was achieved, returned to his farm, refusing the honors usually accorded victorious leaders returning with their military forces.

The name indicated that the Continental Army was a citizen army, led by citizen officers inspired only by patriotism, who would return to their civilian pursuits at the war's end. The organization was comprised of commissioned officers of the Continental Line who had served for a minimum of three years, and Washington was the first to sign the original articles of the Society's Constitution. As membership is passed from father to son, the Society remains in active existence today.

One of the interesting facts in connection with the Cincinnati is that the medal or jewel of the Society, as illustrated herein, was designed by Major Pierre Charles L'Enfant, of the Continental Corps of Engineers, who later planned the Capitol of this country.

The Society voted that "the bald eagle, carrying the emblems on its breast, be established as the Order of the Society, and that the ideas of Major L'Enfant respecting it and the manner of its being worn by the members . . . be adopted."

Major L'Enfant accepted the assignment, and on June 10, 1783, wrote from Philadelphia to General (Baron) von Steuben with two designs and specifications of the proposed medal, including the idea that the medal be made in Paris. He was, subsequently, commissioned by Washington on October 16, 1783, to proceed to Paris to supervise the fabrication of the Eagles, and when completed, a number of Eagles were then transmitted to General Washington.

TO MAJOR-GENERAL HENRY KNOX

Rocky Hill, 16 October, 1783

Dear Sir,

Major Shaw not returning so soon as I imagined, and the subject of your Letter of 28 September not admitting much delay, I take the opportunity of the Post to reply to it.

On referring to the Institution of the Society of the Cincinnaat I find that the Chevr. de la Luzerne, the Sieur Gerard, the Counts D'Estaing, Barras and De Grasse, the Chevalier Des Touches and the Count de Rochambeau with the Generals and Colonels of his Army are to be presented with the Order of the Society.

As it is however proper that these Gentlemen should be made acquainted with the nature of the Society, I propose to write to each of those above named (except the Chevalier de la luzerne who was written to in first instance) and inclose them a Copy of the Institution, at the same time informing them that Major L'Enfant is charged with the execution of the Order, and has directions to furnish them from the first that are finished.

I propose also to inclose a Copy to the Marquis de la Fayette and request him to take the signatures of such of the French Officers in our Service who are entitled and wish to become Members—to receive their month's pay and deliver them the Orders on their paying for them.

These Letters Major L'Enfant will carry with him and deliver to each of those Gentlemen and must be directed to deliver them the Orders so soon as they are compleat, delivering to Count Rochambeau, for the Officers of his Command who will receive them of him—and to the Marquis de Lafayette sufficient for the French Officers in our Service who become Members.

I enclose to you the permission for Major L'Enfant to go to France, and a Certificate of his being a Member of the Society. However, before he sets off, I think it should be well explained and understood by him that the Voyage is not undertaken for the Society but that their business is committed to him only in consequence of his going there on his own affairs, and consequently he is not to be paid any Expenses of the Voyage or his stay—but only such Extra Expense as might in incurred by any person residing in France who transacted the same business for the Society—These are my sentiments—if they accord with yours and the rest of the Gentlemen, and he accepts these conditions I think the sooner he sets out the better.

I will be obliged to you to make out his instructions comprehending the objects I have mentioned above and such other as you may think necessary—and to make the necessary arrangements with him respecting the funds to be furnished. I am told subscriptions have been paid in by those who wish to have Orders—I propose taking seven, for which the Money is ready at any time—and it may not be amiss in this place to inform you that it has always been my intention to present the Society with 500 Dollars—if any part of this is necessary and can be applied with propriety in this business—I have no objection.

Maj. L'Enfant might also be directed to receive from the Marquis the Month's pay of the French Officers in our service who became Members.

I must request you to procure Six or seven Copies of the Institution to be made out neatly, to transmit to the Gentlemen above mentioned; Major L'Enfant can bring them on with him.

I intend immediately to write to the Commanding Officer of each of the State Lines, who have not yet made known their intentions respecting the formations of their State Societies pressing them to determination, for as I wish to adapt the place of the General Meeting to the convenience of all 'till I know which of the State form the Society I cannot fix it.

With great regard,

G⁰. Washington

[Archives of the Great Society]

On the Society's insignia appears as the principal figure Cincinnatus, being presented with a sword and other military objects by three Senators; on a field in the background is shown his wife standing at the door of their cottage, and near it, are a plough and other implements of husbandry. On the reverse, is the sun rising, a city with open gates, and vessels entering a port. Fame appears in the act of crowning Cincinnatus with a wreath.

It was resolved thereafter that "... the thanks of this Convention be transmitted, by the President, to Major L'Enfant, for his care and ingenuity in preparing the aforementioned designs, and the fabrication thereof."

Von Steuben wrote in connection with the Major's journey: "You have sent L'Enfant to France to procure some gold Eagles; but you have forgotten to give him some coppers for his tavern expenses. Mr. R. Morris, General Greene, and myself have made a credit of six hundred dollars, without which the ambassador of the Order would have made his entree into the Philadelphia Jail."

At another meeting in June of 1783, Major General Friedrich Von Steuben informed the Convention that he had transmitted to the Chevalier de la Luzerne, the French Minister, a copy of the Society's INSTITUTION and the votes passed, and that the representative of France had replied "declaring his acceptance of the same and expressing the grateful sense he entertains of the honor conferred on himself, and the other gentlemen of the French Nation, by this act of the Convention."

It was voted, "That the letter of the Chevalier de la Luzerne be recorded in the proceedings of this day, and deposited in the archives of the Society, as a testimony of the high sense this Convention entertains of the honor done to the Society, by his becoming a member thereof."

The first meeting of the officers of the French military was held on January 7, 1784, in the "Hotel" of General Rochambeau, No. 40 Rue du Cherche-Midi, where the General was living when he received word from King Louis to take command of the army about to be sent to America. The French officers holding commissions from the United States Congress held their meeting in Lafayette's house.

General Washington's Eagle of the Society of the Cincinnati.

The meeting of the American officers visiting Lafayette on January 16, concluded by their marching en masse to the Hotel de Rochambeau, where the two groups consolidated into one, and formed a single French Society.

Lafayette wrote to General Knox from Paris on January 8, 1784:

"Our association meets with great success. On Thursday next a sufficient number of Eagles will be made to answer immediate purposes. I intend inviting all the American officers to my house, and to conduct them in a body, with our regimentals, to the General of the French Army, to whom we will present the marks of the association. You will receive many applications relative to an addition to the brotherhood. But as nothing will be decided before the assembly in May, I have time to send you my observations."

From Paris, Colonel Gouvion wrote to General Knox in March, 1784:

"The Order succeeds extremely well in this country, but the news we have from America give me some uneasiness. The American gentlemen who are in Paris, and not members of the Society, are much against it; . . . who went the other day so far as to say that if it did take well in the States . . . would not care whether the Revolution had succeeded or not."

As a pertinent sidelight to opposition to the Cincinnati, it is interesting to note that soon after the formation of the Cincinnati, prominent men and newspapers violently assailed it, but the hostility soon subsided. The same antagonism existed in France for a time. The new building where one of the early meetings was held in this country had been struck by lightning, and someone said that it was an "event ominous of the storm brewing from another quarter against the Cincinnati."

Even Franklin wrote against it in 1784: "Others object to the bald eagle as looking too much like a turkey . . . I wish it had not been chosen as the representative of our country; he is a bird of bad moral character; he does not get his living honestly . . . He is therefore by no means a proper emblem for the brave and honest Cincinnati of America, who have driven all the 'King birds' from our country."

Other leading opponents were Thomas Jefferson, John Adams, Samuel Adams, John Jay, and Elbridge Gerry who averred and charged that an attempt was being made to establish an hereditary aristocracy. Later, however, Franklin became an honorary member, and Adams accepted an invitation to address the Society.

The possession of the Eagle in France at the time of the French Revolution became a great danger, and might be reason enough to condemn the bearer to the scaffold. In September of 1792, a number of political prisoners, including the venerable Duc de Brissac, and other individuals of distinction, were ordered to be transported under escort from Orleans to Paris. Seven loaded wagons, each containing eight prisoners in chains, set out on the fatal journey, headed by Fourmier, a renegade American.

"From the neck of Fourmier's horse," says Lamartine, in his History of the Girondins, "dangled a collar composed of Crosses of St. Louis, EAGLES OF CINCINNATUS, and other military decoration snatched from the breasts of the victims." Arriving at the gates of Versailles, they were attacked by a mob of assassins, and savagely butchered in cold blood.

At the first meeting, General Washington was unanimously chosen President-General, and held that office until his death, when he was succeeded by Major General Alexander Hamilton, who in turn remained President-General until his tragic death. He was succeeded by Major General Charles Cotesworth Pinckney. At his death in 1825, he was succeeded by Major General Thomas Pinckney. He was followed in 1829 by Major General Aaron Ogden of New Jersey. In 1839, Major General Morgan Lewis, and in 1844, Major William Popham, both of New York, were successively elected President-General. Brigadier General Henry Alexander Scammel Dearborn, of Massachusetts, was elected in 1848; Hon. Hamilton Fish, of New York, In 1854; Hon. William Wayne, of Pennsylvania, in 1896; Hon. Winslow Warren, of Massachusetts, in 1902; Hon. John Collins Daves, of North Carolina, in 1932. Bryce Metcalf, of Connecticut, in 1939; Issac Anderson Pennypacker of Maryland, in 1950; Major General Edgar Erskine Hume of Virginia, in 1950; Colonel John Fulton Reynolds Scott of Delaware, in 1952; Colonel Richard Hooker Wilmer of New Jersey, in 1953; Colonel Catesby ap Catesby Jones of Virginia, in 1956; Hon. Blanchard Randall of Maryland, in 1959; Francis Whiting Hatch of Massacusetts, in 1962; Colonel Charles Warren Lippitt of Rhode Island, in 1965; Frank Anderson Chisholm of Georgia, in 1968; Commander Armistead Jones Maupin of North Carolina, in 1971; Lt. Commander Harry Ramsay Hoyt of Pennsylvania, in 1974; Commander John Taylor Gilman Nichols of New Hampshire, in 1977; John Sanderson duMont of New York, in 1980; Catesby Brooke Jones of Virginia, in 1983; and, Reuben Grove Clark, Jr., of Georgia, in 1986.

Each President-General prior to 1950 has held office for life, and in 203 years there were but twenty-eight men elected to that high office. Even more remarkable is that in this period, there have been only fifteen Secretaries-General, the first was Major General Henry Knox.

Among the great leaders of the American Revolution, who became members of the Society besides George Washington were Alexander Hamilton, the Marquis de Lafayette, Henry Knox, Nathanael Greene, Friedrich Von Steuben, Benj. Lincoln, Charles C. Pinckney, John Paul Jones, Israel Putnam, John Schuyler, Horatio Gates, James Monroe, William Moultrie, Thaddeus Kosciuszko, Anthony Wayne, William Sullivan, "Light Horse Harry" Lee, Arthur St. Clair, and many others.

From the early issue of THE NEW YORK DIRECTORY (1786), many members of the Cincinnati are known to have been Freemasons. Those mentioned are George Washington, the Marquis de Lafayette,

General Friedrich Von Steuben, Chancellor Robert R Livingston (Grand Master), John Paul Jones, General Henry Knox to list a few.

On February 24, 1784, the officers of the French Navy who had been admitted to the Order of the Cincinnati, presented General Washington, through his Excellency, the Count d'Estaing, the ranking Naval officer, the Eagle of the Cincinnati richly set in diamonds. The Eagle was sent via the packet ship WASHINGTON, with the following letter of transmittal:

FROM THE COUNT D'ESTAING

Paris, 26th February, 1784

Sir:

It is in the name of all the French Navy that I take the liberty to request Your Excellency to accept an American Eagle, expressed rather then embellished by a French artist.

Liberty (of which it is the happy and august symbol) has risen of itself, supported by wisdom, talents and disinterestedness; by every virtue; by General Washington. Obstacles have only served to increase its strength.

The efforts of a patriotic army were irresistable when seconded by the King's troops, who have shown themselves by their discipline and conduct worthy of the choice of his Majesty. Those with his navy made everything possible.

It appears then to be proper in one of those who unites the titles of soldier and sailor, and whom you inspire with the sentiments of the most profound admiration and attachment, to entreat you to receive with indulgence an homage which must cease to be unimportant when it shall appeal to your sensibility.

One who has had the happiness to be the first of those whom the King sent to America, and who has been the last of those who were designed to lead thither the forces of two great monarchs, thereby acquiring the happy perrogative of being entitled to express, though failtly the sentiments of all his fellow sailors and soldiers.

I have the honor to be, with respect, Sir,
Your Excellency's most obedient and
Most humble servant,

Estaing.

[*Archives of the General Society*]

General Washington was deeply touched by the gift of the Diamond Eagle by the Count d'Estaing on the part of the officers of the French Navy that he thenceforth wore his Eagle instead of the one he purchased.

TO THE COUNT D'ESTAING

Philadelphia, May 15, 1784

Sir:

Any token of regard of whatever intrinsic worth in itself, coming from the Count D'Estaing, must [be] stamped with dignity and respect; but when attended with the esteem and regards of all the Sailors of your Nation, the companions of your honorable Toils in America, is not only agreeably acceptable, it becomes absolutely inestimable. As such I receive the American Eagle, which your Excellency has been pleased to present me in the name of all the Sailors of the French Nation. And at the same time that I acknowledge myself hereby inexpressibly honored by that most respectable Body of men. I beg you to assure them in my name of the very high estimation in which I shall ever hold this particular mark of their regard and attention.

To the Navy of France sir, this Country will hold itself deeply indebted: its assistance has rendered practicable those enterprizes, which without it could not with any probability of success, have been attempted. I feel myself happy in this opportunity thro' your Excellency's favour, of paying to the Officers and sailors of His Most Christian Majesty, this tribute of grateful acknowledgement, which I beg you sir to be so obliging as to convey to them, and at the same time to assure yourself of possessing in my breast, every sentim. of inviolable attachment and respect, with which your character has impressed my mind.

I have the honor, etc.

[*French National Archives, No c^8 1; copy in Washington's Letter Books*]

Washington wore this Eagle at official gatherings of the Cincinnati, and after his death, at Mrs. Washington's request, the diamond Eagle was sent by his heirs to Major General Alexander Hamilton, his successor in the office of President-General.

Upon the tragic death of Hamilton on July 12, 1804, the diamond Eagle was transmitted by his widow to the third President-General, Major General Charles C. Pinckney, who at the triennial meeting of the Society of the Cincinnati in Philadelphia on August 8, 1811, presented the following memorandum:

"That the diamond insignia of the Order of the Cincinnati which had been presented by the marine officers of France, who were members of the Society, to his Excellency George Washington, and by the heirs of the General, had been sent to General Hamilton, was delivered to him (General Pinckney) by Mrs. Hamilton — and as he conceived that this testimonial respect for the immortal Washington, which his heirs had delivered to General Hamilton, and Mrs. Hamilton had been pleased to confide to him, as president-general of the Society, ought, in respectful remembrance of her flattering distinction, to be hereafter considered as appurtenant to the office of president-general on the records of the General Society."

The General Society thereupon resolved that the "respectful and affectionate thanks of the General Society of the Cincinnati be presented to Mrs. Hamilton for this highly acceptable present; and that the wish of the president-general, expressed in his memorandum, respectfully acceded to by the Society."

Thus, the diamond Eagle has been worn by each of the twenty-eight men who have held the office of President-General. It is now held for the Society by three trustees: The President-General, the Secretary-General, and the Treasurer-General; and, is worn on such occasions as the President-General may deem proper.

THE
NEW-YORK DIRECTORY,
CONTAINING

A Valuable and well Calculated ALMANACK;— Tables of the different COINS, fuitable for any State, and digeſted in ſuch order, as to render an Exchange between any of the United States plain and eaſy.

LIKEWISE,

1. The names of all the Citizens, their occupations and places of abode.
2. The members in Congreſs, from what ſtate, and where reſiding.
3. Grand departments of the United States for adjuſting public accounts, and by whom conducted.
4. Members in Senate and Aſſembly, from what county, and where reſiding.
5. Judges, Aldermen, and other civil officers, with their places of abode.
6. Public ſtate-offices, and by whom kept.
7. Counſellors at law, and where reſiding.
8. Miniſters of the goſpel, where reſiding, and of what Church.
9. Phyſicians, Surgeons, and their places of abode.
10. Preſident, Directors, days, and hours of buſineſs at the Bank.
11. Profeſſors, &c. of the univerſity of Columbia college.
12. Rates of porterage, as by law eſtabliſhed.
13. Arrivals and departures of the mails at the Poſt-Office.

BY DAVID FRANKS.

NEW-YORK:
Printed by SHEPARD KOLLOCK, corner of Wall and Water Streets, M,DCC,LXXX,VI.

LIST of the members of the Cincinnatti of the State of New-York.

ALEXANDER M'DOUGALL, Efq; Prefident,
Barton Stuben, Efq; Vice Prefident,
Philip Cortlandt; Efq; Treafurer,
Richard Platt, Efq; Deputy Treafurer,
Robert Pemberton, Efq; Secretary,

George Clinton,	R. Cochran,
Samuel T. Pell,	Rod. V. Hovenberg,
John F. Hamtramch,	Ephraim Woodruff,
Jonathan Hallet,	Jofeph Frilick,
Israel Smith,	Samuel Dodge,
Theodofius Fowler,	B. Vanderburgh,
Henry Vanderburg,	Henry Dubois,
Henry Pauling,	Jacob Wright,
Samuel Dodge,	Benjamin Walker,
Charles Weiffenfelts,	Wm. Stephen Smith,
James Johnfon,	P. Magee,
B. Swartwout,	John Graham,
Samuel Talmage,	Jer. Van Ranffelaer,
Daniel Dennifton,	Aaron Aorfon,
Nehemiah Carpenter	John Marfh,
Chriftopher Hutton,	Ephraim Snow,
William Colbreath,	John Fondey,
Goofe Van Schaick,	Henry Tiebout,
John Gano,	Willes Ryckman,
Daniel Minema,	G. Lanfing,
Abner Prior,	James Gregg,
Michael Connolly,	R. Wilfon,

John C. Ten Broeck,
Samuel Lewis,
Cornelius V. Dyke,
John Furman,
Charles Parſons,
Benjamin Herring,
George Sitez,
Cornelius J. Janſen,
Abram. Hardenburg
Dy Fondey,
Henry V. Woert,
Jacob H. Wendell,
J. Morrel,
Adam Ten Broeck,
Benjamin Gilbert,
John Elliot,
Derik Schuyler,
Leonard Bleecker,
Joſeph Morrel,
C. Sweet,
William Peters,
John Lamb,
Andrew Moodie,
Michael Wetzell,
John Shaw,
Ephraim Fenns,
James Bradford,
Cornelius Swartwout
John Reed,
Iſaac Hubbel,
Henry Cunningham,
Ebenezer Stevens,
Sebaſtian Bauman,
Daniel Niven,
Peter Taulman,
William Price,
John Doughty,
Iſaac Smith,
Jacob Kemper,
Thomas Machin,
Peter Anſpach,
Henry Dember,
Iſaac Guion,
Jonas Addamſon,
R. Burnet, jun.
Caleb Brewſter,
George Fleming,
Joſeph Foote,
Pierrie Regnier,
Geo. J. Denniſton,
William Tapp,
Thomas Hunt,
William Belknap,
John F. Vacher,
Benjamin, Ledyard,
Charles Graham,
Fred. Weiſſenfelts,
John Cape,
Elihu Marſhall,
James Stuart,

Daniel Parker, jun.
James Gilliland,
Abraham Hyat,
Richard Varick,
Ranald S. M'Dougal
John Lawrence,
Simeon Dewitt,
Andrew Englis,
Jacob Reed,
George Leaycraft,
William Leaycraft,
Daniel M'Lean,
William Strachan,
Abraham Legget,
I. Stake,
James Giles,
Peter Neftle,
J. Bagley,
Samuel Hay,
John Cockran,
John Conway,
Edward Dunfcomb,
John D. Crimfhier,
Duncan Campbell,
Aquila Giles,
Marinus Willet,
Peter Vafborough,
Francis Hanmer,
Samuel Logan,
Peter Ganfwoort,
Matthew Clarkfon,
Robert Johnfon,
John Waldron,
Garrit J.V.Wagener
Thos. Fred. Jackfon
William W. Morris
John Smith,
John Green, capt. in
  the navy,
Thomas Tillotfon,
John Bard,
Stephen Graham,
John Grier,
A. White,
Alexander Clinton,
J. Brewfter,
Jonathan Lawrence,
Arthur Thompfon,
Daniel Gans,
Thomas Turner,
Hen. Em. Lutterloh
John Santford,
Morgan Lewis,
David Van Horn,
Teunis V. Wagener,
Silas Gray,
Charles Newkirk,
Tjerck Beckman,
Nathaniel Henry.

Honorary Members.

Lt. Gov. Cortlandt,
Chan. Livingſton,
Chief JuſticeMorris,
Judges, { Yates and Hobart,
James Duane, Eſq;
Judge Platt,
General Morris,
Colonel M'Laughry
Colonel Hathorn,
Colonel Floyd,
Capt D. Williams,
Maj.ThomasMoffat
H. R. Livingſton, Upper Manor,
Wm. Duer, ⎫
J. Lanſing, ⎬ Eſqrs
Philip Pell, ⎭
Dr. S. Gano.

Standing Committee.

Doctor Cockran,
Captain Dunſcomb,
Mr. Brooks,
Colonel Hay,
General Webb,
Colonel Antill,
Captain Reed,
Major Stagg,
Captain Guion.

Delegates for the General Meeting of the Committee.

Baron De Steuben, Colonel Troup. W
General Webb,

The Society, for the ſake of frequent communications, is divided into diſtricts, viz.---the ſouthern and northern diſtricts,-- the former including Long-Iſland, Staten- Iſland, New York-Iſland, the counties of

Weft-chefter, and Orange; The latter including the reft of the State. Thefe diftricts to hold their meetings in New-York and Albany, refpectively, on the laft Monday in March, and firft Monday in November, every year.

For the Southern Diftrict.

Marinus Willet, Efquire, Chairman, Edward Antill, Efq; Dep. Chairman, Jacob Reed, jun. Efq; Secretary.

The Northern Diftrict has not yet made their appointment.

CHAPTER XIII

THE WASHINGTON MASONIC LODGES

This work was originally predicted in an attempt to prove through documentary evidence a theory which had been passed down year after year that Washington Lodge No. 21, Free & Accepted Masons of New York City, New York, was the "Namesake" Lodge of General and Worshipful Brother George Washington. Tradition had inferred this to be a true statement alleging that this Lodge had been the "First," warranted after his death, and was, therefore, in fact his "Namesake" Lodge. For many years the Lodge has enjoyed Masonic intercourse with Fredericksburg Lodge No. 4 of the City of Fredericksburg, in the Commonwealth of Virginia and Alexandria—Washington Lodge No. 22 in the City of Alexandria in the Commonwealth of Virginia, celebrating his birthday, February 22, and his initiation into Masonry November 4, and paying homage on the anniversary of his death each December 14. All of this transpired in the absence of documentary evidence to prove its suspected heritage.

Lists of Masonic Lodges named for Washington appeared in *The Facts About George Washington as A Freemason* by J. Hugo Tasch (1932), *George Washington Freemason* by William Moseley Brown (1952), *Washington Miscellanea* by Harold V. B. Voorhis in Volume VI, Number 3 and *The Washington Masonic Lodges* by William Thomas Moree in Volume IX, Number 1, *Transactions of The American Lodge of Research*.

From the documented information assembled to date, there is no doubt that Washington Lodge No. 21 in New York City is the first Lodge to be warranted after the death of Washington and the "Namesake" Lodge of Washington.

Yes, it's true, Washington Lodge No. 21 Free and Accepted Masons, New York City, was and is the first Lodge to bear the name of Washington warranted after his death, but in a true meaning of the word, "Namesake," how could '21 state it is THE Namesake Lodge, when in fact so many other Lodges had been named for this great American. More, in fact, had been named for him than for any other person.

The first known Lodge to be named directly for Washington during his life time was Lodge No. 14, Chartered by the Grand Lodge of Pennsylvania on 27 December 1769. This lodge withdrew on June 7, 1806, from Pennsylvania jurisdiction, and was chartered as Washington Lodge No. 1, under Delaware jurisdiction. This lodge still exists today.

The first Lodge to be named for Washington after his death was without a doubt Washington Lodge No. 16, of New York City, chartered 5 March 1800. This Lodge is presently No. 21, in the First Manhattan District of New York.

The newest existing lodge to bear his name directly is Washington-Lafayette Lodge No. 176, of Portsmouth, Virginia, U/D 23 June 1947, chartered 12 February 1948, and the newest lodge to bear his name indirectly is Mount Vernon Lodge No. 219, of Alexandria, Virginia, U/D 1960, chartered 1961. It might be interesting to note that this lodge meets in a building on the original land tract of the Mount Vernon estate in Virginia.

By further examination of the lists following, one will observe that foreign Masonic jurisdictions have also taken up the trend and have used the name of the father of our country for lodges under their jurisdictions.

Little doubt exists that for the future many, many more Lodges will be named either directly or indirectly for this noted Masonic brother. We know that our Masonic brothers who are priviledged to belong to a Washington lodge can be justly proud of their association with the name and memory of George Washington.

New York State

Washington Lodge No. 21, F. & A.M., New York City, New York
chartered: 5 March 1800

Chartered as No. 16, 5 March 1800, First Lodge chartered after Washington's death to bear his name. 4 June 1819 number changed to 84. On June 8, 1839, number was changed to No. 21. Only Washington Lodge to have a stone in Washington Monument in Washington, D.C.

Washington Lodge No. 85, F. & A.M., Albany, New York U/D 6 Feb. 1841
chartered: 1841

Washington Lodge No. 240, F. & A.M., Buffalo, New York U/D 28 Oct. 1851
chartered: 2 Dec. 1851

George Washington Lodge No. 285, F. & A.M., New York City, New York
chartered: 2 March 1853

Alabama

Washington Lodge No. 36, F. & A.M., Tuscumbia, Alabama -
chartered: 9 Dec 1836

Arkansas

Washington Lodge No. 1 F. & A.M., Fayettville, Arkansas U/D 24 Dec. 1835

Granted a Dispensation 24 December 1835 by the Grand Lodge of Tennessee, chartered as Washington Lodge No. 82, 30 October 1837. Was one of the four Lodges which formed the Grand Lodge of Arkansas, 21 November 1838, when it was assigned No. 1.

George Washington Lodge No. 231, F. & A.M., Thornton, Calhoun County, Arkansas   chartered: 3 Nov. 1869

California

Washington Lodge No. 20, F. & A.M., Sacramento, California - chartered: 21 Feb. 1852

George Washington Lodge No. 525, F. & A.M., San Francisco, California   chartered: 1922

Colorado

George Washington Lodge No. 161, A.F. & A.M., Denver, Colorado chartered: 16 Sept. 1925

Connecticut

Washington Lodge No. 19, A.F. & A.M., Monroe, Connecticut chartered: 12 Jan. 1791

Washington Lodge No. 70, A.F. & A.M., Windsor, Connecticut chartered: 30 May 1825

Washington Lodge No. 81, A.F. & A.M., Cromwell, Connecticut chartered: 15 May 1856

George Washington Lodge No. 82, A.F. & A.M., Ansonia, Connecticut   chartered: 18 May 1857

Delaware

Washington Lodge No. 1, F. & A.M., Wilmington, Delaware chartered: 27 Dec. 1769

Chartered as Lodge No. 14 under Grand Lodge of Pennsylvania on 27 Dec. 1769. In 1806 withdrew from Pennsylvania jurisdiction and was chartered as Washington Lodge No. 1, 7 June 1806, under Delaware jurisdiction.

District of Columbia

Washington-Centennial Lodge No. 14, F.A.A.M., District of Columbia   chartered: 4 Nov. 1852

Chartered just a hundred years after the initiation of Washington in Fredericksburg Lodge, in the City of Fredericksburg, Virginia

Florida

Washington Lodge No. 2, Quincy, County of Gadsden, Florida
chartered: 27 Sept. 1830
An Original Charter Member of the Grand Lodge of Florida.

Georgia

Washington Lodge No. 19, F. & A.M., Cuthbert, Georgia
chartered: 8 Sept. 1840

Washington Lodge No. 359, F. & A.M., Ellaville, Georgia U/D-1845
chartered: 29 Oct. 1891

Illinois

Washington-Emblem Lodge No. 956, A.F. & A.M., Chicago, Illinois
chartered: 8 Oct. 1912
Emblem Lodge No. 984 was chartered on 13 Oct. 1915 and merged with Washington Park Lodge No. 956, in 1955, and the name was changed to Washington-Emblem.

George Washington Lodge No. 222, A.F. & A.M., Chillicothe, Illinois
chartered: 7 Oct. 1856

Washington Lodge No. 55 A.F. & A.M., Nashville, Ill. U/D-21 July 1847 chartered: 1848
Dispensation granted as Hardin Lodge. Name change to Washington when Charter granted.

Indiana

Washington Lodge No. 13, F. & A.M., Brownstown, Indiana
chartered: 1849
Present Charter date 1849, First Charter date unknown, suspended 1819, again 1822 and 1845. First Lodge in Jackson County, Indiana.

George Washington Lodge No. 325, F. & A.M., Bristol, Indiana
chartered: 1865

Iowa

George Washington Lodge No. 618, A.F. & A.M., Donnellson, Iowa
U/D:10 March 1916   chartered: 13 June 1916

Kansas

Washington Lodge No. 5, A.F. & A.M., Atchinson, Kansas
chartered: 14 July 1856

One of the First Lodges organized in Kansas, but was not one of the group which organized Grand Lodge of Kansas on 17 March 1856.

Kentucky

George Washington Lodge No. 904, F. & A.M., Louisville, Kentucky
chartered: 19 Oct. 1921

Louisiana

George Washington Lodge No. 65, F. & A.M., New Orleans, Louisiana U/D: Feb. 1847
chartered: 4 March 1850

Dispensation granted from Grand Lodge of Mississippi February 1847, Chartered by Grand Lodge of Louisiana, March 1850.

Maine

Washington Lodge No. 37, A.F. & A.M., Lubec, Maine
Date of Precedence: 10 Jan. 1822
chartered: 24 Jan. 1822

Maryland

Washington Lodge No. 3, A.F. & A.M., Baltimore, Maryland
chartered: 28 June 1770

Constituted as Lodge No. 15 by Grand Lodge of Pennsylvania, 28 June 1770. Joined in forming Grand Lodge of Maryland in 1787, receiving title of No. 3. Charter surrendered 1835, but restored 1845. Originally met at Fells Point, but now meets at Masonic Temple, Baltimore.

Massachusetts

Washington Lodge, A.F. & A.M., Lexington, Massachusetts
chartered: 17 March 1796

Originally located at Roxbury, Massachusetts.

Michigan

Washington Lodge No. 7, F. & A.M., Tekonsha, Michigan
chartered: 11 Jan. 1855

Minnesota

Washington Lodge No. 38, A.F. & A.M., West Concord, Minnesota
chartered: 23 Oct. 1861

Mississippi

Washington Lodge No. 3, F. & A.M., Port Gibson, Mississippi
chartered: 9 Apr. 1817

Chartered as Washington Lodge No. 17 by Grand Lodge of Tennessee on 9 April 1817. Rechartered at the organizational meeting of the Grand Lodge of Mississippi as Washington No. 3, in 1818.

George Washington Lodge No. 157, F. & A.M., Charleston, Mississippi   chartered: 22 Jan. 1852

Missouri

George Washington Lodge No. 9, A.F. & A.M., St. Louis, Missouri
chartered: 10 May 1849

Washington Lodge No. 87, A.F. & A.M., Greenfield, Missouri U/D 16 Oct. 1845   chartered: 12 Oct. 1847

Nebraska

George Washington Lodge No. 250, F. & A.M., Lincoln, Lancaster County, Nebraska   chartered: 20 June 1900

New Hampshire

Washington Lodge No. 61, F. & A.M., Manchester, New Hampshire U/D 1 Jan. 1857   chartered: 9 June 1857

New Jersey

Washington Lodge No. 9, F. & A.M., Eatontown, New Jersey
chartered: 14 Nov. 1815

Warrant dated 14 Nov. 1815 was issued to Shrewsbury-Washington Lodge No. 34. Resusitated, renamed and rewarranted 14 Nov. 1843 as Washington No. 9.

Washington Lodge No. 33, F. & A.M., New Jersey
chartered: 10 Nov. 1818

Warranted 10 Nov. 1818 as Washington No. 41. Stricken from Rolls 8 Nov. 1842. Resusitated and renumbered as 33, 10 Jan. 1855.

North Carolina

George Washington Lodge No. 174, A.F. & A.M., RFD #1, Apex, North Carolina   chartered: 5 Dec. 1855

Originally located at Lassiter's Cross Roads in Chathane County. Moved to Bell's Cross Roads in 1882, its present location.

American George Lodge No. 17, Murfreesboro, North Carolina
chartered: 17 Dec. 1789

Ohio

Washington Lodge No. 17, F. & A.M., Hamilton, Ohio
chartered: 6 Jan. 1813
U/D 7 Sept. 1811

Oregon

Washington Lodge No. 46, A.F. & A.M., Portland, Oregon U/D 16 Feb. 1869
chartered: 22 June 1869

Pennsylvania

Washington Lodge No. 59, F. & A.M., Philadelphia, Pennsylvania
chartered: 3 June 1793

George Washington Lodge No. 143, F. & A.M., Chambersburg, Pennsylvania
chartered: 15 Jan. 1816

Washington Lodge No. 156, F. & A.M., Quarryville, Pennsylvania
chartered: 2 Feb. 1818

Chartered at Chestnut Level, now Drumore Centre, Lancaster County. Moved to Quarryville 5 June 1895.

Washington Lodge No. 253, F. & A.M., Pittsburg, Pennsylvania
chartered: 15 March 1851

Washington Lodge No. 265, F. & A.M., Bloomsburg, Pennsylvania
chartered: 15 March 1852

Rhode Island

Washington Lodge No. 3, F. & A.M., Warren, Rhode Island U/D 24 June 1796
chartered: 19 March 1798

Washington Lodge No. 5, A.F. & A.M., North Kingston, R.I. U/D 4 July 1798
chartered: 24 June 1799

South Carolina

Washington Lodge No. 5, A.F. & A.M., (A.Y.M.), Charleston, South Carolina
chartered: 25 Nov. 1798
(1791)

South Dakota

Washington Lodge No. 111, A.F. & A.M., White, Brookings County, South Dakota
U/D 5 March 1891
chartered: 9 June 1891

Tennessee

Washington Lodge No. 159, F. & A.M., Greenfield, Weakley County, Tennessee
chartered: 5 Oct. 1849

George Washington Lodge No. 181, F. & A.M., Louisville, Blount County, Tenn.
chartered: 3 Oct. 1849

Texas

Washington Lodge No. 1117, A.F. & A.M., Dallas, Texas
chartered: 8 Dec. 1916

Utah

George Washington Lodge No. 24, F. & A.M., Ogden, Utah
chartered: 19 Jan. 1921

Vermont

Washington Lodge No. 3, F. & A.M., Burlington, Vermont
chartered: 13 Oct. 1795

No number was assigned until 1801, when it became No. 7, carried as No. 7 until 1849, when renumbered 3.

George Washington Lodge No. 51, F. & A.M., Chelsea, Vermont
chartered: 12 Jan 1860

No. 24 originally chartered 18 Jan. 1804, not reported a working lodge in 1846-7-8-9. Reorganized in 1849. Declared extinct in 1850. Rechartered 12 Jan. 1860, as No. 51.

Virginia

Alexandria-Washington Lodge No. 22, A.F. & A.M., Alexandria, Virginia
chartered: 3 Feb. 1783

Chartered as Alexandria Lodge No. 39 under Pennsylvania 3 Feb. 1783. Rechartered under Virginia as No. 22, 28 April 1788. Renamed 1804. Washington was Charter Master under Virginia jurisdiction.

George Lodge No. 32, A.F. & A.M., Howardsville, Virginia
chartered: 14 Apr. 1791

Chartered at Wariminster 14 April 1791. Charter revived 15 Dec. 1846.

Washington-Henry Lodge No. 344, A.F. & A.M., Mechanicsville, Virginia
U/D 18 Aug. 1922
chartered: 14 Feb. 1923

Washington-Lafayette No. 176, A.F. & A.M., Portsmouth, Virginia
U/D 23 June 1947
chartered: 12 Feb. 1948

Washington

Washington No. 4, F. & A.M., Vancouver, Washington
U/D 31 Oct. 1857
chartered: 18 July 1858
(as No. 22)

George Washington Lodge No. 251, F. & A.M., Seattle, Washington
chartered: 15 June 1922

West Virginia

Washington Lodge No. 58, A.F. & A.M., St. Albans, Kanawha County, West Va.
chartered: 12 Nov. 1873

Wisconsin

Washington Lodge No. 21, F. & A.M., Green Bay, Wisconsin
U/D 23 Dec. 1847
chartered: 16 Dec. 1848

Masonic Lodges in the United States With Names that Relate to Washington

Mount Vernon Lodge No. 428, F. & A.M., Pea Ridge, Arkansas
Mount Vernon Lodge No. 75, A.F. & A.M., Versailles, Connecticut
Mount Vernon Lodge No. 22, F. & A.M., Athens, Georgia
Mount Vernon Lodge No. 31, A.F. & A.M., Mount Vernon, Illinois
New Washington Lodge No. 167, F. & A.M., New Washington, Indiana
Washington Lodge No. 26, A.F. & A.M., Washington, Iowa (chartered 4 June 1851)
Mount Vernon Lodge No. 112, A.F. & A.M., Mount Vernon, Iowa
Mount Vernon Lodge No. 145, A.F. & A.M., Beloit, Kansas
Mount Vernon Lodge No. 14, F. & A.M., Georgetown, Kentucky
Washington-Meredith Lodge No. 355, F. & A.M., Brownsville, Kentucky

Mount Vernon Lodge No. 83, F. & A.M., Logansport, Louisiana
Vernon Valley Lodge No. 99, A.F. & A.M., Mount Vernon, Maine
Mount Vernon Lodge No. 151, A.F. & A.M., Baltimore, Maryland
Mount Vernon Lodge, A.F. & A.M., Malden, Massachusetts
Mount Vernon Lodge No. 166, F. & A.M., Quincy, Michigan
Mount Vernon Lodge No. 99, A.F. & A.M., Mount Vernon, Missouri
Mount Washington Lodge No. 614, A.F. & A.M., Mount Washington, Missouri, 19 Oct. 1911
Washington Lodge No. 21, Blair, Washington County, Nebraska (chartered 24 Feb. 1868)
Mount Vernon Lodge No. 15, A.F. & A.M., Newport, New Hampshire
Mount Washington Lodge No. 87, F. & A.M., North Conway, New Hampshire
Mount Vernon Lodge No. 3, F. & A.M., Albany, New York
Mount Vernon Lodge No. 263, F. & A.M., Java Village, New York
Vernon Lodge No. 1055, F. & A.M., Mount Vernon, New York
Port Washington Lodge No. 1010, F. & A.M., Port Washington, New York
Mount Vernon Lodge No. 143, A.F. & A.M., Bonlee, North Carolina
Mount Vernon Lodge No. 359, A.F. & A.M., Oriental, North Carolina
Washington Lodge No. 675, A.F. & A.M., Washington, North Carolina
Mount Washington Lodge No. 642, F. & A.M., Cincinnati, Ohio
Mount Vernon Lodge No. 64, F. & A.M., Norwalk, Ohio
Port Washington Lodge No. 202, F. & A.M., Port Washington, Ohio
Washington Lodge No. 406, A.F. & A.M., Washington, Oklahoma
Fort Washington Lodge No. 308, F. & A.M., Fort Washington, Pennsylvania
Washington Lodge No. 164, F. & A.M., Washington, Pennsylvania (chartered 1 March 1819)
Mount Vernon Lodge No. 4, F. & A.M., Providence, Rhode Island
Mount Vernon Lodge No. 349, F. & A.M., Sharon, Tennessee
Mount Vernon Lodge No. 691, A.F. & A.M., Mount Vernon, Texas
Vernon Lodge No. 655, A.F. & A.M., Vernon, Texas
Mount Vernon Lodge No. 8, F. & A.M., Morrisville, Vermont
Washington Lodge No. 78, A.F. & A.M., Washington, Virginia (chartered 10 Dec. 1806)
Mount Vernon Lodge 219, A.F. & A.M., Alexandria, Virginia

Washington Lodges
In Foreign Jurisdictions

England

Washington No. 4346, Washington, Durham

Canada
Washington No. 260, A.F. & A.M., Petrolia, Ontario

Brazil
George Washington No. 62, Campos Belos, Goias

Chili
Jorge Washington No. 56, Rancagua

Cuba
Washington, Havana

Guatemala
Jorge Washington No. 28, Quetzaltenango City

France
George Washington No. 69, Military Lodge in Spain

Italy
George Washington No. 585, Vincenza

Puerto Rico
Washington No. 78, Mayaguez

Venezuela
George Washington No. 100, Caracas

Washington Lodges No Longer in Existance

New York

Washington Lodge No. 11 (later 13 and again 11)
Fort Edward, New York
   Chartered: 26 September 1785
Defunct: 1835

Washington Lodge No. 16
Clermont, Colombia County, New York
   Chartered: 20 September 1790
Defunct: 1811

Washington Lodge No. 141
Stephentown, Westchester County, New York
   Chartered: 1806
Defunct: 1818

Washington Lodge No. 220
Blooming Grove, Orange County, New York
   Chartered: 1813
Defunct: 1834

Washington Lodge No. 234 (later 42)
Manneheim, Herkimer (formerly Montgomery) County, New York
   Chartered: 1814
Defunct: 1842

Washington Lodge No. 256
Henderson, Jefferson County, New York
   Chartered: 1815
Defunct: 1834

Alabama

Washington Lodge No. 17
Greensboro, Hale County, Alabama
   Chartered: 10 December 1823
Charter surrendered: 10 June 1825

George Washington Lodge No. 24
Clinton, Green County, Alabama
   Chartered: 16 December 1839
Charter forfeited: 1922

George Washington Lodge No. 62
Chinese Camp, California
   Chartered: 1856
Consolidated 15 September 1919 with Tuolomne Lodge No. 8 and presently existing and operating under that name.

Georgia

Washington Lodge No. 5
For the first time 1787 this Lodge appears in the Grand Lodge Proceedings of Georgia and not again.

Washington Lodge No. 46, F. & A.M.
Pond Town, Scheley County, Georgia
   U/D: 1845
   Chartered: 1846
Surrendered its Charter in 1876.

In 1858, the Lodge moved to Ellaville, the County seat of Scheley County. In 1876, Charter was surrendered to Grand Lodge; from 1877 to 1891, there were no Lodges operating in Scheley County. However, in 1891, a group of Masons petitioned Grand Lodge for a Charter, which was issued 29 October 1891 to Washington Lodge No. 359, which is still in existence at Ellaville, Georgia.

Washington Lodge No. 38
    Chartered: 21 July 1918
Number changed to 15 on 4 December 1820
Defunct: 9 December 1829

Kentucky

Washington Lodge No. 6
Bairdstown (Bardstown), Kentucky
    Chartered: 9 February 1801
Defunct: 7 October 1806
First Lodge established by the Grand Lodge of Kentucky.

Washington Lodge No. 19
Washington, Kentucky
    Chartered: 29 August 1811
Defunct: 24 August 1823

Washington Lodge No. 19
    Chartered: 2 September 1847
Defunct: July 1860

Washington Lodge No. 19
    Chartered: 31 August 1868
Defunct: 1870

Washington Lodge No. 79
North Middletown, Kentucky
    Chartered: 1 Sept. 1824   Defunct: August 1836
    Reinstated: 1838   Defunct: 18 Oct. 1866
    Restored: 24 October 1867   Consolidated 20 January 1953 with Paris Lodge No. 2, still existence at Paris, Kentucky as Paris Lodge No. 2.

Maryland

Washington Lodge No. 59
Denton, Maryland
    Chartered: 1816
Chapter lapsed: 1835

George Washington Lodge No. 94
Westminster, Maryland
    Chartered: 12 May 1851
Charter lapsed: 1882

Massachusetts

Washington Remembered
New Bedford, Massachusetts
    Chartered: 12 September 1803
Charter Surrendered: 5 October 1816

Washington Lodge No. 10 (Traveling Army Lodge)
    Chartered: 6 October 1779
Charter lapsed at end of Revolution.

Traveling Army Lodges are the only ones in the records of Massachusetts that had numbers.

Mississippi

Washington Lodge of the Grand Lodge of Mississippi located at New Orleans, Louisiana
    U/D: 22 February 1847
Withdrew to Louisiana jurisdiction 3 March 1850

Montana

Washington Lodge No. 19, A.F. & A.M.
Gallatin City, Montana
    Chartered: 8 October 1872
Charter surrendered: 3 October 1877

New Hampshire

Washington Lodge No. 13
Exeter, New Hampshire
Dispensation: 28 January 1801
    Chartered: 22 July 1801
Charter surrendered: 9 July 1824

New Jersey

Washington Lodge No. 12
    Chartered: 6 January 1794

Charter surrendered: 1819 or 1820

Shrewsbury-Washington Lodge No. 34
Warrant dated 14 November 1850
Resuscitated, renamed and rewarranted 14 November 1843 as Washington No. 9

Washington Lodge No. 41
Warrant dated November 10, 1842
Stricken from Rolls November 8, 1842
Resuscitated and renumbered No. 33, January 10, 1855

North Carolina

Washington Lodge No. 15
Beaufort County, North Carolina
  Chartered: 24 June 1789
  Dissolved: 24 December 1833

Pennsylvania

Washington No. 14, A.Y.M.
  Chartered: 27 December 1769
  Became one of the Charter Lodges of Delaware 7 June 1806 and renumbered as Washington No. 1

Washington No. 15
  Chartered: 28 June 1770
  It joined with other Lodges in forming the Grand Lodge of Maryland in 1787 receiving the title Washington Lodge No. 3

South Carolina

Washington Lodge No. 5
  Chartered: 25 November 1789 (possibly 1791)
  In 1808 there existed in South Carolina two Grand Lodges, one A.Y.M., the other F. & A.M. Each had a Washington Lodge No. 5. In 1808 an attempt was made to unite the two Grand Lodges. No. 5 A.Y.M. was given No. 7. Several Lodges withdrew to continue as A.Y.M., but Lodge No. 5 remained in the United Grand Lodge as No. 7. In 1817, when the Grand Lodge A.F. & A.M. was formed and all Lodges united under one Grand Lodge, this Lodge retained No. 7. Lodge No. 5 F. & A.M. surrendered its charter on 2 November 1824, and became affiliated with Orange Lodge No. 14, which is still in existence in Charleston, South Carolina. On December 16, 1825, authority was granted to change the number of Lodge No. 7 back to its original No. 5. Although the records show that this Lodge was chartered 1789, it is understood by the South Carolina history that it was originally chartered in 1791 and took the name of Washington in honor of President Washington, who visited the City of Charleston that year.

Tennessee

Washington Lodge No. 17
Port Gibson, Mississippi
Organized 6 October 1817, united with Andrew Jackson No. 15 at Natchez, Mississippi and Lodge No. 33 of Kentucky, to form the Grand Lodge of Mississippi, 7 July 1818

Washington Lodge No. 23
Located at Hazel Green, Alabama
Organized 6 October 1818
Charter surrendered 2 December 1829

Washington Lodge No. 82
Located at Fayetville, Arkansas
U/D 24 December 1835
Organized 3 October 1837, became No. 1 of Grand Lodge of Arkansas on 2 November 1838

Washington Luminary Lodge No. 42
Washington, Tennessee
Organized 3 October 1821
Charter arrested 4 October 1827

Washington Lodge No. 236
Washington, Tennessee
Organized 3 October 1854
Charter arrested 29 January 1904

Texas

Washington Lodge No. 18
Washington, Texas
   Chartered: January 1884
Demised 1887

Vermont

Washington Lodge No. 21
Brenton, Vermont
   Chartered: 15 October 1802
Declared extinct: 1847

Virginia

Washington Lodge No. 26
Botetort, Virginia
   Chartered: 30 December 1786
Ceased: 1802

Washington Lodge No. 99, A.Y.M.
Louisiana, New Orleans County, Virginia
   Chartered: 14 December 1814
Never made a return to Grand Lodge of Virginia and was declared transferred to the Grand Lodge of New Orleans, Louisiana, in 1821. Not recognized by Louisiana.

Washington Lodge No. 121
Martinsville, Henry County, Virginia
Dispensation 22 July 1820
    Chartered as No. 212, 12 December 1820
Ceased: 1837

Washington Lodge No. 57
Berryville, Clarke County, Virginia
    Chartered: 15 December 1840
Ceased: 1855

George Washington Masonic National Memorial, Alexandria, Va.

CHAPTER XIV

THE GEORGE WASHINGTON MASONIC NATIONAL MONUMENT

Alexandria, Virginia

Amid the monuments and museums, the memorials and mausoleums of Washington, a looming structure has managed to elude most tourists and natives for nearly 60 years.

Driving through the heart of Alexandria, Va., one can hardly miss the tower of the George Washington Masonic National Memorial. But the 55,000 tourists who visit it every year hardly compare to the 3,000,000 who go through the Smithsonian Museums, or the 75,000 who peer from the windows of the Washington Monument.

The 440 foot tower stands on 36 acres of land that once was considered for the Capitol of the United States, and across the street from its grassy slopes is the Alexandria Railroad Station, at one time the gateway to the North and South. Just a few feet beyond are the tracks of the Metrorail.

The Memorial was designed after the Pharo at Alexandria, Egypt. The famed lighthouse built by King Ptolemy in 280 B.C. that was once listed among the ancient "Seven Wonders of the World".

The Cornerstone of the Memorial was laid in 1923, and the building was dedicated in 1932.

Today it is open to the public seven days a week, from 9 a.m. till 5 p.m.

Inside may be found the largest Royal Meshed Persian rug in the world, the original Joshua Reynolds painting of Lord Fairfax, murals by Allyn Cox, a collection of rare books, and the only elevators in the world which rise on rails slanting inward 7.1/2 degrees.

As visitors enter the main entrance, he is greeted by a guide who explains the layout of the memorial, and informs them of the tours to the tower and observation deck.

The Guides are all members of the fraternity and well informed on the memorabilia. The visitors first sight is the Great Memorial Hall, at the far end is the beautiful bronze statue of George Washington, standing 17 feet 3 inches, and weighing 8 tons, the statue is flanked by eight granite columns 48 feet in height and weighing 60 tons each. They are the main support of the memorial.

Murals depicting events in the life of Washington line the walls behind the pillars. They were painted by the famous Allyn Cox, a Washington artist who has painted all the murals in the Memorial and many of the murals in the U.S. Capitol, Cox was considered one of the finest muralists in the World. He was a member of Holland Lodge No. 8, in New York City.

Rising above the murals are six stained glass windows installed by Robert Metcalf, honoring such great patriots as, Franklin, Lafayette, Livingston, Warren, Gist, Dr. Dick.

The green granite columns are repeated in the Assembly Room below the Great Hall, which contains the 12 dioramas of Washington's Life, and the 360 year old Persian carpet, the largest one piece rug in the world.

Nearby is a room supported by the Imperial Council of the Nobles of the Mystic Shrine, where miniature mechanized Shriners parade with 1,100 figures, and a scale model of the Taj Mahal.

As visitors ride the slightly slanted elevators to the tower, they see a variety of rooms, each one a different order of architecture. They range from Persian to 15th century England, a Chapel with organ music, the Royal Arch Room with the Egyptian architecture, a glimpse of the Holy of Holies with the ark of the covenant.

The Library, another of the tower rooms, contains several thousand volumes on Masonry, the classics, religion and mathematics. Among its most precious possessions are the Washington family library brought from Mt. Vernon by John Washington, the last of the family to own Mt. Vernon.

The most outstanding item of interest to all visitors is the Observation Deck on the ninth level. The deck surrounds the building and is enclosed with an iron fence to protect the public, unlike the Washington Monument in Washington, from which you have to look out of a window, here at the Memorial to Washington you have the freedom of a walkway and clear vision to all.

Visiting Masonic Brothers, find the memorial occupied by most of the Masonic bodies, and a visiting Mason may enjoy the evening with one of the Masonic bodies which meet in the Memorial regularly. There is always a meeting of one of the lodges on Thursday nights.

The Memorial being supported and operated by all the Grand Lodges in the United States, is of course an open Jurisdiction to all the Grand Lodges. Because of this unique ownership, Lodges from all over the United States are free to visit and use the Memorial and its facilities. They may even hold lodge, make arrangements for banquets, motel accomodations, etc.

As a word of warning, any lodge interested in using the Memorial accomodations should plan well in advance of their program. Almost every Saturday in the Spring, Summer, & Fall months are taken far in advance of the date. Most dates are set a year in advance.

There are two outstanding rooms in the Memorial which hold forth to Historians and Visitors a look into the past. The Replica Room, is an exact duplicate of Alexandria Lodge No. 22 in 1788. It contains all the original furniture and regalia, from the Library Chair from Mt. Vernon, given to the Lodge by Washington when Master of the Lodge, to the meeting house benches purchased from the Presbyterian Church for 10 cents each, after the Church obtained their new pews.

There are wall cases filled with Washington Memorabilia given to the Lodge over the years by members of the family.

The second room of importance to Historians is the Washington Museum in the tower. This room contains memorabilia of Washington and his family. Items such as the Family Bible, Chest of Drawers, Desk, also the family picture by John Chapman.

Visitors are permitted to spend as much time as they wish in these two rooms.

It has been said, and I quote. "The greatest achievement by the Masonic Order in the twentieth century, is the construction of the George Washington Masonic National Memorial."

BIBLIOGRAPHY

Abott, Wilbur C., *New York in the American Revolution*, 1929, Charles Scribner's Sons, New York.

Andrews, William Loring, *New York as Washington Knew it After the Revolution*, 1905, Charles Scribner's Sons, New York.

Bacheller, Irving & Herbert Kates *Great Moments in the Life of Washington*, 1932, Grosset & Dunlap, New York.

Baker, William Spohn, *Itinerary of General Washington, July 15, 1777 to December 23, 1783*, 1892, J. B. Lippencott Company, New York.

Baker, William Spohn, *Character Portraits of Washington*, 1887, Globe Printing House, Robert M. Lindsay, Philadelphia.

Baker, William Spohn, *Bibliotheca Washington*, 1889, Globe Printing House, Robert M. Lindsay, Philadelphia.

Baker, William Spohn, *Medallic Portraits of Washington*, 1885, Robert M. Lindsay, Philadelphia.

Barratt, Norris S., and Sachse, Julius F., *Freemasonry in Pennsylvania 1729-1907*, 1907, New Era Printing Company, Philadelphia.

Bayles, W. Harrison, *Old Taverns of New York*, 1915, Frank Alaben Genealogical Company, New York.

Bell, Charles H., *History of the Town of Exeter, New Hampshire*, 1888, Privately Printed, Exeter, New Hampshire.

Bellamy, Francis, *Private Life of George Washington*, 1951, Thomas Y. Crowell Company, New York.

Bloom, Sol, *A Masonic Tribute to the Sesquicentennial of the Inauguration of George Washington*, 1939, United States Government Printing Office, Washington, D.C.

Bloom, Sol, *Our Heritage; George Washington and the Establishment of The American Union*, 1944, G. P. Putnam's Sons, New York.

Booth, Edward Townsend, *Country Life in America*, Chapter II, George Washington; Tidewater Plantation, 1947, Alfred A. Knopf, New York.

Booth, Mary L., *History of the City of New York*, 1859, W. R. C. Clark & Meeker, New York.

Bolton, Charles Knowles, *The Private Soldier Under Washington*, 1902, Charles Scribner's Sons, New York.

Boudreau, Allan. *George Washington and New York City*, 1989, Masonic Service Association of the United States, Silver Spring, Maryland.

BIBLIOGRAPHY

Boudreau, Allan, *Washington in New York City*, 1989, The Empire State Mason, New York.

Boudreau, Allan, *George Washington and U. S. Postage Stamps*, 1989, Masonic Philatelist, New York.

Boudreau, Allan, *Why The St. John's Lodge Bible ?*, 1989, The New Age, Volume XCII, Number 4, Washington, D.C.

Boudreau, Allan, *Two Hundred Years of Freemasonry in New York*, 1983, Transactions of the American Lodge of Research, Volume XV, Number 3, New York.

Boyden, William L., *Masonic Presidents, Vice Presidents, and Signers*, 1927, Privately Printed, Washington, D.C.

Brewster, Charles W., *Rambles about Portsmouth*, 1859, 2 volumes, Portsmouth, New Hampshire.

Brown, William Moseley, *George Washington Freemason*, 1952, Garrett & Massie, Inc., Richmond, Virginia.

Brown, Wallace, *The Good Americans, The Loyalists in the American Revolution*, 1969, William Morrow & Company, New York.

Bruce, Philip Alexander, *Social Life in Virginia in the Seventeenth Century*, 1907, Reprinted 1968 by Corner House Press, Williamstown, Massachusetts.

Buffington, Joseph, *The Soul of George Washington*, 1936, Dorrance & Company, Philadelphia.

Callahan, Charles H., *Washington the Man and Mason*, 1913, George Washington Masonic National Memorial Association, Washington, D.C.

Callahan, Charles H., *The Memorial to Washington*, 1923, Local Memorial Committee of Alexandria, Alexandria, Virginia.

Carrington, General Henry B., *Washington the Soldier*, 1899, Charles Scribner's Sons, New York.

Claudy, Carl H., *Washington's Home and Fraternal Life*, 1931, The Masonic Service Association of the United States, Silver Spring, Maryland.

Cook, Roy Bird, *Washington's Western Lands*, 1930, Shenandoah Publishing House, Inc. Strasburg, Virginia.

Corbin, John, *The Unknown Washington*, 1930, Charles Scribner's Sons, New York.

Cunliffe, Marcus, *George Washington Man and Monument*, 1958, Little, Brown and Company, Boston.

Cunliff, Marcus, *George Washington and the Making of a Nation*, 1966, American Heritage Publishing Company, New York.

Custis, George Washington Parke, *Recollections and Private Memoirs of Washington, by His Adopted Son*, 1860, New York.

Dangerfield, George, *Chancellor Robert R. Livingston*, 1960, Harcourt, Brace and Company, New York.

Decatur, Stephen, *Private Affairs of George Washington*, 1933, Houghton Mifflin Company, Boston.

Dunn, Robert H., *Old St. John's at Portsmouth and Her Distinguished Colonial Flock*, 1947, Portsmouth.

Eisen, Gustav, *Portraits of Washington*, 1932, 3 volumes, R. Hamilton & Associates, New York.

Engel, Carl, *Music From the Days of George Washington*, 1931, United States Government Printing Office, Washington, D.C.

Fielding, Mantle, *Gilbert Stuart's Portraits of Washington*, 1923, Wickersham Printing Co., Lancaster, Pennsylvania.

Fish, Hamilton Jr., *George Washington in the Highlands*, 1932, Press of the Newburgh News, Newburgh. New York.

Fitzpatrick, John C., *Calendar of the Correspondence of George Washington*, 1915, 4 volumes, United States Governmnet Printing Office, Washington, D.C.

Fitzpatrick, John C., *George Washington Colonial Traveller 1732-1775*, 1927, The Bobbs-Merrill Company, Indianapolis.

Fleming, Thomas J., *Affectionately Yours, George Washington*, 1967, W. W. Norton & Company, Inc., New York.

Flexner, James Thomas, *George Washington: The Forge of Experience (1732-1775)*, 1965, Little Brown and Company, Boston.

Flexner, James Thomas, *George Washington in the American Revolution (1775-1783)*, 1967, Little, Brown and Company, Boston.

Flexner, James Thomas, *George Washington and the New Nation (1783-1793)*, 1969, Little, Brown and Company, Boston.

Flexner, James Thomas, *George Washington, Anguish and Farewell (1793-1799)*, 1972, Little, Brown and Company, Boston.

BIBLIOGRAPHY

Flexner, James Thomas, *Washington The Indispensable Man*, 1974, Little Brown and Company, New York.

Ford, Henry Jones, *Washington and his Colleagues*, 1921, Yale University Press, New Haven.

Ford, Paul Leicester, *George Washington*, 1896, Lippencott, Philadelphia.

Freeman, Douglas Southall, *George Washington,* 1948-1957, 7 volumes, Charles Scribner's Sons, New York.

Frothingham, Thomas G., *Washington, Commander in Chief*, 1930, Houghton Mifflin Company, New York.

Gorham Company, *George Washington: Jean Antoine Houdon, Sculptor*, 1931, Gorham Company, Providence, Rhode Island.

Grand Lodge of Iowa, *Grand Lodge Bulletin*, 1925.

Grand Lodge of New Hampshire, *Proceedings, Volume 1, 1789-1814*, 1860, Concord, New Hampshire.

Grand Lodge of New York, *Early History and Transactions, 1781-1815*, 1876, Masonic Publishers, New York.

Grand Lodge of Pennsylvania, *Reprint of the Minutes, Volume 1, 1779-1801*, 1895, Philadelphia.

Grasse, Francois Joseph Paul, *Correspondence of General George Washington and Comte de Grasse*, 1931, United States Government Printing Office, Washington, D. C.

Guizot, Francois Pierre Guillaume, *Washington* (translated by Henry Reeve), 1860, Murray, London.

Hayden, Sidney, *George Washington and His Masonic Compeers*, 1866, Masonic Publishing Company, New York..

Haworth, Paul Leland, *George Washington, Farmer*, 1915, Bobs-Merrill, Indianapolis.

Hammond, Otis G., Editor, *Letters and Papers of Major General John Sullivan*, 3 Volumes, 1930-39, Concord, New Hampshire.

Harper, Kenton N., *History of the Grand Lodge of Freemasonry in the District of Columbia*, 1911, Grand Lodge of the District of Columbia, Washington, D.C.

Hayden, Sidney, *Washington and His Masonic Compeers*, 8th Edition, 1905, Macoy Publishing Company, New York.

Headley, Joel Tyler, *The Life of George Washington*, 1859, G. & F. Bill, C. A. Alvord, Printer, New York.

Headley, Joel Tyler, *Washington and His Generals*, 1847, Baker & Scribner, New York.

Heaton, Ronald E., *Masonic Membership of the Founding Fathers*, 1974, The Masonic Service Association of the United States, Silver Spring, Maryland.

Heaton, Ronald E., *Valley Forge Yesterday and Today*, 1957, Ronald E. Heaton, Norristown, Pennsylvania.

Heaton, Ronald E., *The Image of Washington, The History of the Houdon Statue*, 1971, Ronald E. Heaton, Norristown, Pennsylvania.

Heaton, Ronald E. and Case, James R., *The Lodge at Fredericksburgh, A Digest of the Early Records*, 1981, The Masonic Service Association of The United States, Silver Spring, Maryland.

Helderman, Leonard Clinton, *George Washington, Patron of Learning*, 1932, The Century Company, New York.

Heusser, Albert H., *In the Footsteps of Washington*, 1921, Privately Printed, Paterson, New Jersey.

Hough, Franklin B., *Washingtonia: or, Memorials of the Death of George Washington*, 1865, 2 volumes, W. Elliot Woodward, Roxbury, Massachusetts.

Hughes, Rupert, *George Washington*, 1927, 3 Volumes, William Morrow & Company, New York.

Hume, Edgar Erskine, *General Washington's Correspondence Concerning the Society of the Cincinnati*, 1941, The Johns Hopkins Press, Baltimore.

Irving, Washington, *Life of George Washington*, 1855-59, 5 Volumes, Putnam, New York,

Irving, Washington, *Life of George Washington*, Edited and abridged by Jess Stein, 1975, Sleepy Hollow Restorations, Tarrytown, New York.

Ives, Mable Lorenz, *Washington's Headquarters*, 1932, Lucy Fortune Press, Upper Montclair, New Jersey.

Johnston, Elizabeth Bryant, *George Washington Day by Day*, 1895, The Cycle Publishing Company, New York.

Jones, Thomas, *History of New York During the Revolutionary War*, 1879, 2 volumes, Printed for the New-York Historical Society, Trow's Printing & Bookbinding Co., New York.

BIBLIOGRAPHY

Kane, Joseph Nathan, *Facts About the Presidents*, 1981, The H. W. Wilson Company, New York.

Kane, Joseph Nathan, *Famous First Facts*, 1981, Fourth Edition Expanded and revised, The H. W. Wilson Company, New York.

Kernochan, Marshall Rutgers, *George Washington's Honorary Membership in the Holland Lodge,* 1949, Transactions of The American Lodge of Research, Volume 5, The American Lodge of Research, New York.

Ketchum, Richard M., *The World of George Washington*, 1974, American Heritage Publishing Company, New York.

Klapthor, Margaret Brown, *G. Washington, a figure upon the stage*, 1982, Exhibit at the National Museum of American History, February 22, 1982 - January 7, 1983, Smithsonian Instution Press, Washington, D.C.

Knollenberg, Bernard, *George Washington, The Virginia Period 1732-1775*, 1964, Duke University Press, Durham, North Carolina.

Knox, Dudley Wright, *The Naval Genius of George Washington*, 1932, Houghton Mifflin Company, Boston.

Lafayette, Marie Joseph Paul Yves Roch Gilbert du Motier, marquis de, *The Letters of Lafayette to Washington 1777-1799*, Edited by Louis Gottschalk, 1944, Privately Printed by Helen Fahnestock Hubbard, New York.

Lamb, Martha J., *History of the City of New York*, 2 Volumes, 1877, A. S. Barnes & Company, New York & Chicago.

Lang, Ossian, *History of Freemasonry in the State of New York*, 1922, Hamilton Printing Company, New York.

Lanier, John J., *Washington The Great American Mason*, 1922, J. J. Little & Ives Company, New York.

Lichtenstein, Gaston, *George Washington's Lost Birthday*, 1924, The William Byrd Press, Inc., Richmond.

Little, Shelby, *George Washington*, 1929, Minton, Balch & Company, New York.

McClenachan, Charles T., *History of Freemasonry in New York*, 4 Volumes, 1888, Press of J. J. Little & Co., New York,

McGroarty, William Buckner, *Washington First in the Hearts of His Countrymen*, 1932, Garrett & Massie, Incorporated, Richmond.

McSpadden, Joseph Walker, *The Story of George Washington*, 1922, Barse & Hopkins, New York.

Marshall, John, *The Life of George Washington*, 1925, 5 Volumes, Compiled Under the Instpection of the Honorable Bushrod Washington, Wm. H. Wise & Co.,New York.

Merriam, George Ernest, *More Precious Than Fine Gold - Washington Commonplace Book*, 1931, G. P. Putnam's Sons, New York.

Moore, Charles, *The Family Life of George Washington*, 1926, Houghton, Boston.

Morse, Jedidiah, *Annals of the American Revolution*, 1824, (Reprinted 1987), White Rose Press, Memphis, Tennessee.

Nettels, Curtis Putnam, *George Washington and American Independence*, 1951, Little Brown, Boston.

Nordham, George Washington, *A George Washington Treasury*, 1982, Adams Press, Chicago.

Nordham, George Washington, *George Washington and the Law*, 1982, Adams Press, Chicago.

Nordham, George Washington, *George Washington's Religious Faith*, 1986, Adams Press, Chicago.

Nordham, George Washington, *George Washington, President of the Constitutional Convention*, 1987, Adams Press, Chicago.

Page, Elwyn L., *George Washington in New Hampshire*, 1932, Houghton, Boston.

Pound, Arthur, *Johnson of the Mohawks, A Biography of Sir William Johnson*, 1930, The MacMillan Company, New York.

Pound, Arthur, *Washington Freeman of Albany*, 1932, Albany Institute of History and Art, The Argus Press, Albany, New York.

Prussing, Eugene E., *The Estate of George Washington, Deceased*, 1927, Little Brown and Company, New York.

Ritter, Halsted L., *Washington as a Business Man*, Introduction by Albert Bushnell Hart, 1931, Sears Publishing Company,Inc., New York.

Roberts, Allen E., *G. Washington, Master Mason*, 1976, Macoy Publishing Company, Richmond, Virginia.

Ross, Peter, *A Standard History of Freemasonry in the State of New York*, 2 volumes, 1899, The Lewis Publishing Company, New York.

Rugg, Henry W., *History of Freemasonry in Rhode Island, 1895*, E. L. Freeman & Son State Printer, Providence.

BIBLIOGRAPHY

Sabine, William W. H., *Murder, 1776 & Washington's Policy of Silence*, 1973, Theo. Gaus' Sons, Inc., Brooklyn, New York.

Sachse, Julius Friedrich, *Washington's Masonic Correspondence*, 1915, New Era Printing Company, Philadelphia.

Sawyer, Joseph Dillaway, *Washington*, 2 Volumes, 1927, The MacMillian Company, New York.

Schouler, James, *Americans of 1776 Daily Life During the Revolutionary Period*, 1906, (Reprinted 1984), Corner House Publishers, Williamstwon, Massachusetts.

Schroeder, John Frederick, *Life and Times of Washington*, 1857, 2 volumes, Johnson Fry & Company, New York.

Scudder, Horace Elisha, *George Washington, an historical biography*, 1924, Houghton, Boston.

Sears, Louis Martin, *George Washington*, 1932, Crowell, New York.

Smith, Thomas E.V., *The City of New York in the Year of Washington's Inauguration 1789*, New York, 1889, Anson D.F. Randolph & Co., New York.

Snowden, James Rose, *A Description of the Medals of Washington*, 1861, Lippincott, Philadelphia.

Sparks, Jared, *The Life of George Washington*, 1839, Published by Ferdinand Andrews, Boston; Printed by Folsom, Wells, and Thurston, Cambridge.

Stephenson, Nathaniel Wright & Dunn, Waldo Hilary, *George Washington*, 1940, 2 volumes, Oxford University Press.

Stevenson, Burton Egbert, *A Soldier of Virginia*, 1901, Houghton Miffin and Company, New York.

Tasch, J. Hugo, *The Facts About George Washington as a Freemason*, 1932, Macoy Publishing Company, New York.

Tebbel, John, *George Washington's America*, 1954, E. P. Dutton & Co., New York.

Thayer, William Roscoe, *George Washington*. 1922, Houghton Mifflin Company, Boston.

Unrau, Harland D., *Here Was The Revolution, Historical Sites of the War for American Independence*, 1976, U. S. Government Printing Office, Washington, D.C.

Upham. C. W., *The Life of General Washington*, 1851, 2 volumes, Office of the National Illustrated Library, London.

Van Dyke, Paul, *George Washington, Son of His Country*, 1931, Charles Scribner's Sons, New York.

Wall, Charles Cecil, *George Washington Citizen-Soldier*, 1988, The Mount Vernon Ladies' Association, Mount Vernon, Virginia.

Washington, George, *The Journal of Major George Washington an account of his first official mission, made as emissary from the Governor of Virginia to the Commandant of the French forces on the Ohio, October 1753-January 1754*, 1754, William Hunter, Williamsburg, Virginia.
(Facsimile edition, 1959, Colonial Williamsburgh, Williamsburgh, Virginia, distributed by Holt, New York).

Washington, George, *The Writings of George Washington*, 1834-37, 12 volumes, Jared Sparks, Editor, American Stationers' Company, Boston.

Washington, George, *The Diaries of George Washington 1748-1799*, 1925, 4 volumes, John C. Fitzpatrick, Editor, Published for the Mount Vernon Ladies' Association of the Union, Houghton Mifflin Company, Boston and New York.

Washington, George, *The Diaries of George Washington*, 1976-79, 6 volumes, Donald C. Jackson, Editor, Dorothy Twohig, Associate Editor, University Press of Virginia, Charlottesville, Virginia.

Washington, George, *Account of Expenses while Commander-in-chief of the Continental Army 1775-1783*, 1917, with annotations by John C. Fitzpatrick, The Riverside Press, Cambridge, Houghton Mifflin Company, Boston and New York.

Washington, George, *The Writings of George Washington*, Collected & Edited by Worthington Chauncey Ford, 1889-93, 14 volumes, G. P. Putnam's Sons, The Knickerbocker Press, New York.

Washington, George, *The Writings of George Washington*, 1933-44, 39 Volumes, John C. Fitzpatrick, Editor, United States Government Printing Office.Washington, D.C.

Washington, George, *The Papers of George Washington, Colonial Series*, 1983- , Volumes 1-6, W. W. Abbot, Editor, Dorothy Twohig, Associate Editor, The University Press of Virginia, Charlottesville, Virginia.

Washington, George, *The Papers of George Washington,Revolutionary War Series*, 1985- ,Volumes 1-3, W. W. Abbott, Editor, The University Press of Virginia, Charlottesville, Virginia.

Washington, George, *The Papers of George Washington, Presidential Series*, 1987- ,Volumes 1-2, W. W. Abbott, Editor, The University Press of Virginia, Charlottesville, Virginia.

BIBLIOGRAPHY

Washington, George, *The Journal of the Proceedings of the President*, The University Press of Virginia, Charlottesville, Virginia.

Weems, Mason Locke, *A History of the Life and Death, virtues and exploits of General George Washington*, 1919, J. B. Lippincott Company, Philadelphia.

Willis, Garry, *Cincinnatus George Washington & The Enlightenment*, 1984, Doubleday & Company, Inc., Garden City, New York.

Wister, Owen, *The Seven Ages of Washington*, 1929, The MacMillan Company, Norwood Press, New York.

Young, Norwood, *George Washington, Soul of the Revolution*, 1932, Robert M. McBride & Company, New York.

Adams, John   73, 94, 96, 105, 125, 164
Adams, Samuel   105
Address, First Presidential Inaugural, April 30, 1789   86-89
Albany Institute of History and Art   55
Albany, N.Y.   9, 54-56, 68
Alexander, William (Lord Sterling)   4, 10, 12
Amboy, Perth, N.J.   2
American Lodge of Research, The, F. & A.M.   108
American Union Lodge   26, 43
Andre, Major John   26, 27, 52
Annapolis, Md.   66
Annual Communication, Grand Lodge of N.Y., June 2, 1790, Robert R Livingston re-elected Grand Master   149
Anthony's Nose   10
Appleby, Joseph (see also G. W.'s Hqs. Phillipsburg, N.Y., near Dobbs Ferry)   26
Apron, Masonic, The, made by the Marquis de La Fayette for George Washington, see Washington Benevolent Society of Philadelphia   137-139
Arnold, General Benedict   9, 25, 52
Association, Washington Headquarter, of the D.A.R.   4, 25
Assumption Bill, The   124
Athenaeum Collection (Boston, Mass.)   132
Attainder, Act of (1779)   5

Ball, The first inaugural, May 7, 1789, N.Y.C.   75
Bard, Doctor John (One of the founders of the New York Hospital)   100, 101
Bard, Doctor Samuel (son)   5, 100, 101
Baskett, Mark (Publisher of the St. John Lodge No. 1 (N.Y.), Holy Bible, G. Washington took oath of office)   83
Bayard, Major William   5
Beacon, N.Y. (formerly Fishkill Landing)   9, 24
Bear Mountain Park Bridge   12
Bemis Heights (see Saratoga National Historic Park)
Bible, Masonic Inaugural, belongs to St. John's Lodge, N.Y.   8, 83, 86
Bibliography   200
Boston Post Road   2, 9, 111
Bowery Lane, N.Y.C.   2
Braddock, Sir, General Edward   1, 5, 59
Brandywine, Pa.   12
Breakneck Hill, N.Y.C.   125
Brewster Forge (Moodna, N.Y.)   10
Brewster House   22
Broglie, Prince of, (Claude Victor)   100
Brooklyn, N.Y.   125; the defense of   7, 8; intense fighting at Cortelyeau House   7; and, at Battle Pass (Prospect Park)   7; the retreat from   7; Gravesend Bay   7; Fort Hamilton   7
Brown, Library, John Carter (R.I.)   139
Bunkers Mansion House (Macomb Mansion)   118, 119
Burgoyne, General John   12, 25, 54

INDEX

Cabinet, Presidential, the first 98, 99
Calvert, Eleanore 5
Capital, Federal, Plans and relocation of the, July 16, 1790, from N.Y.C. 126
Carlton, Sir Guy (see G. Washington's take over of New York City from British) 52
Cedars, The (30 miles from Montreal) 6
Chains, defensive, across the Hudson River during Revolutionary War 10
Chastellux, Marquis de 22
Church Pew, Geo. Washington's, St. Paul's Chapel, N.Y.C. 90
Cincinnati, Society of the 162-180
Cincinnatus, General Lucius Quinctius 166
Clermont, Home of Chancellor Robert R Livingston 12, 13
Clinton, DeWitt 18, 90, 95, 134
Clinton, General George 11, 12, 18, 55, 69, 71, 72, 73, 78, 90, 94
Clinton, Sir, General Henry 53, 54
Clinton, General James 11, 12, 18
Colden, Elizabeth 5
Columbia University (formerly King's College) 95
Columbian Order, The Tammany Society 119
Congress, The Continental 8, 9, 78, 81, 98
Congress, The first United States — its problems 78, 98, 110, 114, 116, 126, 147
Constitution Island 10, 11, 20
Cooper, Myles (President of King's College) 4, 5
Cornwallis, Lord, General Charles 53
Correspondence, Masonic, George Washington's see, Chapter IX
Crown and Thistle Tavern (N.Y.C.), operated by John Thompson ("Scotch Johnny") 2
Crown Point, N.Y. 66
Currency, U.S., value of in 1789 148
Custis, John Parke 4
Custis, Martha (sister of John Parke Custis) 4

Declaration of Independence 7, 9
DeClark, Daniel, see DeWint House
Defenses, Military, Crown Point; Putnam Point; defensive chains across the Hudson River near West Point 10; see Military Forts
Defenses of N.Y.C. and Staten Island, unsuccessful 7
DeLancey, James 5
DeLancey, Peter 5
D'Estaing, Count Charles Hector 163, 164, 172, 173
DeWint House, Tappan, N.Y., also known as The George Washington Masonic Shrine. Built by Daniel DeClark, 1700 26, 52ff
Duportail, General 13

Eagle of the Society of the Cincinatti, see Chapter X
East River 7, 8
Electoral Vote of first national election, 1789 74
Ellison, William, house at New Windsor, N.Y. 19, 20
Evarts, Senator William M. 33

Federal Hall National Memorial, Broad & Wall Streets, N.Y.C. 2, 78, 80, 81, 82, 85, 92
Fish, Lt. Colonel Nicholas 81
Fishkill, N.Y. (now Beacon, N.Y.) 9, 22, 24, 27

a. Mount Gulian   22, 164
b. Verplanck House   9, 22
Fleet, Halifax, The (Howe's Command)   7
Fleming, Major George   32
Forest Dean Mine   10
Forts, Military (N.Y.), Revolutionary War: Fort Clinton   9, 10, 11, 12; Fort Constitution   10, 11; Fort Duquesne   1; Fort Edward   66; Fort Frederick   56; Fort Frontenac   68; Fort George   81; Fort Hamilton   7; Fort Independence   10; Fort Montgomery   9, 10, 11, 12, 20; Fort Plain   67, 68; Fort Schuyler   66, 67; Fort Ticonderoga   66; Fort Washington   8, 125; Fort Niagara
Franklin House, First Presidential Mansion, N.Y.C.   78, 119
Franklin, William (son of Benj. Franklin)   4
Fraunces, Samuel
a. Owner of Fraunces Tavern   6
b. Geo. Washington steward, 1789   95
Fraunces Tavern (N.Y.C.)   19, 33, 70, 71

Gage, General Thomas   5, 7
Genesvoort, Brig. General Peter   55, 57
George Washington Masonic National Memorial, The, Alexandria, Va.   199
Germantown, Pa.   12
Grand Lodges of Free and Accepted Masons, England   44; Massachusettes   47; New Hampshire   108-115; New York   140, 146; in North America (R.:W.:Jeremy Gridley, Grand Master, 1760)   130; Pennsylvania   35ff, 44, 45, 138; Rhode Island   128-136; Georgia   148-151; Supreme Federal Grand Lodge   151
Grand Lodge of Emergency (1780)   36, 44, 149, 151
Gridley, Jeremy, Grand Master, F. & A.M. in North America   130

Halifax Fleet, The   7
Hamilton, Alexander   18, 25, 72, 96, 99, 124f, 125, 126, 171, 173
Harlem Heights, see Manhattan   125
Harrison, George (Provincial Grand Master of New York, 1769   130
Hasbrouck House   19, 21, 22, 65
Hayes, Moses H.   130
Heath, General William   10, 11, 20, 23, 25
Herkimer, General Nicholas   18
Hickey, Thomas, Geo. Washington's bodyguard. Hanged for the attempted murder of George Washington   6
House of Commons, British   53
Howe, Lord, Admiral Richard   7
Howe, General William (brother of Lord Howe)   7
Hudson River Highlands (Cradle of the Republic)   9, 19, 24, 25, 29, 31, 33, 61, 65, 66

Inauguration, first, of George Washington at Federal Hall, April 30, 1789; and procession   72-89
Indians, New York State, Oneidas, Tuscaroras, Iroquis   54, 56-58

Jackson, Doctor Hall, Second Grand Master, N.H.   111, 114
Jay, John, First Chief Justice of N.Y. State; see also Supreme Court, U.S.   18, 76, 81, 82, 94, 96, 99, 102
Jefferson, Thomas   72, 99, 112, 124f, 125f, 134, 164, 170

INDEX

Jenkins, Robert, Deputy Grand Master, R.I. 130
Jones, John Paul 114, 171
Johnson, Sir William, Provincial Grand Master of N.Y. 67
Jumel, Stephen, Post war owner of Morris-Jumel Mansion 4

King's Bridge 2
King's College (now Columbia University) 4
Kingston, New York 12, 27
Knights Templar, N.Y., 1789 147
Kosciuszko, General Thaddeus 13, 171
Knox, General Henry, First Secretary of War, appointed by President Geo. Washington January 1785, 21, 25, 30, 32, 69, 76, 81, 82, 94, 96, 99, 125, 164-171

La Fayette, Marquis de 22, 25, 27, 53, 101, 162, 169, 171
Law and Order Speech by Gen. Geo. Washington to his troops, May 22, 1782 17
L'Enfant, Major Pierre Charles 81, 92, 163, 166, 167
Library of Congress 150
Library, Chancellor Robert R Livingston Masonic 93
Lispenard, Colonel Leonard 5
Livingston, Robert R
  a. Chancellor of the State of N.Y. 18, 67, 77, 82, 83, 92, 96, 118, 145, 146, 149
  b. First Grand Master, F. & A.M., N.Y. 83
  c. Presented oath of office to G. W.'s first inauguration at Federal Hall, N.Y.C. 5, 84
Livingston, Chancellor Robert R Library and Museum, Grand Lodge of New York 93
Lodges, early masonic; Federal No. 5 (N.H.) 111; Holland (N.Y.) 140-143; Independent Royal Arch No. 8 (N.Y.) 147; King David's (Newport, R.I.) 128-132; Livingston (Kingston, N.Y. 1790) 151; St. Andrews (N.Y.) 141, 145; St. Patrick's 141, 145; Steuben, N.Y. 142; Washington (Cleremont, N.Y., 1790) 149; St. John's Lodge No. (N.Y.) 83, 143; St. John's Lodge No. 1 (R.I.) 128
Lodges with name of George Washington 181-197
Long Island, N.Y., Battle of, 7
Macomb's Mansion 118-119
Manhattan, N.Y.C.; Kipps Bay (34th St.) 7, 8; Harlem 7, 8, 69; City Hall Park 8; General Grant National Memorial 8; Fire engulfed British occupied N.Y.C., Sept. 21, 1776, 8; The Battery 7; Bloomingdale 8; Greenwich 8; Fort Washington fell Nov. 16, 1776, 8; Federal Hall (see Federal Hall National Memorial) Macomb's Mansion 118, 119 (later Bunker's Mansion)
  a. Second Presidential Residence (Feb. 1790) 117;
  b. Later Bunkers Mansion House
  c. Demolished in 1928 118, 119
Masonic Correspondence by George Washington 152
Masonic Hall, Grand Lodge of F. & A.M. of the State of N.Y. 84, 120
Masonic Inaugural Bible (St. John's Lodge No. 1) 83, 84
Masonic Shrine, The George Washington, Tappan, N.Y., also known as "The DeWint House" 26, 52ff
Masters, Wardens and Society of F. & A.M., Rhode Island (Legislative Incorporation in 1759) 130, 131
Mc Dougalls, General 18, 25
Mercury, The (N.Y.C. Newspaper) 1, 2
Miflin, General 11, 75
Missouri Lodge of Research 152

— 215 —

Monongahela, Battle of 1
Montgomery, General 18
Monroe, James 72
Moore House, West Point, N.Y. 20, 21
Moore, John 20
Moore, Richard Channing 20
Morris-Jumel Mansion (Washington's Headquarters, 1776) 3, 4, 8
Morris, Roger, Owner of Morris-Jumel Mansion 3, 4, 8, 125
Morris, Gouverneur 18, 123
Morris, Lewis 18
Morris, Robert 126

National Election, First, 1789 74
Newburgh, N.Y. 9, 15-20, 22-24, 28-30, 32, 34, 54, 59, 65, 66, 68, 165
New Hampshire Gazette, 1789 115
Newport, R.I. 27, 128-136
New York Harbour, Occupation of, July 19, 1776, by The Halifax Fleet 7
New York Packet (newspaper - 1789) 95
Nicola, Colonel 15, 17
Noble, Townsend Company - Sterling Furnace Works 10

Old Club of Hulls 5
Order Against Swearing by Gen. George Washington to his Troops 21
Oriskany, N.Y., The Battle of 58

Parsons, General 11, 13
Patroon, The, see Stephen Van Rensselaer 120f
Peekskill, N.Y. 9, 10, 11, 27, 28
Pennsylvania "Ahiman Rezon" 1783 139
Phillipsboro, Manor of (now Westchester County, N.Y.) 2
Phillipse, Frederick 2
Phillipse, Mary 2, 3
Phillipse, Susannah 2
Plan for Defense of N.Y.C. and Staten Island, unsuccessful, 1776 7
Pollopel's Island 10
Portsmouth, N.H. 107-110
Post Roads, The 9, 120
Presidential Mansion, First, Franklin House, Cherry St., New York City 78, 119
Prince of Broglie, Claude Victor 100
Princeton, N.J. 11, 32, 69, 76
Purple Heart, Order of the 22, 65
Putnam, General Israel 8, 12

Queen's Chapel, Portsmouth, N.H., see Pres. Geo. Washington's visit to New Hampshire 113

Ramapo River (Ramapough) 11, 27
Robinson, Beverly 2, 3, 5, 9, 20, 25, 26, 28, 42, 52
Robinson's Bridge 11
Rochambeau, Count de Jean Baptiste 27, 53, 54, 163, 164
Rousselet, Nicholas 10

INDEX

St. John the Baptist, the Festival of 26, 42, 145, 146
St. John the Evangelist, the Festival of 26, 37, 41, 42, 43
St. John's Day, N.Y.C., June 24, 1789 139, 141, 145, 146
St. Leger, Major Barry 54, 55
St. Paul's Chapel, N.Y.C. (Parish) 80, 90ff, 92, 94, 146, 148
Salary as President (1789) 94
Saratoga, N.Y. 9, 57
Saratoga National Historic Park, N.Y., also Bemis Heights (Cite of the Battle of Saratoga) 17, 66
Saratoga, Old, see Schuylerville, N.Y. 67
Schenectady, N.Y. 54, 58, 67
Schuyler, General Philip John 18, 25, 55, 59, 66, 67
Schuylerville, N.Y., (also Old Saratoga) 67
Scotch Johnny, see Crown and Thistle Tavern
Seixas, Moses, First Grand Master, F. & A.M., Rhode Island 131f, 132, 134ff
Shirley, William, British Governor of Massachusetts 2, 3
Sidmun's Bridge 11
Smith, Joshua Hett, see also Treason House 26
Society of the Cincinnati, The, 21, 75, 106, 162ff
Staten Island, N.Y., Lord Howe's Hqs, Halifax Fleet 6, 7
Stavers Tavern, Portsmouth, N.H. 113, 114
Sterling, Earl of, also Lord Sterling and William Alexander 4, 10, 12
Stoney Point, see Treason House 9, 13, 26
Storer, Major Clement, Fifth Grand Master, F. & A.M., N.H. 111
Sullivan-Clinton Campaign, N.Y. 54
Sullivan, Major General John 109, 110, 114, 115
    a. Governor of N.H. 107, 110
    b. First Grand Master, F. & A.M., N.H. 109, 115
Supreme Court, First U.S. (N.Y.C.)
    a. John Jay, Chief Justice 99
    b. Six other Justices 99
Swits, Major Abram 59

Tammany Society, The, see Columbian Order 119
Tappan, N.Y., see George Washington Masonic Shrine 52ff
Tarrytown, N.Y. 27
Temple, The, (New Windsor, N.Y.) 23, 24ff
Temple Hill, N.Y. 15, 23ff, 34
Ten Broeck, Brig. General Abraham 55
Ticonderoga, N.Y. 66
Thomas, General John 7
Thompson, John, see Crown and Thistle Tavern 2
Thompson, Colonel Thomas
    a. Master, St. John's Lodge, N.H. 115
    b. Fourth Grand Master of F. & A.M., N.H. 112, 113
    c. Early Naval Captain of U.S. Frigate "Raleigh" after American Revolution 111
Treason House, also known as Joshua Hett Smith House 26
Treaty of Paris (1783) 54
Trenton, N.J. 11, 75
Trinity Church (Wall St., N.Y.C.) 90, 91, 92
Tryon, Governor William 5, 7

Tuoro Synagogue, Newport, R.I., also known as Congregation Jeshuat Israel   133ff
Truman, Most Worshipful Harry   152

Van Courtlandt House   27, 69
Van Rensselaer, Stephen, The Patroon   120
   a. United States Senator, N.Y.   120
   b. Married to Mrs. Alexander Hamilton's sister, Margaret   120
   c. Grand Master F. & A.M., N.Y. 1825-1828   120
   d. Laid cornerstone (1828) of first Masonic Hall, N.Y.C.   120
Verplanck Point, N.Y.   9, 10, 22, 27, 28
Victor, Claude (Prince of Broglie)   100
Von Steuben, General, Baron Friedrich   22, 96, 165, 168, 171

Washington Benevolent Society of Philadelphia   138, 139ff
   a. The masonic apron made by the Marquise de la Fayette for Geo. Washington   138
   b. Apron now in possession of the Grand Lodge of Pennsylvania   138
Washington, George
   a. Commander-in-Chief, Continental Army   5
   b. Attempted murder of, by Thomas Hickey, 1776   6
   c. Consulted with Continental Congress, Phila., 1776   7
   d. Battle of Brooklyn Heights and retreat   7
   e. Headquarters during Revolutionary War in New York; Morris-Jumel Mansion 3, 4, 8, 125; New Windsor 9, 15, 16, 19, 27, 32; Hasbrouck House 19, 21; Fredericksburg, N.Y., 1778   24, 25, 28, 29; Reed Ferris House, near Pawling, N.Y.   24; John Kane's House, Patterson, N.Y.   24, 25; DeWint House, Tappan, 1780   26, 52ff; White Plains, N.Y., 1776 and 1778   8, 26, 28; Joseph Appleby House near Dobbs Ferry, 1780   29; Van Courtlandt House, 1781   29; Verplanck Point, Peekskill   9, 10, 22, 27, 28
   f. Brief visits to Fishkill (now Beacon), N.Y., 1778   9, 22, 24, 27
   g. Military Encampments, 1780, West Point, Newburgh, and New Windsor; and, his farewell address November 1783. See Chapter II
   h. Occupation and take over of N.Y.C. from British, Nov. 25, 1783   32, 52f, 53
   i. Farewell address to and departure from his officers of Continental Army at Fraunces Tavern   71
   j. Visit to Grand Lodge of F. & A.M. of Pennsylvania   See Chapter III
   k. At Masonic functions, and visits to N.Y. Masonic Lodges   See Chapter VIII
   l. Nominated General Grand Master of Freemasons of the U.S., and reaction   43, 44
   m. Resigned military commission at Annapolis, Dec. 23, 1783   71
   n. Electoral vote, election, 1789   74; Oath on April 30, 1789   83-84; Inaugural address   86-89
   o. Tour of New England as President, visit to Masonic, church, and synagogue events, 1789   See Chapter VI, 90, 102ff, 109, 110, 113
   p. Signed bill into law (July 16, 1790), changing location of national seat of government   126
   q. Visit Tuoro Synagogue, Newport, R.I.   132-135
   r. Honorary membership in Holland Lodge, N.Y.   140, 141
   s. Masonic correspondence   See Chapter IX
   t. Membership in and election as first President-General of The Society of the Cincinnati   See Chapter X
   u. Master, Alexandria Masonic Lodge No. 22 (Va.) while President of the United States   109

INDEX

    v. Tour of Long Island, N.Y., 1790 117-127
Washington (George) Masonic National Memorial (Alexandria, Va.) 198
Washington, John Augustine 25
Washington, Martha 6, 73, 78, 97, 125
    a. Proposed innoculation 6
    b. In Philadelphia, 1776 6
    c. At Newburgh, N.Y. 22
    d. At Inaugural Ball 25, 97
    e. Her grandchildren, Eleanor and Geo. Washington Custis 97
    f. Contribution to Children's Fund, during Masonic Service, St. Paul's Chapel on St. John's Day, N.Y.C. 146-148
Washington Masonic Lodges, The, in the U.S. and foreign countries 181
Washington Valley 20
Watson and Cassoul (Nantes, France) 59
    a. Makers of the famous George Washington Apron 59ff, 64, 152
    b. Now in possession of Alexandria-Washington Lodge No. 22, Alexandria, Va. 59-64
Watson, Elkanah, see Watson and Cassoul
West Point, N.Y. 9, 10, 13, 14, 19, 20, 26, 28, 29, 32, 42, 59, 112
Whipple, William 113
White Plains, N.Y. 8, 10, 28, 29
Wolcott, Oliver 100, 116

Yates, Peter W. 55, 96

                Index prepared by Alexander A. Bleimann